COVERING GOVERNMENT

COVERING GOVERNMENT

A Civics Handbook for Journalists

Rob Armstrong

Iowa State Press
A Blackwell Publishing Company

Rob Armstrong covered government for thirty-two years, most of them for CBS News. From 1989 to 1998 he was senior radio correspondent for CBS News, covering Congress and national politics. Since 1998, he has been a retired professional in residence at Flagler College, St. Augustine, Florida. He is a graduate of the University of Denver, where he majored in history, and also attended the University of Denver College of Law. He is the author of four other books and writes a newspaper column.

© 2002 Iowa State Press
A Blackwell Publishing Company
All rights reserved

Iowa State Press
2121 State Avenue, Ames, Iowa 50014

Orders: 1-800-862-6657
Office: 1-515-292-0140
Fax: 1-515-292-3348
Web site: www.iowastatepress.com

Authorization to photocopy items for internal or personal use, or the internal or personal use of specific clients, is granted by Iowa State Press, provided that the base fee of $.10 per copy is paid directly to the Copyright Clearance Center, 222 Rosewood Drive, Danvers, MA 01923. For those organizations that have been granted a photocopy license by CCC, a separate system of payments has been arranged. The fee code for users of the Transactional Reporting Service is 0-8138-1467-7/2002 $.10.

⊗ Printed on acid-free paper in the United States of America

First edition, 2002

Library of Congress Cataloging-in-Publication Data

Armstrong, Rob
    Covering government : a civics handbook for journalists / by Rob Armstrong.—1st ed.
        p. cm.
Includes index.
    ISBN 0-8138-1467-7
    1. United States—Politics and government. 2. State governments—United States.
3. Local governments—United States. I. Title.
    JK276.A76 2002
    320.473′024′097—dc21   2002005723

The last digit is the print number: 9 8 7 6 5 4 3 2 1

Dedication

For all those along the way
who taught me the importance of the news
and helped me to be a reporter

Contents

Preface

civics (siv' iks) *n.* [*with sing.v.*]: a sub-discipline of political science that studies the structure and workings of government, the role of government in public process and policy issues, and the duties and rights of citizens

It used to be that almost every kid in the country was required to take a class called "civics" some time in late junior high or early high school. In my own case civics was taught along with current events in tenth grade. I was taught by a teacher who knew virtually nothing about the subject that wasn't in the wretched, dull textbook. She dutifully informed the students that civics was the study of how government works and what citizens do in our democracy. I don't think she had a clue what that meant. It was boring and lifeless to her and she imparted that to her students.

Today, only about half of my college students are required to take any form of civics. Painfully few of them remember anything about the class. Nonetheless, for those young men and women who want to be journalists, a working knowledge of civics, the role of government in public issues, how government works, the rights and duties of citizens, is critical.

The news media are the people's watchdog. Arguably, the most important function of the news media is to inform the people about what their government is doing that directly or indirectly affects their lives, regulates their activities, and spends their money.

It is the responsibility of every journalist to know enough about civics — how government operates, what the various officials, legislative bodies, executive departments and agencies, and courts do and how they do it — to provide necessary and factual information to their readers and viewers. Government is not some distant amorphous thing. It is not abstract. It does not function in a vacuum. It is not a bunch of faceless pols in Washington, D.C.

Government (of one level or another) has an enormous impact on our lives. Like it or not, government is around us all the time. Government is your local school board, your county or city zoning authority, your police and fire department. Government imposes taxes, regulates the safety of our food, water, and drugs, protects the nation from foreign threats, and mints our money.

If journalists report inaccurately on the workings of government the nation is weakened, the citizens are less informed than they need to be, and the foundation of the democracy is undermined.

It did not take much deep analysis in the aftermath of the 2000 presidential election to see that while most reporters knew about the Electoral College in a general sense, few had more than cursory knowledge of its structure and history — a serious shortcoming in civics. A contemporaneous, if unscientific, discussion among my own journalism students revealed an equally troubling gap between what they knew about the Electoral College and what young journalists — and citizens — need to know.

Article II Section 1 of the U.S. Constitution clearly gives the various state legislatures the right to determine how members of the Electoral College are picked in each state. There is no uniform national law governing elections, in general, or selection of presidential electors, in particular. That was the reason the entire country focused for a month on Florida's multiple types of voting machines and ballots, alleged voting irregularities, recounts, the role of the Florida secretary of state, the legislature, and the Florida Supreme Court. Why wasn't there a quick, tidy resolution? The short answer is because the Constitution does not provide a quick, tidy solution.

It is difficult to overstate the importance of basic civics, knowing how government works, to journalists. It doesn't matter where you work or what your area of specialization. From small town newspapers to network news reporters in Washington or New York, civics is a part of your daily work. If you don't understand civics it will be impossible for you to explain it to your audience.

Even sports reporters are called upon to report accurately and knowledgeably about civics issues. For example in 2001 they needed to explain the application of the Americans with Disabilities Act to Casey Martin's suit against the PGA Tour for the right to ride a golf cart. They must be conversant with Major League Baseball's special business status because of its congressionally authorized anti-trust exemption. They must be able to explain the FCC rules governing television blackouts of NFL home games.

All journalists are called on daily to help their readers, viewers, or listeners understand civics issues. Reporters covering everything from business and finance to health and medicine, from local schools to crime and courts, from aerospace to agriculture, will be called upon to explain issues involving government and their particular audience.

In the aftermath of the terrorist attacks on the United States, September 11, 2001, journalists were required to explain and clarify such civics questions as the president's overnight creation of a new Cabinet-level position (director of homeland security) and limits on wartime information coming from the Pentagon.

It is fundamental to the American character that citizens have the right to know what their government is doing. The concept not only predates the Revolutionary War, it is part of the reason the colonies split from English rule in the first place. It is embodied in the First Amendment to the Constitution. As James Madison, the fourth president and one of the Constitution's chief architects, stated, "A popular government without popular information or the means of acquiring it is but a prologue to a farce or a tragedy or perhaps both. Knowledge will forever govern ignorance and a people who mean to be their own governors must arm themselves with the power which knowledge gives."

People have a basic right — and, as Madison argues, an obligation — to know about the men and women who are elected and appointed as servants of the people. They have a right to know about government actions that may affect them before they are enacted into law. They have a right to know the various points of view that surround public policy issues. They have the right to know the details of what all facets of government are doing — and not doing — from the president of the United States to their mayor, from the U.S. Congress to their state legislature, county commission, and local school board. They have a right to know what's happening in their courts from the U.S. Supreme Court to their local justice of the peace. And reporters, journalists, the news media are the conduits through which the information is passed. Reporters protect the people's right to know.

In a democracy such as ours, that often means citizens are told a great deal about their leaders — warts, wrinkles and all. Sometimes the media are accused of delving too deeply into the private lives of public officials, revealing too much information in the guise of the people's right to know. But the job of the news media is to report what is factual, not to act as the arbiter of what the public ought to know. We, as citizens, are entitled to know about alleged misconduct, corruption, conflicts of interest, or dereliction of duty on the part of those who serve us. How much information we assimilate is up to us, not up to the people who deliver it.

In postrevolutionary times, the press reported that Benjamin Franklin tippled and had a fondness for the ladies. John Adams was crotchety and churlish. Alexander Hamilton, the first treasury secretary, and James Madison, the first secretary of state, didn't like each other and bickered constantly. And

Thomas Jefferson owned slaves and was widely rumored to have had a romantic affair with at least one of them. How much and what, specifically, the public has a right to know has long been the subject for debate. But the right to know, itself, is a cornerstone of the democracy.

In 1971, in *New York Times Co. v. United States* — the case that has come to be known as the Pentagon Papers Case — Supreme Court Justice Hugo Black wrote, "In the First Amendment the Founding Fathers gave the free press the protection it must have to fulfill its essential role in our democracy. The press was to serve the governed, not the governors. The government's power to censor the press was abolished so that the press could remain forever free to censure the government. The press was protected so that it could bare the secrets of government and inform the people."

A year later Supreme Court Justice William O. Douglas observed, in his dissent in the case *Branzburg v. Hayes*, "The press has a preferred position in our constitutional scheme, not to enable it to make money, not to set newsmen apart as a favored class, but to bring fulfillment to the public's right to know. The right to know is critical to the governing powers of the people. . . . Knowledge is essential to informed decisions."

If newspeople do not know civics, if they cannot report accurately about how government works, it is impossible for them to do their job, to synthesize and clarify those government activities that directly and personally affect the citizens of the country. Journalists are not charged with knowing all the answers. They are charged with knowing the questions, understanding sometimes complex processes, and being able to find the information about the workings of government to make their stories complete.

This book is designed to help journalists. It is a handbook organized and constructed to be user-friendly and informative. It is broken into two major sections: 1) Federal government and 2) State government and local government.

The federal government section roughly follows the U.S. Constitution itself, i.e., legislative branch, executive branch, judicial branch, and extraordinary circumstances such as impeachment and amending the Constitution. There are notes throughout for reporters about important political issues, pitfalls to be avoided, historical anecdotes related to certain civics issues, and useful information for making stories both factually correct and journalistically colorful.

The section on the state and local governments is designed to point out areas of similarity and difference in the vast array of ways in which states, counties, cities and towns operate. Each sub-chapter includes a list of questions reporters must ask in their particular state or locality. The section is designed to raise warning flags for reporters and to make certain that they find out and understand how things work in their state, county, city, or town before they go into print or on the air with erroneous assumptions in the guise of news. For example, almost all local jurisdictions have some sort of school board and zoning commission. But they do not all function the same way. Reporters must ascertain exactly how their board or commission works.

This handbook provides some specific models, delivers examples of how they differ, and offers reporters some guidelines and road maps for answers they need to obtain in their particular locales.

In the back of the book is a complete text of the U.S. Constitution, a list of abbreviations and acronyms, and a compilation of useful web sites. Computer assisted reporting opens new vistas for journalists engaged in covering government, allowing them to seek a deeper understanding of the civics issues with which they work at the click of a mouse. Finally there is a glossary of civics terms with references to where information on the subject can be found in the text of the handbook.

Acknowledgments

As with all of my books, this project simply would not have gotten done without the love, understanding, help, and intellect of my wife, Barbara Stafford. She is my sounding board, my legal expert, my partner, my friend, and a superb editor. She always gets the first crack (and in this case second, third, and fourth cracks as well) at fine-tuning the manuscript. Her insight is without peer; her patience is biblical.

My wonderful research assistant, A. Dawn Rogers, was an outstanding student of mine who blossomed into a full-fledged pro working on this book. Her eye for detail, her dedication, and her tenacity made my job much easier. She provided thousands of pages of documents — raw data — and carefully combed through the manuscript. If there is any error in processing, synthesizing, or analyzing that data it is mine alone. I could not have done this without Dawn.

This project never would have gotten off the ground without the vision and encouragement of Mark Barrett, commissioning editor at Iowa State Press. Thanks also to project manager Lynne Bishop and my marvelous editor, Arnold Friedman.

I am especially grateful to those on whom I prevailed to go through the manuscript with critical and professional eyes, make constructive comments, and tell me where I went astray. My heartiest thanks to CBS News correspondents Howard Arenstein and Bob Fuss, both trusted old friends; and to Fred Brown of *The Denver Post,* whom I have had the pleasure of knowing for more than thirty years.

My students and former students provided a laboratory in which much of this material was tested. My faculty colleagues offered suggestions and encouragement. Special thanks to Flagler College President William T. Abare Jr., whose enthusiasm and encouragement have been deeply appreciated. Thanks also to communications chair Dr. Caroline Dow, Dr. Doug Covert, Dr. Tracy Halcomb, Dr. Virgil Moberg, Dr. Murray Harris, Jim Gilmore, Nadia Reardon, John Lynch, Victor Ostrowidski, Barry Sand, Dan McCook, and Lauren Bosse.

This book would have suffered greatly were it not for the helpful comments, suggestions, and personal encouragement I received from countless working newspeople and former colleagues: Bob Schieffer, John Harge, Tom Mattesky, Kia Baskerville, and Harriet Garber of CBS News; Deborah Potter and Wally Dean of NewsLab; my former boss at CBS, Larry McCoy, who is now with Dow Jones Newswires; Vic Ratner of ABC News; John Bisney of CNN; Jamie DuPree of Cox Broadcasting; Tina Tate and Gail Davis of the House Radio and TV Gallery; Larry Janazich of the Senate Radio and TV Gallery; and Mike Freedman, vice president of information at The George Washington University.

Deep appreciation to my close personal friends Tom Taylor and Sheila Vidamour, and to my sister-in-law and her husband, Meri and Ed Schindler.

And everything I do is a monument to my mother and father, Murray and Freda Armstrong, who have given me a lifetime of nurturing, caring, commitment, patience, and, most of all, love.

Section I
The Federal Government

Overview

So the Declaration of Independence has been signed; the Revolutionary War has been fought and won; the American colonies have shaken off the yoke of the English monarchy; and now they are faced with the most daunting challenge of all — how this new nation will govern itself. As professor Crane Brinton discussed at length in his classic analysis, *The Anatomy of Revolution,* the success of a revolution rests on replacing an old paradigm with a new one. Revolutions have historically failed when the new paradigm turns out to be the same or worse than the old.

The framers of the U.S. Constitution knew that they did not want a government for the new nation that smacked of what they viewed as the tyranny of King George III. They wanted no nobility, no authoritarianism, and no isolation of the government from those governed. James Madison, one of the chief architects of the Constitution, turned to the history of representative government in the colonies for guidance. In Madison's home state of Virginia, the House of Burgesses, a popularly elected legislative body, met first in 1619, and continued for more than 150 years before the American Revolution. It became the model for the House of Representatives.

Under the royal system, the governor of a colony was appointed by the king and the upper chamber of the legislature was appointed by the governor. The switch to complete popular representation took place in all thirteen colonies within two years of 1776.

The former royal colonies quickly adopted a semi-democratic system of government after the Declaration of Independence was signed. They adjusted the royal model in accordance with the suggestions of the Continental Congress. They all had a governor, a two-chamber legislature, and a court system. This tripartite structure would become the model for the Constitution of the United States of America.

In 1787 the Constitution established three coequal branches of the federal government — the legislative branch, the executive branch, and the judicial branch. It was an ingenious concept in the late Eighteenth Century; no nation had such a governmental structure and there was substantial debate at the time about whether it would work in the short term and survive in the long term.

As defined by the Constitution, the legislative branch consists of the House of Representatives and the Senate. The structure of the two bodies resulted from a compromise between the big states and the small states, and represents a political dynamic that survives to this day. The makeup of the House is determined by the population of each state, the bigger the state the more representatives it has. No state can have fewer than one representative. In the Senate, the Constitution makes all states equal with each state allotted two senators, a means of protecting the interests of smaller states.

Today, representatives and senators are elected directly by the citizens of each state, although that was not the way it was originally set up. At first only the House was popularly elected and then only by white males. Senators were chosen by the various state legislatures. (See Chapter 2, sections 2.1 and 2.2.)

The executive branch is symbolized by the president of the United States, but it extends well beyond one individual. It is a vast structure that includes the vice president, the Cabinet departments, and nearly sixty independent agencies, such as the Food and Drug Administration and the Federal Communications Commission. The Constitution delineated the primary function of the executive to implement and enforce laws enacted by Congress, followed by appointing key officials, negotiating treaties, and receiving ambassadors, along with the president's role as commander-in-chief of the military.

It is doubtful the framers of the Constitution envisioned the power of the modern presidency and all that surrounds it. They could not contemplate the sheer size of the executive branch with thousands of employees. They would not believe the impact and reach of the executive branch's power to make and implement the rules and regulations known as administrative law. Advocates of limited executive authority, such as Jefferson, would chafe at the power of the office itself to persuade and dissuade, promote and diminish, encourage and discourage, and approve and disapprove of the actions of the other branches of the U.S. government and governments around the world. It is a far cry from the presidency under George Washington or John Adams.

The president and vice president together are elected only indirectly by the citizens of the country; the actual selection of the president and vice president is made by the Electoral College. (See Chapter 3, section 3.1.) All other department and agency heads are appointed by the president, but must be confirmed by the Senate as a part of its constitutional requirement to advise and consent to such selections. (See Chapter 3, sections 3.6 and 3.7.)

The judicial branch is divided into three levels, although only one was described in the Constitution. The highest court in the land is the Supreme Court of the United States. All other inferior tribunals are the result of legislation passed by Congress, starting almost immediately in 1789 with a system of trial courts.

The Supreme Court currently has nine justices, including the chief justice of the United States. The number nine is not contained in the Constitution. Over the years Congress has provided for six and seven justices, the odd number finally being favored to avoid tie votes. The current nine-justice makeup of the Supreme Court dates to a law enacted in 1948. (See Chapter 4, sections 4.1 and 4.2.)

The middle level of the federal court system is the Court of Appeals. It became apparent by the late 1800s that the Supreme Court was handling too many cases. One court could not hear every appeal in the United States and the justices wanted and needed a greater level of discretion about what appeals they would and would not consider. Thus, the Court of Appeals was established to ease the burden of the Supreme Court.

District courts are the lowest level of federal courts and handle all trials — criminal and civil, jury and non-jury. Federal judges and Supreme Court justices are appointed for life by the president and each must be confirmed by the Senate, with the exception of U.S. magistrate judges who are appointed by the district courts and serve eight-year terms. (See Chapter 4, section 4.3.)

Madison and his constitutional collaborators had a deep distrust of autocracy. The constitutional structure of the U.S. government deliberately and ingeniously creates a separation of powers, unlike the English monarchy in which virtually all powers were vested in one institution, the paradigm the framers of the Constitution wanted to replace.

Along with the separation of powers, the Constitution establishes a series of checks and balances which prevents any one branch from becoming too powerful. Madison referred to the two as complementary. The Senate's mandate to "advise and consent" is one such check. The fact that laws cannot be passed without the approval of both the House of Representatives and the Senate is another, along with the congressional power to allocate and spend all federal money, known as the power of the purse.

Judicial review is one of the most important checks and balances and is unique to the American system. It allows the federal courts and ultimately the Supreme Court to rule on the constitutionality of actions by other branches of government. The doctrine of judicial review was established in 1803 in the landmark case *Marbury v. Madison*. While the words "judicial review" do not appear in the Constitution, the six Supreme Court justices at the time interpreted some of the murky language to give the court the right to order executive branch officials to do their legal duty. The great irony of the case is that the Supreme Court ruled against Secretary of State James Madison, the same man who helped create the system of checks and balances in the first place.

Journalists should be aware that it is not all as neat as it seems. There are many areas in which the powers of the branches overlap, where there is unresolved conflict about which branch has the ultimate power or authority. One such example is the use of the U.S. military and the War Powers Act. (See Chapter 5, section 5.1.) Congress has the express and sole authority to declare war, but the president is expressly the commander-in-chief of the country's armed forces. Ever since Jefferson, presidents have dispatched troops without congressional consent. Congress has passed legislation to rein in the commander-in-chief. And so far the courts have not acted to resolve the conflict.

Key Points

- The Constitution provides for three branches of government: legislative, executive and judicial.
- The legislative branch is made up of the House of Representatives and the Senate.

- The executive branch includes the president, vice president, cabinet departments and independent federal agencies.
- The judicial branch is made up of the Supreme Court of the United States, the Courts of Appeals, and district courts.
- Separation of powers assures equality among the branches and guards against one branch becoming too powerful.
- Checks and balances give the three branches of government oversight over each other and assure separation of powers.
- Judicial review gives the federal courts the power to determine whether other branches of government have acted within the bounds of the Constitution.
- The president is required to seek the advice and consent of the Senate, giving that body the ability to reject presidential nominees for top executive branch jobs and federal judgeships.

The Legislative Branch

Article I of the Constitution establishes the two legislative bodies of the United States, the Senate and the House of Representatives. It is significant that the framers of the Constitution determined that the legislative branch be the first branch to warrant consideration in the Constitution itself. The framers envisioned a government in which the Congress makes the laws; the executive branch enforces the laws; the judicial branch interprets the laws.

Together the Senate and House of Representatives are the Congress. Together, they are constitutionally empowered as the only body to enact the country's statutory laws — with or without the signature of the president or over the president's objections, or veto. (See section 2.5.) The executive branch can make rules and regulations (known as administrative law) but only in departments and agencies specifically authorized to do so by Congress and as delineated by statutory laws enacted by Congress. (See Chapter 3, section 3.8.) The courts in effect make law by interpreting the constitutionality of the laws passed by Congress, the states, and by ruling on the legality of actions of the other branches of government. But the only way a statutory law, sometimes known as a public law, may come into being in the United States is through the action of Congress.

Congress also has other important functions. In addition to making the nation's laws, Congress exercises oversight over federal agencies, investigates public policy issues, oversees the coining and minting of money, and deals with taxation. Tax laws must originate in the House of Representatives. Impeachments must originate in the House. The Senate must give advice and consent on the appointment of top executive department officials, federal judges, and ambassadors, as well as on pending international treaties.

2.1 Makeup of the House of Representatives

The House of Representatives is defined in Article I Section 2 of the Constitution. There are 435 members of the House. It is reapportioned every ten years based on population figures from the U.S. census. States that gain population gain House seats; states that lose population lose House seats. Originally, there were only sixty-five representatives, based on a rough ratio of one representative for every thirty thousand people. The total number of representatives expanded with each census and as new states were added to the union. On August 8, 1911, Congress enacted a law (which took effect in 1913) to freeze the number of representatives at 435, where it has remained ever since. Today, the ratio of House representation is one representative for roughly every 650,000 people.

The Constitution requires House members to be at least twenty-five years old, to be U.S. citizens for at least seven years, and to be living in the state from which they were elected. All 435 representatives are elected every two years. If a vacancy occurs it is up to the governor of the affected state to call for a special election to fill the position.

Apportionment of representatives is based on the population of the states that elect them. No state can have fewer than one representative. Every ten years, following the results of the federal census, the apportionment of seats is reviewed and where states have gained or lost population the number of representatives from that state is adjusted. Each congressional district has roughly the same number of people. The boundaries of each district are drawn by individual states. (See Chapter 8, section 8.7.) That process is known as reapportionment.

When state legislatures create congressional or legislative districts in odd or convoluted shapes for political purposes it's called gerrymandering. Gerrymandering got its name from James Madison's vice president, Elbridge Gerry. During Gerry's term as governor of Massachusetts, his party created one oddly-shaped district that looked like a salamander in a bid to protect the seat of a member of Gerry's party. It was dubbed a gerrymander, named for the governor. (Gerry pronounced his name with a hard "G" as in "gary"; the political process is pronounced as if written with a "J" as in "jerry.")

The original apportionment rules set up by the Constitution were changed over the years. For example Article I Section 2 said slaves and Indians (Native Americans) not taxed could not be counted in determining a state's population. The part of that section concerning slaves was eliminated in 1868 when the Fourteenth Amendment was adopted. Among other things, that important post–Civil War amendment applied the provisions of the previous thirteen amendments to the various states and prohibited states from omitting former slaves in the census figures used to calculate apportionment. (Women were not made full citizens until 1920, when they were given the right to vote by the Nineteenth Amendment.)

The Speaker of the House is that body's presiding officer. The Constitution requires a Speaker to be elected by the members of the House. As a practical matter, the leader of the majority political party is elected Speaker because the majority party has the most votes. The Speaker is second in the line of presidential succession behind the vice president. This is not the result of a constitutional requirement, but the result of a law enacted by Congress in 1945.

Congress had adjusted the line of succession to the presidency twice previously — first in 1792 and again in 1886. When Harry Truman became president after the death of Franklin D. Roosevelt in 1945, he believed an elected official should be in the line of succession behind the vice president. (The secretary of state had been third in line until then.) So Congress changed the law to make the Speaker of the House third and the president pro tem of the Senate fourth in line to succeed the president.

The Speaker usually presides over the House only for major events. The Speaker appoints a Speaker pro tem (always a member of the Speaker's own political party) to preside over most day-to-day business.

The rules of the House provide for election of several support officials, including the clerk of the House, the chaplain, and the sergeant at arms. The House sergeant at arms serves in even numbered years as chair of the Capitol Police Board and alternates with the Senate sergeant at arms as the Capitol's chief law enforcement officer. Capitol Hill — the Capitol building, its surrounding grounds and buildings, including the Supreme Court building — has its own police force apart from that of the District of Columbia.

The chamber, or hall, of the House of Representatives is divided in half by an aisle that runs from the entrance to the well. The well is the carpeted area in front of the multi-tiered dais on which the Speaker's chair is the highest point, and below which such support officers as the clerk and parliamentarian sit. Looking at the House chamber from the Speaker's chair, the Democrats sit to the right of the aisle, the Republicans sit to the left, giving rise to the concept of which side of the aisle one is on. The same kind of carpeted aisle divides the Senate chamber, with Democrats on the right and Republicans on the left looking at the Senate chamber from the president's chair.

The framers of the Constitution knew that the House would be the most political of the two chambers of Congress. It was the only part of the government to be directly elected when the Constitution was enacted in 1787. (Senators were chosen by their state legislatures.) The House term was deliberately limited to only two years so citizens could replace their representatives in relatively short order if they were unhappy with them.

The House also includes five non-voting members, not counted among the 435 representatives. Delegates from American Samoa, the District of Columbia, Guam, and the U.S. Virgin Islands are each elected for terms of two years. The resident commissioner from Puerto Rico serves a four-year term. All take part in floor debate and committee hearings. While they may not vote on the floor of the House on legislation, resolutions, or other House actions, they do cast votes in the committees to which they are assigned.

Key Points

- Congress is the nation's only statutory lawmaking body.
- It is made up of the House of Representatives and the Senate.
- Members must be at least twenty-five years old and are elected for two-year terms.
- House seats are up for election every even numbered year.
- The Speaker of the House is the presiding officer of the House and is second in line to succeed the president, behind the vice president.
- The Speaker is always a member of the majority political party.
- Districts are reapportioned every ten years to reflect population changes as reported by the census.

2.2 Makeup of the Senate

The Senate is the smaller of the two legislative chambers. It almost always works more slowly than the House and takes great pride in its deliberateness and thoroughness of debate. It is made up of one hundred senators. Article I Section 3 gives each state two senators, with one vote each. They serve six-year terms, with a third of the Senate being elected every two years. Senators, like representatives, must be U.S. citizens and live in the state from which they are elected. Senators, however, must be citizens for at least nine years and be at least thirty years old. Senators were not popularly elected until the Seventeenth Amendment was made a part of the Constitution in 1913. Until then, senators were selected by the various state legislatures.

The vice president of the United States is the president of the Senate, a largely ceremonial post save for the fact that the vice president can vote to break ties. The Constitution also requires that the Senate elect a president pro tempore (usually called the president pro tem). Traditionally, that position is filled by the longest-serving senator in the majority political party. Most day-to-day business of the Senate is conducted with a designee of the majority party as presiding officer, often one of the more junior members in terms of Senate seniority. The presiding officer does not participate in debate while he/she is serving as acting-president pro tem.

The Senate elects several support officials each session, including the secretary of the Senate who, among other things, is charged with requisitioning money from the U.S. treasury to pay senators, maintaining the physical facility, paying the support staff, and overseeing the budget allotments for each senator to run his or her office.

The Senate sergeant at arms is also an elected support officer, charged with keeping order in the chamber and alternating with the House sergeant at arms as the chief law enforcement official of the Capitol building and grounds.

Key Points

- Senators must be at least thirty years old, citizens of the United States for nine years, and are elected for six year terms.
- One-third of Senate seats are up for election every two years.
- The vice president of the United States is president of the Senate, but may vote only to break ties.
- Traditionally, the president pro tempore is the longest serving member of the majority party.

2.3 Political Parties and Who's in Charge

The majority political party in the House and Senate runs things in their respective chambers. The term "majority party" is different in the U.S. Congress than in parliamentary governments, such as Britain. In parliamentary systems, the majority party runs both the legislative and executive branches of government. In the U.S. the majority party can be the same for the House, Senate and president — as it was in the first two years of the Clinton administration. It can be divided with the House and Senate of different parties than the president or the House controlled by one party and the Senate controlled by another.

History has shown that the larger the majority for either party in a house of Congress, the more iron-fisted that party becomes in exercising its control. The majority picks the chairs of each committee; the majority picks the support officials of each chamber; the majority determines the legislative agenda; and the majority determines what issues and bills will come up for committee consideration.

When the Senate is in the hands of one party and the House is in the hands of the other, generally minimal legislation is passed, unless there is some kind of national emergency. The same is true when the White House is controlled by one party and the Congress is controlled by the other. Since the end of World War II the voters have frequently opted for divided government, including during parts of the Eisenhower, Nixon, Reagan, Bush, and Clinton administrations. In the election of 2000, voters elected an evenly split Senate, fifty Republicans and fifty Democrats. With the tie-breaking power of the Republican vice president, the Senate was under Republican control. But early in the session, Republican Sen. James Jeffords of Vermont switched from the Republican party to Independent, delivering the Senate to the Democrats.

Political analysts and historians generally agree that when voters opt for divided government, it is a way to express the sentiment that they don't necessarily want to see very much changed. Occasionally, divided government results in legislative paralysis that Washington reporters have come to call "gridlock." When gridlock occurs, even necessary legislation gets stymied.

In both the House and Senate, seniority plays a key role within the political parties. Members who serve the longest usually have the most clout and the best committee assignments. In the majority party, committee and subcommittee chairs are generally the most senior senators and representatives. In the minority party, the position of ranking member is based on seniority. Committee assignments are tied to seniority. Also, the more senior a member the better, more spacious, and more aesthetically pleasing (the view, the architecture) his/her office assignment will be.

In the 1990s there was a primarily conservative movement to limit the number of terms members could serve, in effect an effort to abolish the congressional seniority system. Several states enacted term limit legislation. In 1995, a group of term limit cases reached the Supreme Court under the umbrella name *U.S. Term Limits, Inc. v. Thornton*. The high court struck down term limits legislation affecting federal elections. In the 5-4 decision, Justice John Paul Stevens wrote: "State imposition of term limits for congressional service would effect such a fundamental change in the constitutional framework that it must come through a constitutional amendment . . ."

In the House, the Speaker is the majority party's top official. In addition, there is a majority leader, second in command behind the Speaker, followed by the majority whip. On the opposite side is the minority leader along with the minority whip. The whip is the assistant to the party leader. The office and the term are borrowed from the British Parliament, where the whip was the person charged with maintaining party discipline. In addition to party discipline the whips in the U.S. House and Senate traditionally have been the chief nose-counters. Part of their job is to know how every member is going to vote on every issue and to try to persuade members not to vote against positions established by the party leadership. Today, both sides in the House and Senate have several assistant whips.

In the Senate, the most powerful senator is the majority leader. As with the House, the majority party runs the Senate, picking committee chairs, setting the legislative agenda, determining what will come before committees, and picking the support officials of the body. Senate Republicans and Democrats have slightly different leadership structures. The number two Republican is the assistant leader, followed by the chief deputy whip and the conference chair. The number two Democrat is the whip, followed by the deputy whip and the conference secretary.

Key Points

- Whichever political party is in the majority runs things in the House and Senate.
- The Speaker of the House is always the top leader of the majority party in that body, followed by House majority leader and majority whip.
- The most powerful senator is the majority leader.
- Both chambers' committee chairs and support officers are picked by the majority.
- The majority party controls the legislative agenda, determining what bills go to committees, what hearings are held, and what measures come to the floor for a vote.
- Divided government occurs when different parties are in the majority in the House and Senate or when the majority party in Congress is different from the party of the president.

2.4 How a Bill Becomes Law

Any senator or representative may introduce legislation. The fact is that thousands of pieces of legislation are introduced each session. Most are never considered at all. Of those that make it into the process — being given a number and assigned to a committee — most never make it to committee hearings. Some die as a result of hearings. Some that are voted out of committee don't have enough votes for passage and lose on the floor of the House or Senate. Some are vetoed by the president and die for lack of the two-thirds majority in both the House and Senate needed to override a veto. And only a very few ever become law.

Reporters who cover Congress hear the phrase "I'm introducing a bill to . . ." countless times in the course of an average month on the job. Often it is just a way for a representative or senator to draw attention to a pet issue, project, or concern, especially if the member is in the minority party. Reporters know that the party in the majority has immense influence when it comes to which bills will move and which won't. Bills introduced by the majority have a better chance of consideration than bills introduced by the minority. Bills introduced by a committee chair have a far better chance than bills introduced by rank-and-file members.

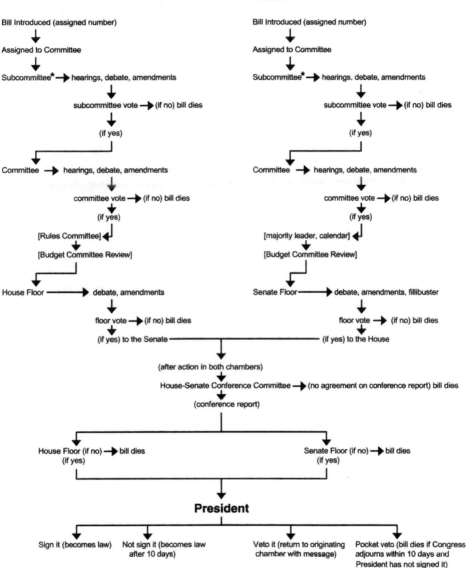

House

Bill Introduced (assigned number)
↓
Assigned to Committee
↓
Subcommittee* ➔ hearings, debate, amendments
                    ↓
            subcommittee vote ➔ (if no) bill dies
                    ↓
                (if yes)
                    ↓
Committee ➔ hearings, debate, amendments
                    ↓
            committee vote ➔ (if no) bill dies
                (if yes)
                    ↓
[Rules Committee]
↓
[Budget Committee Review]
↓
House Floor ────────➔ debate, amendments
                        ↓
                floor vote ➔ (if no) bill dies
                (if yes) to the Senate ──────────────

Senate

Bill Introduced (assigned number)
↓
Assigned to Committee
↓
Subcommittee* ➔ hearings, debate, amendments
                    ↓
            subcommittee vote ➔ (if no) bill dies
                    ↓
                (if yes)
                    ↓
Committee ➔ hearings, debate, amendments
                    ↓
            committee vote ➔ (if no) bill dies
                (if yes)
                    ↓
[majority leader, calendar]
↓
[Budget Committee Review]
↓
Senate Floor ────────➔ debate, amendments, fillibuster
                        ↓
                floor vote ➔ (if no) bill dies
                (if yes) to the House

(after action in both chambers)
↓
House-Senate Conference Committee ➔ (no agreement on conference report) bill dies
↓
(conference report)

House Floor (if no) ➔ bill dies   Senate Floor (if no) ➔ bill dies
(if yes)   (if yes)

President

Sign it (becomes law)   Not sign it (becomes law   Veto it (return to originating   Pocket veto (bill dies if Congress
                         after 10 days)   chamber with message)   adjourns within 10 days and
                                                                                       President has not signed it)

*occasionally the full committee acts without subcommittee action

Figure 2.1.   How a bill becomes a law.

Committees are the turbines that make the congressional machine function. Congressional committees are where the bulk of the work of Congress gets done, including legislation, oversight, and investigation. While there is a lot of talk about "floor debate" the fact is that much of what happens on the floor of the House or Senate is speech-making and posturing; the real debate, most of the fine tuning of legislation, takes place in committees and subcommittees. Committee and subcommittee chairs are picked by the leadership of the majority party, usually based on seniority.

Beyond their pivotal role in the lawmaking process, it is in the committees of the House and Senate that hearings are held on important issues of public concern. Witnesses are examined. Controversies are discussed at length. When a question of oversight (the authority of the Congress to review and examine the operations of the executive and judiciary branches) arises, that oversight is conducted by committees and subcommittees.

To outsiders the political structure of Congress sometimes seems unfair. For example, it is not unusual for a bill introduced by a minority senator or representative to die because the majority leadership refuses to assign it to a committee. Sometimes even though it is assigned to a committee, the chair (always a member of the majority party) will refuse to schedule hearings for it. It's not uncommon for a popular bill introduced by a minority member, a bill that enjoys enough bipartisan support to be voted out of committee, ultimately to be killed by the actions of the majority leadership. That can be done by not bringing it to the floor at all. Or if it does get on the calendar the majority leader may deliberately schedule it for floor action so late in the session that it dies because the clock runs out and Congress adjourns before there's a vote. There are also a host of procedural mechanisms that the majority leaders can use to derail legislation they don't like.

Even a bill that makes it all the way through the process in one chamber may die for any of the previously cited reasons when it gets to the other chamber. An example is President George W. Bush's economic stimulus package that sailed through the Republican-controlled House in 2001 but stalled in the Democratic-controlled Senate in 2002. A modified version that bore little resemblance to the original finally was approved and became law.

Nonetheless, once a bill has been introduced (in either the House or the Senate) the process begins. Formally, the introduction of a bill involves placing a written copy of the proposed legislation into a box called the hopper. With the exception of tax bills, which must originate in the House, a piece of legislation can start in either chamber.

Once in the hopper, the bill is assigned a number. (Numbers preceded by H.R. [House Resolution] mean House origination; bills beginning S.R. [Senate Resolution] mean Senate origination; and J.R. [Joint Resolution] means joint origination.)

After being numbered they go to the committee of jurisdiction, where the chair will turn it over to a subcommittee or determine that it should go to the full committee for hearings. For example, if a representative introduced a bill dealing with the Internet it would go to the House Commerce Committee and be assigned to the Telecommunications Subcommittee. Witnesses will be called to testify for and against the bill. If the measure affects a government agency or department, officials of that agency or department will be called to offer their analysis of the pending bill and its impact. (Occasionally a bill deals with a matter so important or urgent that the subcommittee will be circumvented and the process will go directly to the full committee.)

As a practical matter, members of Congress and their staffs know that one of the best ways to get a bill into committee and into the hearing process is to curry favor with the chair of the committee of jurisdiction. A bill the chair likes has a much better chance than one the chair does not like.

Once hearings are finished, the subcommittee will vote on the measure. If a majority of the subcommittee approves it then the bill goes to the full committee, where there may be more hearings. There will be a full committee vote on the bill and, if it passes by a majority, it will go to the floor of the House or Senate. The last step before a bill has its final committee vote is called mark-up, a process in which the committee goes through the bill word by word to perfect the language.

Bills are subject to amendment all through the process. Amendments can be attached in subcommittee, committee, or on the floor.

After mark-up and the final committee vote, the process varies slightly in the House and Senate. In the House, the bill makes a stop at the Rules Committee prior to floor action. This committee may place time limits on debate or limit the number of floor amendments. This is usually worked out in advance by the majority leadership and the chair of the House Rules Committee. The House Rules Committee action is often a rubber stamp of what the Speaker wants. In the Senate, the process of scheduling bills for floor action (placing them on the calendar) is in the hands of the Senate majority leader and his/her staff.

In addition, the budget committee of whichever chamber is considering the bill will look at the measure to see that it conforms with spending limits set for each fiscal year.

When a bill is passed by a majority on the floor of the House or Senate it is then sent to the other body, where it is again assigned to a committee. Full committee and/or subcommittee hearings will be held. Amendments may be added. And if the measure succeeds in winning a majority in the subcommittee and full committee it then goes to the floor for more debate, amendments, and a vote.

Unless the bill finally passed is identical (yes, word for word), it then goes to a House-Senate conference committee where differences will be resolved and one single version of the bill, called a conference report, will emerge. That conference report is then sent back to the House and Senate, starting in the chamber where the bill originated. The conference report will be voted on.

At this point, the conference report can be approved, rejected, or referred back to committee "with instructions." This is effectively telling the conference committee that its version is not acceptable and must be reworked.

Final passage occurs when the conference report is approved by the full House and Senate and it becomes an enrolled bill. That simply means that an identical measure has passed both chambers. But it is still not the law of the land. The measure must then go to the president. If the president signs the bill it becomes law. If the president sends the bill back to the chamber in which it originated within ten days stating his objections to it — the procedure outlined in Article I Section 7 of the Constitution — the bill has been vetoed. It must then be passed by two-thirds majorities in both chambers to override the President's veto and become law. (See section 2.5.)

Key Points

- A bill may be introduced in either the House or Senate, save for tax bills that must originate in the House.
- Once introduced, a bill is assigned to a committee of jurisdiction and usually passed to a subcommittee.

- The subcommittee holds hearings, engages in debate, considers amendments, and votes; subcommittee approval by majority vote sends the bill to the full committee.
- Approval by a majority vote of the full committee sends the bill to the floor.
- Approval by a majority vote on the floor sends the bill to the other chamber where it undergoes a similar process.
- Amendments may be attached at any point in the process in either chamber.
- If the two bills are not identical they go to a House-Senate Conference Committee to resolve the differences.
- The conference committee refers the identical version of the bill, called a conference report, back to the full House and Senate.
- When the conference report is passed by both chambers it then goes to the President.
- A bill is vetoed when the President sends it back to the originating chamber with a statement of his objections.
- It requires a two-thirds majority vote of both chambers to override a presidential veto.

2.5 Presidential Vetoes and Congressional Overrides

The fact that there is a role for both the legislative and executive branches of government in enacting laws is one of those Madisonian checks and balances. When Congress passes a bill, there are four possible presidential actions:

1. The president can sign it;
2. The president can let the bill become law without his signature;
3. The president can return it to the chamber where it originated, stating his objections, known as a veto;
4. If Congress adjourns before the measure is signed or vetoed, the president can let it die by not signing it, a condition known as a pocket veto.

If the president does not approve of a bill he must, within ten days (excluding Sundays), send it back to the chamber in which it originated. Merely rejecting a bill is not enough. A presidential veto requires both a formal return of the bill and a written explanation as to why he

TABLE 2.1.   **House and Senate Committees**

House Committee	Jurisdiction
Agriculture	Farming, livestock, dairy, nutrition, food inspection, oversight
Appropriations	Responsible for specific determination of where the government spends money; counterpart of Senate Appropriations Committee
Armed Services	Military affairs and policy, all services, military bases, weapons systems, manpower, procurement, oversight
Banking and Financial Services	Monetary policy, capital markets, securities, financial institutions, banking and securities crime, oversight and investigation
Budget	Projection of federal spending and revenues; counterpart of Senate Budget Committee
Commerce	Energy, power, telecommunication, trade, consumer protection, oversight and investigation
Economic and Education	Employer-employee relations, schools, worker training, oversight and investigation
Government Reform	Watchdog over government activities
House Oversight	Internal watchdog
International Relations	Foreign policy, international trade, oversight of the State Department
Judiciary	Crime, constitutional law, administrative law, courts, impeachment, anti-trust, oversight
Resources	Energy, natural resources, fisheries, wildlife, forestry, water, national parks, oversight
Rules	What gets to the floor, rules of debate, rules of procedure, oversight of House facilities and operations
Science	Research, environment, space, technology, oversight
Small Business	Regulatory reform, exports, government programs, rules and regulations, oversight
Standards of Official Conduct	House Ethics Committee
Transportation and Infrastructure	Aviation, maritime transport, highways, trucks, the auto industry, railroads, mass transit, oversight
Veterans Affairs	Benefits, health care and treatment of military veterans, oversight and investigation
Ways and Means	Tax writing committee where tax bills originate
Select Intelligence	CIA, NSA and other U.S. intelligence and counter-espionage activities, oversight

Senate Committee	Jurisdiction
Agriculture, Nutrition and Forestry	Farming, dairy, livestock, commodities production, conservation, rural policy, food inspection, oversight
Appropriations	Responsible for specific determination of where the government spends money; counterpart of the House Appropriations Committee
Armed Services	Military affairs and policy, all services, weapons, military bases, manpower, oversight and investigation
Banking, Housing and Urban Affairs	Financial institutions, securities, community development, securities and banking crime, cities, oversight and investigation
Budget	Oversight of projected government spending and anticipated revenues; counterpart of House Budget Committee
Commerce, Science and Technology	Telecommunications, aviation, technology, space, highways, manufacturing, census, oversight and investigation

TABLE 2.1.   (Continued)

Energy and Natural Resources	Energy research and production, public lands, water, power, oversight
Environment and Public Works	Pollution, nuclear safety, waste control, drinking water, EPA, oversight, no investigations
Finance	Taxation, Social Security, international trade, health care, fiscal and monetary policy; counterpart of House Ways and Means Committee
Foreign Relations	Foreign policy and international operations, State Department oversight, advice and consent on ambassadors and treaties
Governmental Affairs	Oversight of government and the District of Columbia
Indian Affairs	Native American policy, oversight
Judiciary	Advice and consent on confirmation of federal judges, crime, law enforcement, courts, oversight and investigation
Health, Education, Labor and Pensions	Employer-employee relations, schools, workplace safety, vocational training, public health, aging, children, oversight and investigation
Rules and Administration	What gets to the Senate floor, rules of debate, oversight of Senate facilities and operations
Select Committee on Ethics	Oversight of the conduct of senators
Select Committee on Intelligence	CIA, NSA, intelligence gathering and counter-espionage, oversight and investigation
Small Business	Economic and financial opportunity, rules and regulations, competition, oversight
Veterans Affairs	Health care, benefits and veteran's policy, oversight and investigation
Joint Committee	**Jurisdiction**
Joint Committee on the Library	Oversight of the Library of Congress
Joint Committee on Printing	Oversight of the Government Printing Office
Joint Committee on Taxation	A general policy body that holds hearings and makes recommendations but is not authorized to send bills to either chamber
Joint Economic Committee	A general policy body that holds hearings and makes recommendations but is not authorized to send bills to either chamber

objects, which is called a veto message. Both steps are specifically required by the Constitution.

A presidential veto is not absolute. It may be overridden or, in the flowery language of Congress, the bill may be approved "the objections of the president notwithstanding." A two-thirds majority of both chambers is required to override a presidential veto. When a vetoed measure is passed in both chambers by the requisite two-thirds majorities, it automatically becomes law. While every post–World War II president has had at least one veto overridden, it is an extremely difficult task to obtain a two-thirds majority in both the House and the

Senate. Presidents tend to win far more veto fights than they lose, and a presidential veto is a powerful tool in the legislative process and serves as an executive check over Congress.

A bill does not require the president's signature to become law, although historically this circumstance has been extremely rare. If the president neither signs the bill nor vetoes it as described in the Constitution, it becomes law anyway in ten days, unless the Congress adjourns within that ten day period, making it impossible to send the bill back with a veto message.

In the case of congressional adjournment, the president can let a measure die without a formal veto. This informal method of vetoing a bill is often called a pocket veto, so named for the image of a president or state governor simply receiving a bill from the legislative branch, tucking it into his pocket, and letting it die.

Key Points

- Four possible things can happen when a bill approved by Congress is sent to the president: he may sign it, veto it, not sign it and let it become law, or pocket veto it.
- If a president vetoes a bill it is returned to the same chamber in which it originated with a written message explaining the president's objections.
- The statement of the president's objections is known as a veto message and is a Constitutional requirement.
- It takes a two-thirds majority in both the House and Senate to override a presidential veto.
- The president must sign a bill, or veto it within ten days (not counting Sundays) when Congress is in session, or it becomes law anyway.
- If Congress adjourns within ten days of passing a bill and the president does not sign it, the bill dies; this is often referred to as a pocket veto.

2.6 The Authority of Congress

Although the power of Congress to enact laws is extremely broad, legal challenges to the authority of Congress fill hundreds of volumes. Ever since the decision in *Marbury v. Madison* the federal courts have played an active role in reviewing the actions of Congress. (See Chapter 4, section 4.2.)

One general area where congressional authority to legislate has been challenged frequently in the courts involves the commerce clause. Article I Section 8 provides for Congress to regulate interstate and international commerce. Such congressional regulation of commerce has been the subject of legal debate since the Constitution was signed. States argue that they have legitimate interests in regulating and even taxing interstate commercial activities that take place within their borders.

Generally, the courts have tended to side with Congress except in those rare cases in which it can be demonstrated that state interest supercedes the national interest. For example, federal courts upheld a few state laws that banned trucks with double tractor-trailers on the grounds that the state highways were too narrow and thus unsafe for such rigs. On the other hand the federal courts have uniformly rejected state taxes on products produced or grown in other states if there is no tax on similar products produced or grown within the state.

The courts have looked to whether the state laws in question place an undue burden on interstate or international commerce, whether state laws chill commerce to protect local business and economic ventures, and whether state laws promote local economic concerns ahead of broader national concerns, such as public health and safety.

In addition to the commerce clause, the courts have supported congressional legislative actions falling under the clause in Article I Section 8 that specifically provides for passage of any law that "shall be necessary and proper for carrying into execution" the powers enumerated in that section. State challenges to federal laws under the "necessary and proper" clause have not fared particularly well.

In the early 1800s, Congress set up a national bank. The state of Maryland decided that it would tax the bank. The issue went to the Supreme Court and in 1819 Chief Justice John Marshall wrote in *McColloch v. Maryland* that while a national bank was not specifically mentioned in the Constitution it fell within the "necessary and proper" wording. The Maryland state tax was declared unconstitutional.

The Constitution gives Congress the authority to declare war and names the president as commander-in-chief of the military. The overlap of functions has generated controversy since the Jefferson administration. (See Chapter 5, section 5.1.)

Key Points

- There have been many court challenges to the congressional authority to enact statutory laws.
- The commerce clause has generated enough challenges to fill legal volumes.
- States have an uphill battle in commerce cases as the federal courts have usually sided with Congress.
- The courts generally have looked to a test of whether the national interest outweighs the state interest in rendering their rulings.
- The courts have given Congress wide latitude when examining whether a law falls within the constitutional language allowing legislation which is "necessary and proper."

2.7 The Budget, Authorization, and Appropriation

Congress has the power of the purse, but government spending involves three key steps. First is the budget, which is a blueprint of estimated government revenues (how much money is coming in) and projected expenditures for a fiscal year. Second is authorization, a series of bills that specifically earmarks spending levels for all government branches, departments, agencies, and programs. And third is appropriation, which is the actual expenditure of federal dollars to pay for everything from salaries to submarines.

The modern budget ritual in Washington evolved after World War I, but draws on the intent of the framers of the Constitution to reserve the power of the purse to Congress. Foremost, the framers wanted the branch closest to the people, the Congress, to take the lead in collecting (see section 2.8) and spending tax dollars, but with checks and balances by the executive branch. The men who wrote the Constitution all had vivid memories of being ruled by the British monarchy with the powers to tax and spend vested, unchecked, in the hands of one person. Article I Section 9 states clearly: "No money shall be drawn from the Treasury, but in consequence of appropriations made by law."

Every year since 1921, when Congress passed the Budget and Accounting Act, the president has been required to submit an annual report to Congress projecting how much money the government will spend and how much revenue the government will collect in the coming fiscal year. The federal fiscal year runs from October 1 through September 30. The president's report is due fourteen days after Congress convenes each January. This is commonly known as the president's budget message.

Every year Congress receives the president's budget message and every year the document goes into the House and Senate Budget Committees, where it disappears and is replaced by the congressional version of how and where money should be spent and how much revenue will be collected.

The budget committees draft, debate, and vote out their own versions of a budget resolution. Those draft resolutions go to the two chambers where they are debated, amended, and voted on. Following those votes the House and Senate Budget Committees work together in a type of giant conference committee to produce a single document, called a concurrent budget resolution. The concurrent budget resolution anticipates how and where money should be authorized and appropriated in the coming fiscal year. It also estimates revenues, and when projected spending exceeds government income it will provide for the government to borrow money to cover the shortfall. It is important to remember that, since the concurrent budget resolution is not a law, it is only a blueprint that does not earmark (authorize) spending or draw money from the treasury (appropriate) for government use. Authorization and appropriation come later in the process.

To underscore the congressional power of the purse, the concurrent budget resolution does not require the president's signature. But neither does the resolution have the force of law. It is, in effect, only a recommendation that is usually changed substantially when the actual budgetary lawmaking begins. All authorization and appropriation bills go through the same process as every other piece of legislation, including the possibility of a presidential veto. (See section 2.4.)

Once the concurrent budget resolution has been passed, authorization begins. House and Senate committees vested with the power to earmark money by the rules of each chamber set funding levels needed for various departments, programs, and agencies. The legislative action of authorization sets the stage for the final phase of the budget process — appropriation — which actually codifies in law the number of dollars to be drawn from the treasury for the authorized expenditures.

It sounds nice and tidy, but more often than not the process that begins in January is still incomplete when the clock tolls midnight on September 30, and the federal fiscal year draws to a close. Technically, at that point, all programs, departments, and agencies that have not had funding appropriated for the new fiscal year run out of money.

Usually, Congress and the White House agree to stopgap measures known as continuing resolutions, which keep the programs, departments, and agencies that have run out of money temporarily funded until the appropriation process is complete. Continuing resolutions are usually enacted for a specific period of time (such as five business days). Frequently more than one continuing resolution is needed while the negotiations continue toward appropriating the funds to run all government agencies, departments, and programs.

Occasionally, congressional leaders or the president (almost always when they are in different political parties) have threatened to let the government shut down. Even less frequently they have allowed it to shut down for a few hours late at night or over a weekend to prove their point or to flex their political muscles. Reporters who cover Congress generally dismissed such brinkmanship as a bluff.

That all changed in 1995. The 104th Congress — fresh from the Republican landslide in the previous year's congressional elections which put the G.O.P. in the majority in both the House and Senate — and President Clinton, a Democrat, were stalemated over several appropriation bills. (About half of the appropriation bills had been passed and signed into law, but half were not.) Congress and the president could not agree on the bills and time was running out on several short-term continuing resolutions.

After two weeks of unsuccessful and often bitterly partisan negotiations, those government departments and agencies covered by the disputed appropriation bills were forced to close their doors. They included the departments of Labor, Health and Human Services, Housing and Urban Development, Veterans Affairs, Education, Commerce, Justice, the Environmental Protection Agency, and NASA, as well as national parks, monuments, and the Smithsonian museums. In all more than a quarter million non-essential federal workers — those deemed not critical to national security or public health and safety — were furloughed. The shutdown lasted from November 14 until November 20.

What started as a battle of wills between the Democratic president and the first Republican Congress in decades, turned into a nasty political fray in which each side blamed the other for the lack of agreement and the unprecedented government shutdown.

Public opinion polls showed increasing public anger and frustration. No new Medicare, Social Security, and veterans benefits applications were being processed. There was a likelihood that Social Security and other benefit checks would not be sent on time. Finally, legislation appropriating money was passed, the president signed it, and the crisis abated. Nonetheless, there was political fallout. President Clinton successfully used the government shutdown to tar his subsequent Republican opponent, Bob Dole — who had been Senate majority leader during the shutdown. Clinton waltzed to easy reelection in the 1996 election. In the same election the Republican majority in both the House and Senate diminished.

Since then, nobody in Congress or the White House has even whispered about shutting down the government as a result of an appropriation impasse. That doesn't mean it might not happen again.

Key Points

- Every January the president is required to send his budget to Congress.
- Congress makes changes to the president's budget and ultimately passes a concurrent budget resolution, a recommendation for spending in the next fiscal year.
- House and Senate committees then pass legislation authorizing the specific programs, departments and agencies on which federal money should be spent.
- Following authorization comes the process of appropriation, which provides money from the federal treasury for those authorized programs, departments and agencies.
- The federal fiscal year extends from October 1 to September 30.
- If Congress has not finished its appropriation work by October 1, Congress and the White House usually agree to continuing resolutions to provide temporary funding until the appropriations laws are passed and signed by the president.

2.8 Taxes

Most people don't particularly like paying taxes, but taxation is an absolute necessity for the successful function of government. The founding fathers knew that in devising the framework of the new nation's government, provision must be made for the money to operate it. Article I Section 8 expressly delivers the responsibility to Congress to "lay and collect taxes."

Colonial anger over "taxation without representation" was one of the bedrock issues that spawned the American Revolution. England's King George III levied a duty on tea, and almost everything else, in the colonies in the form of a unilateral declaration called "The Stamp Act." To many of the colonists that was the final insult they would suffer from a government an ocean away. The memories of that prerevolutionary anger were fresh when the framers addressed it in the new nation's Constitution. They codified the requirement that all tax bills must originate in the House of Representatives, the only institution of government at the time directly elected by the people. As a result, taxation would originate in the body closest and most immediately responsible to the citizenry.

Initially, the government raised most of its money from tariffs on imports and exports, usage fees, excise taxes (levies on specific commodities), and limited sales and property taxes. Not until 1913, when the Sixteenth Amendment became part of the Constitution, did Congress have the authority to tax personal or business income.

The committee of jurisdiction in the house for all tax bills is the House Ways and Means Committee, traditionally one of the most powerful committees in Congress. The Senate Finance Committee deals with tax matters in that body and is usually considered a fraction less powerful than House Ways and Means.

Tax bills work their way through the House and Senate in the same manner as any other legislation, with amendments possible anywhere along the way. Assuming approval at every step, which as a practical matter seldom happens, movement of a tax bill goes from a Ways and Means subcommittee to the full committee, to the House, to a Senate Finance subcommittee, to the full committee, to the Senate, to a House-Senate conference committee, and on to the president. The chair of the House Ways and Means Committee is usually the chair of the conference committee impaneled to work out the differences in versions of a revenue package.

As with any other bill, the final language passed by the House and Senate must be identical. Any tax bill can be vetoed by the president and requires a two-thirds majority in both the House and Senate to override.

While tax rates have gone up and down over the years, Congress has raised taxes more often than it has lowered them. Nonetheless, tax rates were reduced dramatically under President Ronald Reagan, and in 2001 Congress took the unusual step of both reducing taxes and giving taxpayers a refund, fulfilling a campaign pledge of President George W. Bush.

One historical footnote: Congress has jealously guarded its power of the purse, the power to raise revenues and spend money. President Franklin D. Roosevelt was the first president to veto a tax bill and, even though Congress was controlled by his own Democratic party, the veto was quickly overridden.

Key Points

- All tax bills must originate in the House of Representatives.
- The powerful House Ways and Means Committee is the first committee of jurisdiction in tax matters.
- The Senate Finance Committee deals with tax bills in that body.
- Movement of tax bills is the same as any other bill, with amendments possible at any step in the process.
- As with other bills, tax measures can be vetoed and require a two-thirds majority in the House and Senate to override a presidential veto.
- The federal income tax did not become part of the Constitution until 1913 when the Sixteenth Amendment was ratified.

2.9 Other Congressional Functions

Aside from the power of the purse and the power to enact laws, Congress is charged with other responsibilities all connected with insuring domestic tranquility, providing for the common defense, and promoting the general welfare of the nation. Some of those duties are specifically required by the Constitution, for example: keeping a journal of the proceedings of the House and Senate so citizens may know what's going on in their national legislature; setting up courts below the level of the Supreme Court (see Chapter 4, section 4.3); establishing a post office; coining and minting money; declaring war (see Chapter 5, section 5.1); and impeachment (see Chapter 5, section 5.2).

The Senate's responsibility to provide advice and consent in presidential nominations and approval of international treaties is firmly enshrined in Article II Section 2. The president "shall have power, by and with the advice and consent of the Senate to make treaties, provided two-thirds of the senators present concur; and he shall nominate, and by and with the advice and consent of the Senate, shall appoint ambassadors, other public ministers and consuls, judges of the Supreme Court, and all other officers of the United States."

Historically, presidents have been scrupulous in seeking Senate consent. They have been less diligent in seeking or accepting senatorial advice.

The Constitution also sets out a procedure for impeachment involving both the House and Senate (see Chapter 5, section 5.2).

While the words "oversight" and "investigation" do not appear in the Constitution, they have taken on a critical role in the House and Senate. Oversight generally involves congressional inquiry into the administration and functions of executive agencies and departments and has a governmental connotation. Congressional investigations are not limited to actions of the government and can encompass almost any public issue or controversy. Recent investigations have included the tobacco industry, Internet pornography, campaign finance reform, and whether the government of Switzerland secretly collaborated with Nazi Germany during World War II. In some cases the committee action involves both oversight and investigation simultaneously.

Oversight and investigation responsibility is usually delegated to the committee with jurisdiction over the subject matter in the House and Senate. For example, hearings on irregularities in FBI investigative procedures were held separately by both the Senate and House Judiciary Committees. Abuses in the federal food stamp program (a program of the Department of Agriculture) was handled by the House Agriculture Committee and the Senate Committee on Agriculture, Nutrition, and Forestry.

Congress has routinely and vigorously exercised its oversight and investigative functions since the early 1970s. Before that Congress had at best a spotty record on oversight and investigation. After the Communist witch-hunts of the early 1950s involving Republican Sen. Joseph McCarthy of Wisconsin and, on the other side of the Capitol, the House Un-American Activities Committee, Congress ventured into oversight and investigation only tentatively for nearly two decades. When the Watergate scandal erupted as the result of a 1972 break-in at Democratic National Headquarters in Washington, Congress investigated. That investigation led to the start of impeachment hearings against President Richard Nixon and ultimately, in 1974, Nixon's resignation.

In the aftermath of the Challenger disaster, both the House and Senate held hearings to investigate what happened and to oversee the practices of the space agency, NASA. During the savings and loan crisis of the 1990s, Congress moved to investigate. When President Clinton summarily fired the White House Travel Office staff in 1993, House and Senate committees quickly held hearings involving both oversight and investigation.

Occasionally, there are complaints that a congressional investigation has overstepped its proper role. Some members of Congress have expressed concern about the potential legal conflict created when congressional committees and criminal investigators explore the same case.

In 1987, Congress launched an investigation into whether the Reagan Administration gave help to a group of anti-government rebels in Nicaragua, called the Contras. Such help to the Contras would be in violation of a statutory law, known as the Boland Amendment, which prohibited such aid. During its investigation Congress granted limited immunity from future prosecution to a young Marine lieutenant colonel named Oliver North who had worked for President Reagan's National Security Council. The condition for the grant of immunity was that his testimony before Congress could not be used against him in any future criminal case.

North was subsequently indicted for, among other things, lying to Congress and went on trial in 1990. He was convicted by a federal jury, but appealed the conviction on the grounds that his immunized testimony before Congress had, in fact, been used against him at trial. The Court of Appeals agreed and threw out the conviction. The debate continues over whether Congress should have acted less aggressively in its investigative capacity in favor of not thwarting the legal process.

Another controversy about the propriety of a congressional investigation arose after the presidential election in 2000. On election night, the national TV networks and major news organizations embarrassingly and wrongly called and retracted the election results in several states. Florida's results were called and retracted twice.

Shortly after it convened in January 2001, Congress summoned major news executives to testify about the coverage of election night events. Louis Boccardi, president of the Associated Press, challenged the right of Congress to hold the hearings at all. In his opening statement before the House Energy and Commerce Committee, Boccardi said, "We believe that such an official government inquiry into essentially editorial matters is inconsistent with the First Amendment."

While he and other news executives thought the House committee had overstepped its bounds, nobody suggested a court challenge to the hearings. If they had proceeded to challenge the right of the committee to hold hearings, their case likely would have been rejected out of hand. The courts have steadfastly refused to diminish, dilute, or even venture into any area that would conflict with the constitutional authority of Congress to make its own rules. Among those rules is a broad authority to investigate matters of public concern.

Key Points

- In addition to passing laws, Congress is constitutionally charged with keeping a journal of its proceedings, establishing courts inferior to the Supreme Court, coining and minting money, and establishing the post office.
- While not specifically delineated in the Constitution, oversight of executive agencies and departments and investigating issues of public concern are key congressional functions.
- Congress is also charged with declaring war (see Chapter 5.1) and conducting impeachment proceedings (see Chapter 5.2).

2.10 Limits on Congress and Members

Despite the broad scope of the Congress, its power is not limitless. Article I Section 9 places specific restrictions on what Congress may do. Congress is prohibited from taxing or putting a duty on exports from one state to another. Congress may not take money from the U.S. treasury without first passing a law authorizing it to do so (see section 2.7). Congress is required to publish a record of revenue and expenditure on a regular basis.

Congress is forbidden from enacting *ex post facto* laws, those that are passed after the fact and change the legal consequences. For example making something illegal that was once legal and imposing punishment for those who committed the act while it was, in fact, legal is an *ex post facto* law.

Congress is also expressly prohibited from granting titles of nobility.

Beyond the specific language of Article I Section 9, Congress is also prohibited from interfering with or legislating with regard to the constitutional duties and powers vested in the president or the Supreme Court.

In addition to constitutional limits, congressional rules place other restrictions on members. Both the House and Senate have strict rules regarding outside income, gifts, and financial disclosure. The two sets of rules are not identical, but both chambers prohibit members from accepting salaries or commissions from private corporations or institutions, speaking fees, or appearance fees. Members may receive book royalties, but only with the approval of the ethics committees. Members may not accept gifts other than those valued at less than fifty dollars — including tangible goods, trips, meals, vacations, and entertainment tickets. All members of Congress are required to file annual financial disclosure forms detailing their assets, such as stocks, bonds, securities, trusts, real estate, other real property, and corporate interests.

Violation of these rules constitutes an ethics violation and can result in sanctions, including reprimand (a mild rebuke), censure (a public humiliation carried out in the chamber of the member involved with the member made to face his/her colleagues during the ordeal), and expulsion from Congress. Both chambers have committees to deal with misconduct on the part of members. In the Senate it is the Select Committee on Ethics and in the House it is the Committee on Standards of Official Conduct. Most of the work of the ethics committees is done in private, but occasionally an ethics case becomes public.

One of the most notable recent cases involved former Democratic Speaker of the House Jim Wright of Texas. He resigned in 1991 amid charges he was given large speaking fees, in violation of House ethics rules, for what he claimed were promotional appearances for a book he wrote. His chief accuser, later Republican Speaker of the House Newt Gingrich of Georgia, alleged Wright would give speeches to corporate or lobbying groups. The groups would buy cases and cases of Wright's book, in effect delivering speaking fees in the form of royalties, a maneuver to get around House ethics rules. Two years later Gingrich would face his own ethics violation charges, also involving a book, royalties, and expenses for promotional appearances.

Key Points

- The actions of Congress and its members are not without restriction.
- The Constitution prohibits Congress from taxing what states export to other states, getting treasury dollars without passing a law, or conferring any title of nobility.
- Congress is also restricted from interfering in the constitutional functions of the other branches of government.
- Ethics rules, including financial disclosure requirements and limits on gifts and outside income, place restrictions on members of Congress.
- The House and the Senate each have a committee on ethics to deal with allegations of member misconduct.

2.11 House and Senate Rules

The Constitution specifically allows the House and Senate, individually, to make and enforce their own rules of procedure and conduct for members. Neither the courts nor the executive branch have ever tried to interfere with congressional rules and rule-making. Both chambers have standing committees on rules.

The House and Senate are highly formal in the way that they conduct business. The rules of both prohibit members from addressing each other directly during floor action. Usually members address each other through the presiding officer, always called Mr. or Madam Speaker or Mr. or Madam President.

Virtually every word spoken on the floor of the House or Senate is preserved for posterity in the Congressional Record. The Congressional Record is not a constitutional requirement but has been a tradition since the early 1800s. The Constitution only requires each chamber to produce a journal from time to time. The Congressional Record is published daily, with annual editions bound and indexed. Reporters looking for information about what went on during a specific debate find the Congressional Record an excellent place to start the search.

In the House, members often seek permission, usually in the form of a unanimous consent resolution (see Chapter 2.12) to "revise and extend" their remarks. That means that under the rules of the House what a member says on the floor may be changed, altered, edited, and/or elongated in the Congressional Record. As a result the Congressional Record's version of what was said may not be what was actually said.

Both the House and Senate provide rules for a colloquy, but this procedural ritual bears no resemblance to a conversation or discourse. Under House and Senate rules a colloquy allows one member to ask another a question or a series of questions on a given issue usually in a highly scripted form. ("Would the senator explain . . ." or "Does the amendment proposed by the gentlewoman from Florida intend . . .") A colloquy is generally used to clarify a certain point in a piece of legislation for inclusion in the Congressional Record.

Congresses are numbered. For example, the 100th Congress convened in 1987. Each Congress consists of two sessions. The first session of a new Congress convenes on the first Tuesday in January of odd numbered years, the second session begins in even numbered years. (The Twentieth Amendment specifies January 3 as the first meeting day of Congress, but provides for Congress to change that by law.)

The Constitution, Article I Section 5, provides that neither chamber can adjourn for more than three days without the consent of the other. That is usually done as a matter of courtesy and custom, but has occasionally (usually when the two chambers are controlled by different political parties) required one or the other chamber to hold *pro forma* sessions during a recess. That usually means the chamber is called to order and immediately adjourned without any business being conducted.

Section 6 gives representatives and senators what is generally called a congressional privilege. That means that apart from serious crimes, treason or breaching of the peace, they can't be arrested (for such things as speeding) while they're doing their official duties. The congressional privilege is in effect when Congress is in session or when members are on their way to or from a congressional session. They are also immune from such civil laws as libel and slander for anything they might say on the floor of the House or Senate. (The rules of each body prohibit personal or physical attacks against other members.)

Key Points

- The Constitution expressly authorizes each chamber of Congress to make its own rules.
- The rules of Congress require a significant amount of ritual and formality, including a prohibition on members addressing each other directly on the floor of either chamber.
- Every word spoken on the floor of the House and Senate is recorded in the Congressional Record.
- Congresses are numbered, with each congressional session lasting one year, with each Congress having two sessions.
- A new Congress begins on the day in January when Congress first meets in odd numbered years.
- Members of Congress are immunized against arrest for other than felonies, treason or breach of the peace while they are performing their official duties or on their way to or from a congressional session.

2.12 Practices and Procedures of Congress

Both chambers of Congress conduct virtually all of their floor debate and votes in public. The sessions of both chambers are televised nationally on C-SPAN I and C-SPAN II, the cable television networks created specifically to carry the proceedings of Congress.

The House and Senate each have provisions for voice votes in which the yeas and nays are called out aloud, each side vocalizing in unison, and with the presiding officer determining which side won, usually based on volume. As a result, in most cases beyond minor matters, recorded votes are demanded. There is no proxy or absentee voting in either chamber. Members must be present to cast votes.

In the House, recorded votes are taken by an electronic voting device, utilizing voting cards that look very much like credit cards. How representatives vote is illuminated on a giant electronic tote board high above the Speaker's chair. The electronic tally is also available to the clerk in the form of a printout.

The Senate is a little more old-fashioned. Recorded votes in the Senate require the clerk to call the roll of the senators. Each senator must physically go to the well of the Senate chamber and cast his/her vote aloud.

Despite the greater number of members, the House generally operates in a much more streamlined manner than the Senate. The House Rules Committee almost always sets finite limits on floor debate for most bills and resolutions. The number of amendments members are allowed to offer from the floor is also usually limited. Time limits for debate and amendments are set by the Rules Committee before a bill goes to the House floor. (A fairly common example would be a bill limited to two hours of floor debate, always equally divided between supporters and opponents, with four amendments, limited to fifteen minutes of debate each, equally divided between supporters and opponents.)

The process of bringing a bill to the floor of the House always starts with what is called a "vote on the rule." In theory, that is the point at which members dissatisfied with the limitations on debate time and the number of amendments allowed could change the rule or send it back to the Rules Committee for modification. The reality is that the majority party in the House controls the Rules Committee and with very few exceptions the "rule" that's sent to the floor passes with ease. In those rare cases where a rule is defeated or returned to committee reporters should start looking for fractiousness or even open rebellion within the ranks of the majority party.

The Senate, on the other hand, considers itself the world's greatest deliberative body, and works its way through legislation very slowly. Senate rules provide for time limits on debate only in the case of budget resolutions. Otherwise a bill can be on the floor of the Senate for weeks, sometimes with a hundred or more amendments.

If one word, unique to the lexicon of Congress, has entered the national vocabulary it is "filibuster." Filibuster derives from a rule of the U.S. Senate that allows any senator to speak for as long as he/she wishes on a piece of legislation. It is a delaying mechanism aimed at killing a particular piece of legislation or blocking a presidential nomination. Originally both the House and Senate could engage in filibuster, but the House changed its rules to prevent the legislative logjam that inevitably would accompany unlimited debate in a body that large.

Until 1917 the Senate had no mechanism for ending a filibuster or cutting off debate at all, although several suggestions for changes in

Senate rules had been made as early as the 1840s. In 1917 the Senate adopted a rule called "cloture" that allowed debate to be closed. Modern cloture requires an affirmative vote of three-fifths of the Senate, or sixty votes, to end debate and bring a matter, itself, to a vote.

Historically filibusters were used only on a limited basis. In the 1930s, Louisiana Democrat Huey Long once held the floor for fifteen hours reading Shakespeare, the Bible, and the telephone book in an effort to talk a bill to death. The record for the longest filibuster is held by Sen. Strom Thurmond of South Carolina (once a Democrat who became a Republican). Thurmond talked for just over twenty-four hours in an effort to kill the Civil Rights Act of 1957.

It was not until the mid–1980s that the filibuster became an ordinary instrument of legislative strategy in the Senate. In the late–1980s and 1990s filibusters became so common that when most newspeople started counting noses to see if a particular bill or amendment would pass in the Senate, they looked for the magic number of sixty, the number needed to invoke cloture. The practical effect of the modern filibuster is to require a super-majority, not just fifty-one votes, in the Senate to pass almost any bill.

In both the Senate and the House, there is a common expediting procedure known as unanimous consent. Unanimous consent allows for such things as approval of a temporary presiding officer or approval of the journal of the previous day's proceedings without a formal roll call or electronic vote. In the House and Senate the language is virtually identical. In the House an example might be:

MEMBER: Mr. Speaker I ask unanimous consent that the House stand adjourned until the hour of 12 o'clock noon, tomorrow, and that following approval of today's journal there be a period of morning business of thirty minutes, equally divided, and that members be allowed to speak for a period of up to one minute therein.

SPEAKER: Objection? No objection. So ordered.

A unanimous consent request can be derailed by the objection of just one member. In that case, a vote of the full chamber is required, a roll call in the Senate and a vote by electronic device in the House.

Key Points

- A voice vote is the collective calling-out of first the yeas and then the nays by members, with the presiding officer determining the outcome based on volume.
- A recorded vote in the House is taken by an electronic voting device.
- A recorded vote in the Senate is a roll call in which each senator votes aloud and the vote is recorded by the clerk.
- There is no proxy or absentee voting and in order to vote senators and representatives must be present in their respective chambers.
- In the House, rules are usually set by the Rules Committee to limit the amount of time allotted to debate on any single bill and to limit the number of amendments permitted from the floor.
- The Senate has a historic tradition of not limiting debate, and thus takes much longer to pass a bill than the House.
- A filibuster is a procedure unique to the Senate allowing unlimited debate, usually used when a senator or group of senators wants to kill a bill by talking it to death.
- Cloture is the Senate rule requiring a three-fifths vote (sixty senators) to cut off debate and end a filibuster.
- Unanimous consent is a procedural action allowing routine matters to be decided as long as no member voices objection.

2.13 Notes for Reporters Covering Congress

Virtually all Washington reporters working for legitimate news organizations, as well as freelancers who obtain a letter of sponsorship from a legitimate news organization, may get Capitol Hill credentials. (A Capitol Hill pass also allows a reporter to enter and cover the Supreme Court, which is across the street from the Capitol.) Over the years security has been tightened periodically and background checks for reporters have become more rigorous. The procedure was stiffened in the wake of the Oklahoma City bombing, following the terrorist attacks of September 11, 2001, and once again in 2001 after anthrax was found in the office of Senate Majority Leader Tom Daschle of South Dakota and Democratic Sen. Patrick Leahy of Vermont.

Congress exercises its constitutional right to set the rules for news coverage on Capitol Hill, but has been careful not to encroach on the

First Amendment by acting as the credentialing authority. That authority is vested in committees of gallery members (reporters, producers, photographers and the like). The news galleries on Capitol Hill include the House Press Gallery, House Radio and TV Gallery, Senate Press Gallery, Senate Radio and TV Gallery, and the Press Photographers' Gallery.

Visiting reporters and photographers may obtain temporary credentials by contacting the appropriate gallery in advance.

Covering Capitol Hill is like covering a small city. The physical area is thirty-five city blocks square and includes the Capitol building itself, the House and Senate office buildings and annexes, the Library of Congress, and the Supreme Court building. It has its own police force.

The "House side" of Capitol Hill is everything south of the center point in the Capitol rotunda; the "Senate side" is everything to the north.

Without a special parking pass, parking on Capitol Hill for anybody is impossible. Most reporters, photographers, and camera crews that do not have parking passes usually take a taxi or the Metro (Washington's subway).

Even those with parking passes are subjected to rigid security measures imposed after the September 11, 2001, terrorist attacks on the United States. Drivers are required to open their trunks or the backs of their SUVs or vans. The undercarriage of each vehicle is inspected with mirrors attached to long poles. Occasionally dogs trained to detect explosives are used to inspect vehicles.

Inside the Capitol complex, reporters must know the rules or risk running afoul of the Capitol police. Reporters with pad and pencil can go almost anywhere and approach members or staffers. The use of cameras and audio recorders is limited. No cameras or recorders are allowed in the House or Senate chambers, although all proceedings of the House and Senate are available for broadcast or recording from C-SPAN or the internal congressional cable system. The only time outside cameras are allowed on the floor of either chamber is for national telecasts of important joint sessions of Congress (which take place in the House Chamber) such as the president's annual State of the Union Address.

It has been a longstanding tradition in the U.S. Congress that most House and Senate committee hearings are open to the news media and the public. This tradition was codified into law in the 1970s, in the post–Watergate period, when Congress enacted a federal sunshine law (also known as an open meeting law). Today, all fifty states along with the federal government have sunshine laws (see Chapter 8, section 8.10).

In most congressional hearings, audio and video coverage is permitted. In order to prevent a jungle of microphones in front of members or witnesses, news microphones are not permitted to be placed in hearing rooms. Instead recording devices, including the audio for TV cameras, must be plugged into fixtures containing an array of audio plugs, called mult boxes. Most hearing rooms are equipped with mult boxes providing access to the room's own sound system.

News conferences are uniformly open to camera and audio coverage. In addition, cameras and microphones can be used in any of the studios of the House and Senate radio and TV galleries.

Cameras and microphones may not be used in the halls of the Capitol or the various office buildings unless stakeout permission has been obtained from a representative or senator, or unless a representative or senator has specifically granted an interview in a location outside his or her office. The majority of interviews with members of Congress are done in their offices and are usually set up through their press secretaries. (Occasionally, a reporter, photographer or camera crew from a member's home state or district will be allowed to follow the member around. This must be set up in advance and the member's staff will notify the Capitol police. Even then, no coverage is allowed on the floor of the House or Senate or in any of the cloakrooms — two private rooms just off the floors of both chambers reserved for Republican members on one side and Democrats on the other.)

Hand-held cameras and microphones can be used in most locations on the Capitol grounds, but tripods and microphone stands may be set up only in specifically designated locations.

These rules are not permanent and irrevocable; they may be changed (and have been from time to time) by the Rules Committees of the House and Senate.

In addition reporters should be aware of four congressional support offices that are non-partisan and can be extremely useful. The Government Printing Office, for example, prints virtually every official document of the U.S. government and will sell and ship copies. Some of the documents are not cheap, but many are worth the expense in order to have original material at hand. Some, but not all, GPO material is available on the web.

The Congressional Research Service was originally for the exclusive use of members of Congress and their staffs, but the CRS web site can be extremely useful. When working on economic or budget stories, the Congressional Budget Office and the General Accounting Office can be extremely useful (see Table 2.2).

Key Points

- Reporters, photographers and camera crews wishing to work on Capitol Hill must obtain credentials.
- There are strict rules with regard to where cameras and microphones may be used in the Capitol building and on the Capitol grounds.
- Members of Congress may grant interviews almost anywhere they wish.
- Floor action in both the House and Senate is almost always open to news coverage, but audio and video recording must be taken from C-SPAN or the internal Capitol cable system.
- Congressional support offices can be extremely useful to reporters searching for documents.

2.14 Lobbyists and Lobbying

The Constitution does not mention lobbyists or lobbying, although the concept and practice were well known before 1787. Even in the royal courts of Europe, people would attempt to influence lawmaking by trying to get close to the various courtiers who had the ear of the monarch. Valuable gifts and even cash were often provided in exchange for the courtiers' influence.

The practice continued in colonial legislatures, and took no time at all to gain a foothold in the new Congress. Lobbyists were allowed virtually everywhere, except on the House and Senate floors. When the new House chamber, the one in use today, was added to the U.S. Capitol, a huge, airy room with a balcony facing Independence Avenue was constructed immediately behind the House chamber. It is known as the Speaker's Lobby and for years it was the preferred hangout for lobbyists waiting to buttonhole representatives as they came off the House floor. The Speaker's Lobby has since been closed to lobbyists and is now open only to members, top staff, and credentialed journalists.

TABLE 2.2.   **Congressional Support Offices**

Congressional Budget Office FHOB (House Annex 2), Room 413 2nd and D Sts., SW Washington, DC 20515 phone: 202-226-2600 web site www.cbo.gov	Analyzes the federal budget and provides information to Congress about all federal departments, agencies, and programs.
Congressional Research Service 101 Independence Ave., SE Washington, DC 20540 phone: 202-707-5700	An arm of the Library of Congress. Provides research to members and their staffs.
General Accounting Office GAO Bldg., 441 G St., NW Washington, DC 20548 phone: 202-512-3000	Investigates the executive branch and its agencies and programs at the request of members of Congress. (Not all reports are made public. Check GPO web site, below.)
Government Printing Office 732 North Capitol St. Washington, DC 20402 phone: 202-512-0000 web site www.access.gpo.gov	Prints virtually all public documents of the U.S. Government. (There are GPO bookstores in major cities around the country.)

The majority of lobbying in Washington involves the legislative branch and attempts to influence virtually every piece of legislation considered. But that is not to suggest that countless hours and dollars are not spent by lobbyists attempting to influence the executive branch, especially the federal regulatory agencies.

Anybody may act as a lobbyist, except federal judges and top elected and appointed officials of the executive and legislative branches of government. All lobbyists working on Capitol Hill must register with the clerk of the House or the secretary of the Senate and obtain a lobbyist's credential to work in the Capitol.

The old European lobbyist's practice of gift-giving in exchange for legislative action extended to outright bribery in the U.S. Congress in the mid–1800s. There are examples of members receiving bags of cash or packages of gold in exchange for their votes. Over the years lobbyists have attempted to sway the votes of senators and representatives with everything including cash gifts, lavish junkets, family vacations, expensive meals, large campaign contributions, and promises of employment when a person leaves Congress. Lobbying and political corruption have been kindred spirits despite the efforts of a few crusading journalists and the rise of public interest lobbying organizations which work against corporate influence.

In 1876 Congress enacted the first of a long series of lobbying regulations aimed at identifying lobbyists and limiting their excesses. In 1936 Congress required maritime lobbyists to register with the Commerce Department before attempting to influence legislation. In 1938 Congress required anyone lobbying for a foreign government to register with the Justice Department. In the ensuing years, Congress has required lobbyists to obtain credentials to work inside the Capitol and limited the amount and nature of gifts lobbyists may give.

Lobbyists claim that their work is constitutionally protected and Congress has not disagreed. In attempting to regulate lobbying practices and the lobbyists themselves, Congress has taken pains not to tread on the First Amendment protection of the "right to petition the government for redress of grievances."

Today lobbying is one of the major industries of Washington, D.C., although many lobbyists prefer such euphemistic titles as "legislative consultant." Lobbying firms abound and some huge and prestigious law firms are devoted to the fine art of lobbying. Modern lobbyists bristle at the old image of a nefarious character slipping in and out of congressional offices with expensive gifts and suitcases full of cash.

They do not deny that some lobbyists are extremely well paid. During the 1992 presidential campaign Independent candidate H. Ross Perot labeled the portion of K Street in Washington where many lobbying firms are located as "Gucci Gulch," after the expensive Italian shoes favored by many lobbyists. The most highly paid lobbyists ply their trade on behalf of some of the country's biggest corporate interests. But other lobbyists work for organized labor, social and political interest groups, and even foreign governments.

Lobbyists are often on different sides of an issue and it is not uncommon for a senator or representative to meet over breakfast with a lobbyist for one position on a bill and at lunch with another lobbyist with an opposite position on the same bill.

By definition a lobbyist is a person hired by corporations, groups, organizations, and the like to influence legislation and/or executive rule-making. Members of Congress, congressional staff members, officers of the House and Senate, and top executive branch officials may not serve as lobbyists while they are in the employ of the U.S. government. Rules governing senior executive branch employees impose specific time limits on how long a person must be out of government before they may engage in lobbying activities. The time limit varies depending on the level at which the individual served.

Some scholars, analysts, and newspeople argue that the most powerful lobbyist in Washington is the president. The White House has an office of legislative affairs to influence legislation on behalf of the president. Even though this is arguably lobbying, in a general sense, it does not fall within the legal definition of lobbying as defined in Title 2 of the United States Code.

The actual level of influence lobbyists exert is open to argument. Journalist Jeffrey Birnbaum, in his 1993 book *The Lobbyists*, asserts that lobbyists, especially those working for corporate and business interests, have enormous clout in official Washington and often manage to affect subtle changes in legislation. Others suggest that the real power of the lobbyists is exaggerated, because of their sheer numbers and the fact that they are often working against each other, which tends to have a neutralizing effect on their overall influence.

Lobbyists seldom manage to put their imprint on an entire bill or act, but they are often highly effective in causing minor alterations that can have tremendous financial and policy consequences for their clients. Changing so much as a single word in an amendment can result in millions of dollars for one corporate interest or another. A nuance or slight alteration can amount to a huge success for a labor union or interest group. These are measurable successes for lobbyists.

Less measurable are the results that accrue for a corporation, interest group, or labor union from access to lawmakers by their lobbyists. For some clients it is a success if their lobbyist manages to get a personal meeting with a senator or representative simply to plead the client's case. Failure for a lobbyist is to be ignored. One frustrated lobbyist during the extended debate over the 1996 Telecommunications Act lamented over a cup of coffee that she'd had a terrible day. "Only two senators returned my phone calls," she said.

A controversial practice that has gone on for a long time, but which has drawn a great deal of publicity in the last two decades, is what has come to be known as the legislative revolving door. Former members of Congress (both those who retire and those who are defeated for reelection), along with top congressional aides, frequently leave government only to go to work for one of Washington's many big lobbying organizations. They invariably make more money than they did in government and they are in effect hired because of their contacts.

Washington lobbyists will tell you privately that the size of their paycheck is in direct proportion to the size of their Rolodex, the number of members of Congress who know them on a first name basis, and how quickly they get their phone calls returned. A former member of Congress is on a first-name basis with all of his/her former colleagues, knows many of their individual peccadillos, and has everybody's unlisted phone number.

Average citizens simply cannot compete with a giant corporation or labor union when it comes to gaining access to members of Congress. Unless the citizen happens to be a big campaign contributor, a letter to a representative or senator will probably never be read by the addressee. A phone call will probably be channeled to an aide, sometimes as low-level an aide as a part-time, unpaid student intern.

While much of the bribery and personal gift-giving that dominated lobbying in bygone days no longer happens, money still plays a critical role, and even then the amount given by individuals seldom rises to the level of that contributed by corporations, interest groups, and unions. For the most part it is unregulated "soft money," campaign contributions to political parties or organizations that can help a candidate with such things as producing issue ads or buying television time. An individual may give a few dollars or even a few hundred; some of these corporate interests give tens of thousands. And their lobbyists make that known to the politicians they seek to influence.

Reporters should be aware that the issue of campaign finance reform, especially limitations on soft money donations, is devoutly opposed by most corporate and interest group lobbyists. Placing limits on soft money contributions would constrain the clout of some of Washington's top lobbyists. Republican Sen. John McCain of Arizona and Democratic Sen. Russ Feingold of Wisconsin worked unsuccessfully for years on a bill to reform campaign financing, particularly soft money contributions, and high-powered lobbyists did all that they could to drive a stake through its heart.

The unlikely catalyst for action on campaign finance reform legislation came on December 2, 2001, with the collapse of the energy giant, Enron Corporation — which gave tens of millions of dollars in soft money campaign contributions to both political parties. Enron's access to key politicians was substantial and each revelation about the circumstances of Enron's bankruptcy proved increasingly embarrassing for the politicians who accepted Enron's money.

Among the allegations: Enron illegally shredded pertinent financial documents after an investigation of the bankruptcy was announced. Top corporate executives allegedly used their inside knowledge of the company's financial troubles and sold their company stock reaping windfall profits, while employees were prohibited from selling their stock and watched their retirement accounts dwindle as the price of Enron stock plunged from more than seventy dollars per share to less than a dollar per share. Enron's auditor, the accounting firm Arthur Andersen, was also a consultant to Enron and provided advice on how to hide millions of dollars in losses in offshore partnerships.

More than half of the members of the eleven congressional committees that launched investigations of Enron had taken contributions from the company or from Arthur Andersen. Many raced to give the money back or donate it to Enron workers who lost their retirement savings. And as Congress convened in January 2002 new life was breathed into what had been moribund campaign finance reform legislation that would limit the kind of soft money contributions Enron gave.

The House passed the bill in February; the Senate followed suit in March, and President Bush signed it. The bill became law seven years after McCain and Feingold started work on it. And as this book goes to press the future of the 2002 Campaign Finance Reform Act remains uncertain as several groups have begun court challenges.

Key Points

- A lobbyist is a person hired by a corporation, interest group, labor union, or foreign government to try to influence legislation.
- Lobbying has been part of the legislative process since the first Congress convened in 1789.
- Congress has periodically tried to restrict the practices of lobbyists from cracking down on bribery, to credentialing lobbyists who work in the Capitol, to making agents of foreign governments register.
- Top government officials including the president, cabinet officers, members of congress, congressional aides and federal judges may not be employed as lobbyists while they are in office.

- There are specific time limits on how long top executive branch officials must be out of government before they may undertake lobbying activities.
- The so-called legislative revolving door involves a former top congressional staffer or former member of Congress going to work as a lobbyist with the goal of influencing his/her old colleagues.
- Campaign finance reform legislation to limit so-called soft money is opposed by lobbyists because it would diminish their clout and access to politicians.

The Executive Branch

The president of the United States is the country's chief executive officer. The president is commander-in-chief of all the military; he is the chief negotiator in all foreign diplomacy; he is the chief law enforcement official of the nation; and he is charged with overseeing all executive departments and agencies of the government including their policy-making, rule-making, and enforcement. Since the dawn of the nuclear age the president has been at the top of the chain of command in launching nuclear weapons. He is the principal architect of both domestic and foreign policy. Some historians and scholars posit that today the president of the United States is the single most powerful individual in the world.

There was never a doubt that George Washington would be the first president. The man who led the fledgling nation's army through the Revolutionary War was the only choice. There was, however, considerable discussion about what to call the new leader. "George" was a bit informal. Some suggestions went to the other extreme ranging from "serene highness" to "excellency." In the end, Congress settled for "Mr. President" and it has been that for more than two centuries.

Article II Section 1 sets it out very succinctly. "The executive power shall be vested in a president. . . . He shall hold his office during the term of four years." The Twenty-second Amendment was added to the Constitution in 1951, limiting a president to two terms, a response to mounting concerns about a dynastic presidency after Franklin D. Roosevelt won an unprecedented fourth term in 1944.

To be president a person must be at least thirty-five years old and a natural-born citizen of the United States. (Naturalized citizens — those born as citizens of other countries who become U.S. citizens — may serve in Congress, in the president's Cabinet, or on the Supreme

Court, but may not be president.) The same qualifications apply to the vice president.

The framers of the Constitution did not want the president and vice president to be residents of the same state, and prohibit members of the Electoral College from voting for candidates for the two offices from the same state. Before the 2000 election, Republican vice presidential nominee Dick Cheney switched his residence from Texas (where his running mate George W. Bush was from) to Wyoming to avoid the problem. But it is technically possible for that to be circumvented if a sitting vice president is disqualified, dies, or resigns and his/her successor is appointed. It has never happened that way. In recent times, when Vice President Spiro Agnew resigned, Gerald Ford was named to succeed him. President Nixon was from California and Ford was from Michigan.

The Twentieth Amendment, which became part of the Constitution in 1933, sets January 20 as the day on which the president will be sworn in. If January 20 falls on a Sunday, the new president takes the oath privately on that day and the public ceremony is held the following Monday. The only inaugural function specified in the Constitution is the wording of the oath of office itself.

3.1 Electing the President

The framers of the Constitution devised a system of government untried anywhere in the world. Privately, men such as Alexander Hamilton worried about whether it would work, whether there would be a smooth transition from one leader to another, whether the untried system would endure. They were concerned that if an orderly transfer of power did not ensue, the Constitution would fail and the young country would be thrust into anarchy or civil strife, thus the Revolution would have failed.

Constitutional architect James Madison had faith that the system would work, despite its unique structure. Time has proved that his trust was not misplaced. In fact the constitutional scheme worked and grew stronger as power was passed from Washington to John Adams to Thomas Jefferson and onward.

The U.S. system is often loosely and incorrectly described as a "democracy." While citizen representation was always paramount, the United States was never designed to be a popular democracy in which all officials were voted on directly by the citizenry. The term used by Jefferson, Madison, and others to describe the system was "republican government," in which the president would be elected only indirectly by the people. To that end, the Constitution provides for an Electoral College to pick the chief executive.

Electors are picked by the states to vote for president and vice president. The number of electors are the same as the number of members each state is entitled to in Congress, a minimum of two senators and one representative. As an example, Connecticut has two senators and six representatives for a total of eight electoral votes. Today, there are 538 electors — 435 members of the House, plus 100 senators, plus 3 electors from the District of Columbia. (The Twenty-third Amendment added in 1961 gives D.C. representation in the Electoral College.) It takes a majority, or 270 electoral votes, for a candidate to be elected president.

The electors vote in their respective state capitols and send their sealed ballots to the president of the U.S. Senate, who opens them, tallies the votes, and certifies the results in front of the entire Congress. The person receiving the most votes for president is elected. The anomaly of the system is that it is entirely possible for a presidential candidate to win the popular vote and not be elected president. That was the case in 2000 when Democrat Albert Gore won the popular vote, but Republican George W. Bush won the electoral vote and became the forty-third president.

The Constitution specifically gives the right to establish and administer election rules to the state legislatures. That includes setting up the practices and policies for picking members of the Electoral College. The intent of the framers of the Constitution in establishing an electoral college was to minimize the likelihood of the most important official in the country being elected by popular political whim while at the same time providing some measure of accountability to the voters of each state. Madison, in *Federalist Paper Number 39,* defended indirect election of the president, noting that electors serve for a specific and limited period of time and that there is popular consent to their service at least at some level.

The language of the Constitution is not specific with regard to either choosing electors or binding their votes. As a result there is no uniformity. Some states have laws requiring electors to vote for the person receiving the majority of popular votes in the state. Others select a slate of electors pledged to each candidate on the ballot and, based on the popular vote within the state, empower the electors pledged to the person receiving the highest number of votes. Still other states put slates of electors on the presidential election ballot, either grouped with the candidates they support or labeled as supporters of a given candidate. Finally, there are states that do not put legal bounds on electors, and simply rely on the tradition that electors vote for the person receiving the most popular votes in a state. Less than a handful of electors in U.S. history have not voted as the voters of their state did.

Nonetheless, during the postelection turmoil in 2000, when there was a mathematical possibility of a tie vote in the Electoral College, there was some quiet exploration by Democratic candidate Albert Gore's camp regarding electors who might vote other than for the winner of the popular majority in states that do not legally bind electors. The Gore campaign was concerned about the election being decided by the House of Representatives, which had a Republican majority. The Twelfth Amendment clarified the original constitutional language of Article II Section 1 and set the stage for Gore's concern.

After electors meet in their various state capitols to cast their votes, the tally sheets are sent to the president of the Senate, the sitting vice president. (Ironically, in 2001, when the votes were counted, that was Albert Gore.) If the Electoral College vote is a tie or if no candidate wins a majority, then the election of the president falls to the House of Representatives. The result is not determined by a majority vote of the 435 members of the House. Each state delegation meets to vote separately and each state then receives one vote for president, which does not eliminate the possibility of a 25–25 tie vote in the House.

Regardless of what happens in the House, the Senate is required to vote for vice president, picking from the two people receiving the largest number of votes on the separate vice presidential ballots submitted by the Electoral College. If the House fails to elect a president, the person elected vice president would serve as president under the rules of presidential succession. It's never come to that.

It came close in 1876, the only election in which Congress was called on to decide the outcome. The race was between Democrat Samuel Tilden and Republican Rutherford B. Hayes, but the exact circumstance did not fall within the conditions the Constitution envisioned. After widespread bribery, intimidation, and vote fraud, three states — South Carolina, Louisiana, and Florida — each sent multiple sets of electoral tally sheets to the president of the Senate, with no indication which of the sheets accurately reflected the will of the voters in those states. While the Constitution provided for the president of the Senate to certify the electoral vote count, there is no provision for disputed or multiple electoral tallies. And so the Democrat-controlled House and the Republican-controlled Senate wrangled over the process.

Finally an electoral commission was established, made up of an equal number of Republicans and Democrats from the House and Senate. Originally the commission was to consist of seven Republicans and seven Democrats with one independent Supreme Court justice as the commission's fifteenth and tie-breaking member. But at the last minute that independent justice was appointed to a Senate seat and he was replaced on the commission by a Republican. That changed the dynamics of the commission and thus allowed the outcome to turn on partisanship. The key votes were all along party lines and Rutherford B. Hayes was selected as president. It remains unclear to this day who actually would have won the election were all the irregularities stripped away.

Key Points

- The president must be at least thirty-five years old, a naturalborn citizen, and is elected for a four-year term.
- The Twenty-second Amendment limits an individual to two terms as president.
- The president is not popularly elected but instead is indirectly elected by the Electoral College.
- The Constitution leaves the manner of selecting electors up to the various state legislatures and there is no uniformity in the process.
- Many states require electors to vote for the person receiving the largest number of popular votes in the state for president.
- A few states do not bind their electors and rely on the tradition of electors adhering to the popular vote.
- Electors meet in their state capitols on a date established by a national law to vote on the president and vice president.
- Electors send the tally of their votes to the president of the Senate, who certifies the results.
- If the presidential votes result in a tie, or in the case of more than two candidates on the ballot nobody wins a majority (270 electoral votes), the House of Representatives meets to elect the president.

- Each state delegation gets one vote in the House, for a total of fifty votes.
- It falls to the Senate to elect a vice president.
- If the House fails to elect a president, the vice president selected by the Senate will become president under the rules of presidential succession.
- Only one presidential election in history, in 1876, was decided by Congress.
- It is possible for one candidate to win the popular vote but lose the electoral vote, in effect creating a minority president.

3.2 The Power of the Presidency

On the heels of the Revolutionary War and with all the things they disliked about the English monarchy fresh in their minds, the authors of the Constitution took pains to limit the express powers of the president, lest there be a future inclination to turn the country into an autocracy. It is no accident that Article I, about Congress, is made up of ten sections and fifty-three separate paragraphs. Article II, about the executive branch, is shorter, less specific, and is made up of only four sections and thirteen paragraphs.

From George Washington through World War I, there was a steady evolution of the office. Arguably, the modern role of president was defined in the aftermath of the Great Depression and World War II and was solidified in the dawn of the nuclear age and through the Cold War. The president of the United States emerged as one of the two most powerful figures in the world, sharing the mantle with the leader of the former Soviet Union. With the downfall of communism and the breakup of the Soviet Union, the U.S. president has become the sole most powerful leader on earth.

With it all, the system of checks and balances the framers incorporated into the Constitution has proved effective over more than two centuries. The power of the president remains far from absolute. Congresses have regularly rebuffed modern presidents, changing legislation they propose, passing bills they don't like, spending money in ways of which they do not approve, and overriding presidential vetoes.

Reporters need to be aware that the power of the president is, nonetheless, tremendous and that the influence of the president is felt throughout the entire federal government.

First, the president appoints every major officer and official of the executive branch and the judicial branch. While the Senate is charged with giving the president advice and consent on such nominations, the fact is that most presidential nominations are easily confirmed. The nominations that make news are those the Senate sits on, delaying or killing them. At the end of Democrat Bill Clinton's administration, for example, the Republican Senate refused to act on the confirmation of dozens of federal court judges, awaiting new nominations from what they hoped would be a Republican president.

The Senate puts some presidential nominees through brutal confirmation hearings. President George H. W. Bush's nomination of former Republican Sen. John Tower to be secretary of defense saw Tower go down to defeat at the hands of the full Senate amid charges of alcohol abuse and "womanizing" on the part of the nominee. Supreme Court Justice Clarence Thomas's confirmation involved more than a week of high drama including allegations of sexual harassment. Thomas was ultimately confirmed. President Clinton's first nominee to be attorney general, Zoe Baird, withdrew her name in the midst of Senate Judiciary Committee confirmation hearings when it was revealed that she had failed to withhold taxes and Social Security from the check of the woman she hired as a nanny for her children. These are notable in that they are exceptions.

Second, as a result of his appointments, the president has a lock on what rules and regulations are proposed and adopted, and how they are enforced by the various departments and agencies under his control. Every executive agency and department is authorized by Congress to make and enforce rules, known as administrative law. (See section 3.8.) While Congress makes the statutory laws, a president is not completely hamstrung if Congress gets in his way. Modern presidents have used executive orders and the rulemaking authority vested in the executive branch to stage end-runs around Congress when Congress stalls or rejects Presidential initiatives. It is commonly called "executive action." President Clinton used this technique regularly to circumvent the Republican Congress. President George W. Bush started using executive action when it became apparent that parts of his agenda would stall in the Democratic Senate.

In addition to implementing administrative rules and regulations, executive action also includes so-called recess appointments. That involves temporarily appointing people, usually those whose Senate confirmations are on hold or delayed, to senior executive jobs while

Congress is in recess. The appointments are for a specific period of time. After that the president must resubmit the nomination to the Senate.

Executive action also allows a new president to abolish or change rules and regulations that don't suit his agenda or fit with his policy goals. President George W. Bush delayed or canceled implementation of a host of last-minute rule and regulation changes authorized by President Clinton in the final days of his administration.

Unlike statutory laws passed by Congress, executive actions are not permanent. What can be done by executive action can be changed without notice by a new administration. But it has proven to be an effective and powerful tool for shaping the direction and policy of the executive branch by a new president.

Third, when it comes to encouraging congressional action, there's no political clout quite as effective as that of the White House — any White House. The president has the ability to summon virtually any senator or representative at any time for personal persuasion. President Lyndon Johnson used to call it "jawboning." Others call it "arm-twisting." Whatever you call it, it is extremely difficult for members of Congress to resist the personal persuasion of the president of the United States, regardless of one's political posture. It is especially difficult if the congressperson is a member of the president's own political party.

As a practical matter, it is dangerous to one's political health to make any president too angry. Moreover, if you are a senator or a representative, especially in the president's own political party, the time is almost certain to come when you will want a favor. You might want the president to visit your state or district to speak, to help you raise campaign funds, to support a pet project, or to appoint you or one of your constituents to a top executive job. Even for members of Congress who are not in the president's party, it is not easy to move legislation without presidential support.

Politicians don't like to talk too much about it publicly, but if you are a member of Congress who has done something to offend the president (voting against him, opposing his position on various issues, refusing to come to a jawboning session) the paybacks can be extremely uncomfortable. Say you want the administration to support a federal project being put in your district. Even before you cast your vote or make your statement against the president's position, someone in the administration will likely let you know that the president is deciding to put that project so dear to your heart in the district of a representative who has voted with him instead of in yours. The White House — every administration — can and does play hardball.

Scholars have obtained significant insight into the intensity of behind-the-scenes pressure from the Oval Office tapes secretly recorded during the Johnson administration. President Lyndon Johnson, a former Democratic senator from Texas, can be heard using blunt and sometimes rough language in telling lawmakers what he wants them to do and what he'll do if they defy him.

Fourth, the president's voice is always heard. Republican President Theodore Roosevelt referred to the presidency as a "bully pulpit." When presidents want to generate support for their policies or positions, they can take their case directly to the American people. They can do this by making speeches or personal appearances. They can hold news conferences, most of which are broadcast nationally, at which they are likely to be asked about a particular issue. Or, in the case of major national events, they can request time from the broadcast networks to address the nation.

There is no law requiring the networks to provide such time and there have been a significant number of occasions when presidential requests have been refused. Various administrations have grumbled privately that networks put profits above the national interest when they refuse to interrupt highly rated shows for a presidential speech or news conference.

Fifth, the executive branch may be the most powerful lobbying organization in the world, even though technically the president and his staff are not lobbyists. Lobbyists are individuals paid by groups, corporations or labor unions to influence legislation or rulemaking. (See Chapter 2, section 2.14.) Every person in the executive branch is there to serve the president and further his agenda, his policies, and his legislative priorities. In addition to the president and vice president, the executive branch can muster a cavalcade of the most powerful individuals in the country to gin up support for a major public policy position, from Cabinet secretaries to sympathetic members of Congress to supportive individuals in the private sector (movie stars, sports stars, high profile corporate executives, and the like).

And finally, the president has the authority to grant pardons to people convicted of felonies and misdemeanors.

While the constitutional powers of the president are limited and specific, the real, *de facto*, power of modern presidents extends well beyond those limitations.

Key Points

- While the framers of the Constitution sought to limit the powers of the executive branch, presidential power is extensive.
- The president appoints the heads of all executive departments and agencies.
- The president has nearly absolute influence over the introduction, adoption, and implementation of non-statutory rules and regulations (administrative law) within the executive departments and agencies.
- When Congress stalls or blocks the president's agenda, executive action, including administrative rules, regulations, and recess appointments, can result in something of an end-run around Congress.
- The White House can exert major pressure on members of Congress to support the president, sometimes accompanied by old-fashioned political arm-twisting.
- Members of the president's own political party in Congress are especially vulnerable to White House pressure.
- The president can always take his case for a policy position or agenda item directly to the American people.
- The White House can muster tremendous public relations campaigns in support of the president's agenda.
- The president has the power to grant pardons.

3.3 State of the Union Address

Article II Section 3 of the Constitution requires the president to "give to the Congress information of the state of the union, and recommend to their consideration such measures as he shall judge necessary. . . ." Historically, this provision was subject to wide interpretation. The first two Presidents — George Washington and John Adams — liked giving speeches and appeared personally before Congress to deliver their reports. Thomas Jefferson, who was not particularly fond of public speaking, sent Congress written messages on the state of the union.

The state of the union message has traditionally been delivered in the early days of the new session of Congress, now usually in mid-January.

Not until Woodrow Wilson's presidency, in 1913, did it become an annual custom for the president to deliver his state of the union message in person. It was not formally named the State of the Union Address until Franklin Roosevelt's last such appearance in 1945.

Today, the State of the Union Address has become an important fixture in the president's arsenal of weapons in presenting and promoting his agenda before the public. While the constitutional requirement is for a message to Congress, all presidents of the television age have used the occasion to speak to a much broader audience and have taken the opportunity to lay out their legislative, economic, and policy agendas for the coming year to the nation.

Journalists should note a recent trend regarding State of the Union Addresses: the proliferation of standing ovations. Standing ovations have long been traditional at the beginning and end of each address. But starting with President Reagan and increasing perceptibly under Presidents Bush, Clinton, and Bush, the State of the Union Address has become a political clapathon. During the speech itself the president is interrupted by applause scores of times. Sometimes it's more like a sporting event than a somber occasion of state. Whenever the president says something that pleases his own party, that side of the chamber will jump up with thunderous applause, while opposition party members remain seated and silent. Only when the president says something that's popular on a bipartisan basis is he acknowledged by applause from both sides of the aisle.

After the speech representatives and senators rush to waiting reporters to react to what they've heard. But the reaction is generally predictable. Members of the president's own party will eagerly declare why the speech was among the greatest of all times, often reciting lines fed to them by the White House Press Office; and members of the opposition party will express their disappointment and point out its flaws.

The opposition party is generally given time to respond by many, but not all, radio and television networks.

Key Points

- The Constitution requires a regular report on the state of the union from the president to Congress.
- Today the State of the Union Address is usually given in mid-January.
- The annual tradition of delivering a speech began with Woodrow Wilson; until 1913 presidents did it in person if they were so moved or sent a written message if that was their desire.
- Television age presidents use their State of the Union Addresses to present their legislative agendas for the year both to Congress and to the nation at large.

3.4 Top Aides and Advisors to the President

To much of the world, the Oval Office is a symbol of the U.S. presidency and its immense power. What the world sees, however, is just the tip of the iceberg with regard to the office of the president. Literally hundreds of men and women work for the president, from his personal secretary to speech writers to schedulers to the president's personal physician.

Despite the constitutional connection between the president and vice president, the vice president often has not been one of the president's closest advisors. The nature of the relationship depends, to a great extent, on the chemistry between the two men. For example, Franklin Roosevelt did not view Harry Truman as a key advisor, nor did Roosevelt include Truman in key executive decisions. When Roosevelt died, Truman knew little about the Manhattan Project in which the U.S. was developing a nuclear weapon. Richard Nixon was not a particularly close confidant of Dwight Eisenhower; John F. Kennedy never completely trusted Lyndon Johnson. On the other hand, Bill Clinton and Al Gore had a very close relationship until it was strained by the presidential scandal involving Monica Lewinsky. And George W. Bush has a very close relationship with Vice President Dick Cheney.

For almost every president, the chief of staff is his top advisor, usually a close personal friend or close professional colleague. The job of White House chief of staff is demanding and draining. For most presidents, the chief of staff is the first person other than his wife he sees in the morning. Chiefs of staff are often required to work fifteen to twenty-hour days, seven days a week. It is not at all unusual for a president to have several chiefs of staff during a term, simply because of the pressure and mental demands on the individual in the job.

Presidents have also relied heavily on the men and women they appoint to the positions of counselor to the president, national security advisor, chair of the president's Council of Economic Advisors, and press secretary. Some turn to political allies such as pollsters or political strategists for advice. One of Bill Clinton's closest friends throughout his sometimes troubled presidency was James Carville, who had been one of his campaign managers in 1992. The exact nature of each relationship varies from president to president.

It is not unheard of for presidents to seek advice and counsel from outside the White House. There is nothing in the Constitution that requires a presidential confidant to be on the government payroll. Richard Nixon often turned to his friend Bebe Rebozo. George W. Bush regularly consults his father, former President George H. W. Bush.

First ladies of the United States have had varying roles in public policy and advising their husbands. Franklin Roosevelt gave his wife, Eleanor, an extraordinary and (to that time) unheard-of role as his eyes and ears to the world. F.D.R. was confined to a wheelchair and thus limited in his mobility; Eleanor Roosevelt was his unofficial emissary traveling on his behalf and reporting back to him about the details of what she saw. As a result, Eleanor Roosevelt's imprint was all over the social policy of the Roosevelt administration.

Jacqueline Kennedy was among the first presidential wives to have her own public agenda, aside from that of her husband. How much actual policy clout a first lady has relates directly to the relationship between husband and wife. Nancy Reagan had as much direct influence as almost any modern first lady. Insiders reported that President Reagan rarely made any major policy decision without discussing it with his wife first. Other highly influential first ladies include Rosalyn Carter, Barbara Bush, and Hillary Clinton.

President Clinton is the only president formally to have put the first lady in charge of a major public policy initiative. During the first year of his administration, he decided to let her direct development of a national health care plan, a key element of his 1992 campaign. Congressional Republicans were highly critical of Mrs. Clinton and her role and ultimately the health care plan was soundly defeated. The decision turned into an early policy and public relations disaster for the Clinton administration.

Key Points

- The vice president is not necessarily the president's top advisor.
- Usually the White House chief of staff is the closest personal advisor to the president.
- First ladies have played key roles as advisors to their husbands with Eleanor Roosevelt, Rosalyn Carter, Nancy Reagan, Barbara Bush, and Hillary Clinton all acting as key presidential advisors.
- Other top-level presidential advisors include the counselor to the president, national security advisor, chair of the president's Council of Economic Advisors, and the White House press secretary.
- Presidents are not limited to their official circle for advice and counsel and often turn to personal and political friends outside government.

3.5 Notes for Reporters Covering the White House

Every reporter, producer, photographer, or television camera crew member covering the president of the United States must obtain a White House press pass issued by the Secret Service. Everyone applying for a White House press pass undergoes a thorough background check. (Yes, they'll talk to your boss, former boss, high school principal, neighbors, and ex-spouses.) After all, aside from the president's immediate staff, nobody is closer to the president on a daily basis than the White House press corps.

Temporary passes are given on a daily basis to newspeople not holding permanent credentials, provided they have been through a preliminary background check and are listed in the security computer. Visiting news media — newspeople from outside Washington — will undergo a brief Secret Service interview before being allowed onto the White House grounds.

Security has always been tight around the White House. It underwent a major review after the bombing at the federal building in Oklahoma City. And ever since the 2001 terrorist attacks on New York and Washington security has been extraordinary around the president. Everyone entering the White House security perimeter passes through a magnetometer. Equipment, briefcases, purses, and so on are thoroughly searched and X-rayed. Newspeople traveling with the president undergo a full security sweep, including bomb-sniffing dogs and individual pat-downs, before each leg of a trip.

The White House pressroom is not a single room at all. It's actually a rabbit warren of cubicles and booths, in a series of rooms on two floors, with the briefing room as its hub. The briefing room is smaller and far less palatial than it looks on television. It's a long, thin room with a camera platform at one end and a small stage at the other, with rows of seats in between. It ranges from crowded on an average day to standing room only on a busy day. All seats in the briefing room are assigned. By tradition, the wire services and the major TV networks have front row seats. Major daily newspapers, such as *The Washington Post* and *The New York Times* are next, along with the news magazines such as *Time* and *Newsweek*.

Regulars have assigned booths or work spaces in the press complex. Visiting newspeople are advised to bring their own cellular phones and laptop computers, and be prepared to work any place they find an empty seat. Camera crews have assigned locations on the north lawn where TV reporters do their standups and live shots.

The president's press office — where press assistants, deputy press secretaries, and the press secretary him/herself work — is through a door to the side of the stage where White House briefings and some presidential news conferences take place. That door also leads to the West Wing where the Oval Office, the Cabinet Room, and the offices of the President's top aides are located. The level of access for newspeople, how deep they are allowed to penetrate into the West Wing, varies from administration to administration. During the first Bush administration newspeople had almost unrestricted access to the office of press secretary Marlin Fitzwater. If his door was open, reporters could knock and go in at will.

The Clinton administration tried to restrict access to anything but the "lower" press office (so called because it is a step below the actual entrance to the West Wing), except by invitation. That policy was quickly adjusted both as a result of protests from reporters and a spate of unfavorable news stories in print and broadcast about candidate Clinton preaching openness and President Clinton retreating from it. The office of the press secretary is only a few steps from the president.

Reporters regularly cover events within the inner sanctum, but only in limited numbers.

There's no doubt that one of the most famous rooms in the world is the Oval Office. The Oval Office is the heart of the West Wing of the White House. Traditionally, it has been the president's ceremonial office. We see it on television when the president greets visiting heads of state, signs bills into law, or meets some kind of hero or celebrity. Most Oval Office events are covered by a small rotating pool of White House newspeople. The White House press office determines the size of the pool; the news organizations determine the specific members (reporters, camera crews, still photographers, and the like).

The room itself looks out on the White House rose garden and south lawn. A few presidents have used the Oval Office as their working office, but most modern presidents have opted to use a smaller room down a short hallway just off the Oval Office as their private study and workspace.

President Franklin Roosevelt used the Oval Office to deliver his radio fireside chats. Virtually every president of the television age has used the Oval Office as the stage from which to address the nation on a vast array of topics, including John F. Kennedy's assessment of the Cuban missile crisis, Richard Nixon's resignation, and George H. W. Bush's announcement of the end of the Persian Gulf War. It was on his desk in the Oval Office that Harry Truman had the famous sign: "The buck stops here!"

When Truman was in office, access to the president was far more open than it is today. The entire White House press corps would follow Truman around the White House grounds on his daily walks and have one-on-one contact with him. Today, the size of the White House press corps dictates limited coverage of most presidential events.

In addition to Oval Office events, a pool of reporters, photographers, and camera crews rotates daily coverage of everything concerning the president. A pool rides on Air Force One, the presidential aircraft. A pool is present in every presidential motorcade. A pool is often invited to cover the beginning of important White House meetings such as with the Cabinet, members of Congress, foreign dignitaries, business executives, and civic leaders. A pool covers state dinners.

The pool is usually made up of the wire service reporters, a newspaper and magazine still photographer, a radio reporter with audio recorder, a network TV reporter, and at least one network TV crew. The print reporter's first job is to give a written summary of what happened at the event to all the other members of the press corps. The audio and videotape is distributed to all the other networks immediately after the event, if it is not fed live. No pool member's news organization can use the material before it is distributed to everyone else in the White House press corps.

Getting an interview with the president is never easy and competition is fierce among news organizations. It is more difficult for visiting newspeople than White House regulars to secure interviews, unless of course it is campaign season and the visiting reporter is from a state the president needs to carry to win re-election.

Visitors who want to cover the White House temporarily must obtain permission from the White House press office, which also handles interview requests for top White House officials. The vice president and first lady have their own press offices if visitors specifically want to cover either of them or their top staff.

Key Points

- Any newsperson who wants to cover the White House must be cleared by the Secret Service.
- Security around the White House and around the president is extraordinarily tight.
- Seats, work spaces, and the like in the White House press room and briefing room are all assigned.
- Most White House events are covered by rotating "pools" of reporters and technicians.
- Members of any White House pool have a responsibility to distribute written accounts, sound, and video to all other members of the White House press corps before they can use the material themselves.
- Visiting media people must obtain advance approval from the press office to cover White House events or to set up interviews.

3.6 The Cabinet

There is no specific provision in the Constitution for the president's Cabinet, but it dates back to the administration of George Washington. Washington's Cabinet included the secretary of state, secretary of the treasury, attorney general, and secretary of war. (The War Department was changed to the Department of Defense in 1947, after World War II.) Washington included the chief justice of the United States in many of his top level consultations, but it is notable that he did not include his vice president, John Adams. In fact, the vice president did not sit regularly with the President's Cabinet until Richard Nixon was invited to participate by President Eisenhower in the early 1950s.

One function of the president is to name the heads of the executive departments. The number of departments has changed over the years as some have been added and others expanded or consolidated. At present there are fourteen Cabinet departments. All nominees for top department positions — usually with titles such as secretary, under-secretary, and assistant secretary — must be confirmed by the Senate before they may take office.

The heads of those departments form the Cabinet, which advises the president, proposes and implements executive policy, and even provides political advice and counsel to the president. Most modern presidents have taken an active role in developing, implementing, and articulating the public policies each of the executive departments will follow.

While Congress is constitutionally charged with enacting statutory laws, the executive departments also establish, usually with varying degrees of public input, rules and regulations that have the force of law. These non-statutory laws encompass the general category of administrative law and include rules, regulations, and orders. (See section 3.8.)

For the most part, presidents select Cabinet officials with whom they are politically and philosophically aligned, although there are examples of presidents selecting Cabinet secretaries who are not members of their own political party. Democrat Bill Clinton, for example, named Republican Sen. William Cohen of Maine to be secretary of defense, and Republican George W. Bush retained former Democratic representative and Clinton Cabinet officer Norman Mineta of California, moving him from the post of commerce secretary to secretary of transportation.

The Cabinet, itself, is not limited to the heads of the various executive departments. Presidents have the discretion to elevate other senior officials to cabinet level as they see fit. Under Presidents Nixon, Ford, Carter, Reagan, Bush, Clinton, and Bush, Cabinet status has been given at various times to the United Nations ambassador, the director of the Office of Management and Budget, the U.S. trade representative, the chairman of the president's Council of Economic Advisors, the director of the Environmental Protection Agency, the president's national security advisor, the administrator of the Small Business Administration, and the director of the Office of Science and Technology Policy. Right after the September 11, 2001, terrorist attack on the United States, President Bush created a new Cabinet-level position — director of homeland security.

The vice president is also a member of the Cabinet. The president's chief of staff usually attends Cabinet meetings, along with any other executive branch officials the president may choose to invite.

Key Points

- The tradition of a Cabinet goes back to George Washington.
- The role of the president's Cabinet is to advise the president on policy and political issues.
- The vice president is a member of the Cabinet.
- Other top presidential advisors such as the White House chief of staff usually sit in on cabinet meetings.
- The heads of the executive departments are named by the president and must be confirmed by the Senate.
- There are currently fourteen Cabinet departments.
- The department heads are all members of the Cabinet along with such other senior government officials as the president chooses to elevate to Cabinetlevel rank.

3.7 Independent Agencies

In addition to the Cabinet and his personal White House staff, the president is responsible for nearly sixty independent agencies. This roster includes relatively minor agencies such as the American Battle Monuments Commission and critical entities such as the Central Intelligence Agency, the Federal Reserve System, and the Securities and Exchange Commission. The heads of agencies (usually with the title administrator) and members of commissions (with the title commissioner or commission chair) all require Senate confirmation before they take office.

Many of these independent agencies, like executive departments, have the authority to enact and enforce administrative law in the form of rules and regulations. Agencies such as the Environmental Protection Agency, the Federal Communications Commission, the Federal Trade Commission, and the Securities and Exchange Commission have tremendous rule-making and enforcement authority in areas that affect most of our daily lives. The EPA, for example, regulates such things as air and water pollution and can sanction

TABLE 3.1. **Executive Departments**

Department	Areas of Responsibility
Department of Agriculture	Farming, rural development and economics, animal and plant health inspection, forest service, food stamps, nutrition
Department of Commerce	Census, patents and trademarks, National Weather Service, exports including restricted goods, imports including unfair trade practices, National Oceanic and Atmospheric Administration, travel and tourism
Department of Defense	Army, Air Force, Marines, Navy, National Guard, National Security Agency, Defense Intelligence Agency, weapons systems, military bases
Department of Education	Oversees federal assistance to state and local agencies in charge of primary and secondary schools, standardized testing, literacy, national standards, continuing education, vocational training
Department of Energy	National security, oil and gas, nuclear energy, energy policy and research, electricity, experimental production
Department of Health and Human Services	Social Security, National Institutes of Health, Centers for Disease Control, health care research, Food and Drug Administration, Public Health Service, health policy, surgeon general
Department of the Interior	National Park Service, Bureau of Indian Affairs, reclamation, land management, Fish and Wildlife Service, geological survey, conservation, mining
Department of Justice	Marshals service, FBI, Bureau of Prisons, federal criminal and civil prosecution, defense of actions against the U.S. government, drug enforcement, federal prisons, U.S. attorneys
Department of Labor	Fair labor practices oversight, Bureau of Labor Statistics, Occupational Safety and Health Administration, labor-management relations
Department of State	All U.S. relations with other nations, treaty monitoring and negotiation, U.S. foreign service, international negotiations, dispute resolution and diplomacy, embassies and consulates, office of protocol
Department of Transportation	Roads, highways and surface transportation, maritime transportation, railroads, air transportation, Coast Guard, Federal Aviation Administration
Department of the Treasury	U.S. mint, Bureau of Engraving and Printing, Internal Revenue Service, customs service, U.S. Secret Service, the Treasury of the United States, comptroller of the currency
Department of Veterans Affairs	Veterans benefits, V.A. hospitals, health care, veterans services and education, national cemeteries

those who violate the rules. The FCC regulates radio, television, cable, and the Internet, and has a list of enforcement tools including imposing fines and denying the renewal of broadcast licenses. The FTC regulates deceptive advertising, and the SEC regulates the stock markets. Both have significant enforcement authority.

Other independent agencies are quasi-private enterprises. These include AMTRAK, also known as the National Railroad Passenger Corporation, and the U.S. Postal Service.

Key Points

- There are nearly sixty independent agencies that come under the aegis of the executive branch.
- Administrators, commissioners, and other top officials of independent agencies must be confirmed by the Senate.
- Many but not all of the independent agencies have the capacity to make administrative law, as do the other executive departments.

TABLE 3.2.   **Independent Executive Agencies**

Advisory Council on Historic Preservation	National Endowment for the Arts
Agency for International Development	National Endowment for the Humanities
American Battle Monuments	National Indian Gaming Commission
Central Intelligence Agency	National Mediation Board
Commodity Futures Trading Commission	National Railroad Passenger Corporation
Consumer Product Safety Commission	National Science Foundation
Corporation for National Service	National Transportation Safety Board
Environmental Protection Agency	Nuclear Regulatory Commission
Equal Employment Opportunity Commission	Nuclear Waste Technical Review Board
Federal Deposit Insurance Corporation	Office of Federal Housing Enterprise
Federal Election Commission	Oversight
Federal Emergency Management Agency	Office of Personnel Management
Federal Energy Regulatory Commission	Office of Special Counsel
Federal Housing Administration	Overseas Private Investment Corporation
Federal Housing Finance Board	Peace Corps
Federal Labor Relations Authority	Pension Benefit Guaranty Corporation
Federal Maritime Commission	Postal Rate Commission
Federal Reserve System	Railroad Retirement Board
Federal Retirement Thrift Investment Board	Securities and Exchange Commission
Federal Trade Commission	Selective Service System
General Services Administration	Small Business Administration
Government National Mortgage Association	Tennessee Valley Authority
Institute of Museum and Library Services	Thrift Savings Plan
Merit Systems Protection Board	U.S. Agency for International Development
National Aeronautics and Space Administration	U.S. Arms Control and Disarmament Agency
National Archives and Records Administration	U.S. Information Agency
National Commission on Libraries and	U.S. International Trade Commission
Information Services	U.S. Office of Government Ethics
National Council on Disability	U.S. Postal Service
National Credit Union Administration	U.S. Trade and Development Agency

3.8 Administrative Law and Executive Rule-Making

Congress vests most executive departments and independent agencies with the power to make rules and regulations, implement those rules and regulations, and enforce those rules and regulations. This is a wide-ranging authority growing out of the fact that it would be impossible for Congress to legislate the detailed operations of each executive department and agency. Congress thus enacted statutory laws authorizing department and agency rule-making. The body of law that has grown out of executive rule-making, along with the legal precedents established through challenges to those rules, is known as "administrative law."

Executive branch rule-making authority is designed to implement, enforce, and interpret acts of Congress, implement policy, and regulate or protect a general public interest. An example is the 1996 Telecommunications Act, passed by Congress and signed by President Clinton. Included in that act are broad changes involving radio station ownership and the cable television business. It fell to the Federal Communications Commission to make the rules and regulations necessary to implement the 1996 Telecommunications Act. Under the act and previous acts of Congress, the FCC has a broad range of enforcement powers, including the refusal to grant new or renew existing broadcast licenses, the power to revoke broadcast licenses, injunctive authority, the right to fine, require restitution, and require payment of fees.

Other regulatory agencies with broad enforcement powers include: the Food and Drug Administration, which regulates food safety and the pharmaceutical industry; the Federal Aviation Administration, which regulates airlines and air travel; the Securities and Exchange Commission, which regulates the stock and financial markets; and the Occupational Safety and Health Administration, which regulates workplace safety.

Agencies have wide discretion with regard to what rules to enforce and what rules not to enforce, what and how to change or revoke rules, and what level of sanctions or penalties to impose. This executive authority can and does change frequently when the presidency changes hands. What has come to be known as "executive action" has become an expedient way for presidents to circumvent Congress. (See section 3.2.)

Unlike statutory law, which can only be changed by the action of Congress, administrative law can be amended, adjusted, revised, and/or stricken when an administration changes policy, when there is a change of administration, or by a superceding act of Congress.

Federal regulatory authority, and the resulting body and practice of administrative law, has an often profound impact on nearly every aspect of our lives. Regulatory laws do not have the permanence of statutory laws enacted by Congress, but federal rules and regulations are law and can be enforced with most of the penalties available to enforcement of statutory law — including imprisonment, fines, injunctive relief, confiscation of property, and loss of licenses.

When departments and agencies determine to put new rules and regulations into place, the usual procedure requires public hearings and comment both during the drafting process and prior to implementation of the rule or regulation. Public comments can be in the form of oral testimony and/or written communication with an agency. When a new rule or regulation is put into place, public notice must be published along with the text of the rule or regulation. This is done in the Federal Register.

Rules and regulations may be challenged. Administrative law judges, or people designated to serve in that capacity, are a part of most departments and agencies. Many departments and agencies also have panels to hear appeals of decisions by administrative law judges. Ultimately, agency administrative law decisions may be appealed to the federal courts. Many rules and regulations generate litigation as a result of claims that the rule or regulation is outside the scope of the congressional authority granted to the department or agency making the rule.

In addition to court challenges, Congress itself can act to alter executive rule-making. Congress authorizes departments and agencies to make and enforce rules and Congress can change or revoke that authority.

When a person or organization is charged with violating a rule or regulation, the case goes before an administrative law judge within the agency that issued the rule or regulation. Jury trials are not part of administrative law procedure. Evidence is heard, as in other court proceedings. Those charged with violations are always entitled to an attorney, although unlike criminal actions where an attorney will be appointed without cost, the parties are responsible for obtaining their own counsel. Administrative law judges, like other judges, often (but not always) have subpoena power to compel the production of documents, evidence, or testimony.

If one of the parties to an administrative law action believes a judge's decision is in error, the decision can be appealed. The first step is usually to an appellate body within the agency. If further appeal is sought, the case can be petitioned to U.S. District Court, then to the Court of Appeals, and finally a petition for a writ of certiorari may be submitted to the U.S. Supreme Court.

The scope of administrative law is enormous and is embodied in an entire volume — Title 5 — of the U.S. Code.

Reporters must be aware that the number and nature of federal regulations is the subject of hot political debate. The Libertarian Party, for example, regularly places candidates on state and national ballots who want to do away with almost all federal rules and regulations, including those dealing with public health and safety, drugs, transportation, food and agriculture, small business, corporate America, and banking and finance.

Ronald Reagan ran for the White House in 1980 on a pledge to limit and/or eliminate rules and regulations he viewed as unduly burdensome — a process and policy known as "deregulation." Deregulation has been a priority for all subsequent presidents.

Key Points

- Executive departments and agencies have the power to make rules and regulations and that power comes from Congress.
- The body of law encompassing executive rule-making and legal precedents resulting from challenges to or actions under such rules and regulations is called administrative law.
- Administrative law implements, enforces, and/or interprets acts of Congress or protects a general public interest.
- Agency rules and regulations have an impact on nearly every area of our lives.
- Administrative law cases are heard first before judges within the agency that made the rule or regulation.
- Administrative law judges can issue subpoenas, compel production of documents, witnesses, and evidence.

- Sanctions under administrative law can include prison, fines, confiscation of property, and loss of licenses.
- Rules and regulations, along with the decisions of administrative law judges, can be challenged, starting with agency appellate panels and then in the federal courts.
- Limiting or eliminating some federal rules and regulations has been the policy of most recent administrations and is called "deregulation."

3.9 Notes for Reporters Covering Executive Departments and Agencies

Reporters assigned to cover stories involving federal departments and agencies should brace themselves for intense security and allocate appropriate time for the process. In the wake of the September 11, 2001, terrorist attack on the United States, access to most federal buildings was severely restricted.

In the last quarter century there have been a series of benchmark events that caused federal law enforcement authorities to ratchet-up security around government offices — both in Washington and around the country. The two assassination attempts against President Gerald Ford, the Iranian hostage crisis, John Hinkley's attempt on President Ronald Reagan's life, the Oklahoma City bombing, and the 2001 terrorist attacks on New York and Washington have generated unprecedented security.

Visiting news media will have a much more difficult time gaining access than will those reporters, photographers, and camera crews who are appropriately credentialed and cover various agencies and departments on a regular basis. In many buildings, briefcases, camera gear, audio recording equipment, laptop computers, and the like will be screened by security personnel before admission is granted.

The key departments all issue their own press credentials, although having a White House press credential eases the way because the Secret Service background check is already in place. (See section 3.5.) The Pentagon, State Department, Justice Department, and Treasury Department all issue their own press passes to reporters regularly assigned to them. A White House or Capitol Hill press credential will usually be enough to get newspeople into the other agencies and departments. Most buildings have public telephones, but visiting news media are always well advised to have their own cellular phones.

Visiting reporters can set up interviews with individual officials or through the various press and information offices of the departments and agencies. In all cases the secretary (or attorney general or other top official) has his/her own press secretary. Most departments and a few of the bigger independent agencies have pressrooms inside their headquarters. Visitors need to make arrangements with the press or information offices of each department and/or agency if they desire to cover such public events as hearings, presentations, and/or news conferences. Each has rules about where cameras and microphones may be used and it is up to visiting reporters to find out what the rules are.

Many major news organizations assign reporters to cover specific agencies. Reporters assigned to these beats usually become experts in the various areas they cover. It is not unusual for a news organization to assign a reporter with a law degree to cover the Justice Department, or a reporter with a pilot's license to cover the Federal Aviation Administration, the Department of Transportation, or the National Transportation Safety Board.

There are literally hundreds of specialty publications, including magazines, newspapers, newsletters, web sites, radio programs, television, and/or closed circuit or syndicated industry broadcasts that assign reporters to cover departments and agencies.

Local news organizations generally do not assign reporters to cover federal agencies on a regular basis, although there are exceptions. The local news organizations in Washington, D.C., often treat federal news as local news and assign reporters accordingly. Journalists working in rural areas in which a dominant industry is farming, ranching, dairy, or poultry will likely be well acquainted with the local USDA officials. Reporters who work near military bases will know top officers in the chain of command as well as other personnel at the bases. Newspeople in places large and small where NASA has facilities will make it their business to know about the agency and its local impact. Reporters in Houston may cover the Johnson Space Center; reporters from all over Florida cover stories about the Kennedy Space Center; reporters in Pasadena, California, cover the Jet Propulsion Laboratory; and newspeople in New Mexico cover the White Sands Testing Facility. All over the country reporters whose territory includes national parks or forests know the local Interior Department and Park Service officials.

Key Points

- Be prepared for extremely tight security around federal offices in Washington and the rest of the country.
- Several key executive departments (Justice, State, Defense, and Treasury) have their own press credentials.
- Visiting reporters will be admitted for interviews with officials provided they have appointments and some form of identification.
- Many departments and agencies have pressrooms, but access is often limited to newspeople accredited to the particular department or agency.
- The rules regarding news coverage vary from agency to agency and reporters should check with the respective press or information offices.

The Judiciary Branch

The federal judiciary has three tiers. U.S. District Courts (the civil and criminal trial courts) form the lowest tier or level; the Courts of Appeals are the middle level; and alone at the top is the U.S. Supreme Court. Unlike the other two branches of government, which have endured with only minor modification since the Constitution was adopted in 1787, the judiciary branch has evolved and changed over two-plus centuries, both in structure and in the power of the courts within the overall U.S. government.

4.1 Development of the Judiciary

Article III Section 1 of the Constitution did not provide much more than an outline, a sketch of the federal judiciary. The only tribunal specifically described in the Constitution is the U.S. Supreme Court. The framers were far more vague regarding the judiciary than in their lengthy delineation of the duties, responsibilities, and prohibitions on the House and Senate or the executive branch. The defining sentence is: "The judicial power of the United States shall be vested in one Supreme Court, and in such inferior courts as the Congress may from time to time ordain and establish." The Constitution was silent on such important questions as the number of Supreme Court justices, the nature of the "inferior" courts Congress may establish, and the jurisdictional scope of the judicial branch.

It did not take Congress long to fill in some of those gaps regarding the federal courts. In 1789 Congress passed and President Washington signed the first major judiciary act. Among other things the Judiciary Act of 1789 established the number of Supreme Court Justices at six, which allowed the Supreme Court itself to sit for the first time in February 1790. The act provided for one chief justice and five associate justices of the Supreme Court. Congress added a seventh member to the court in 1807 to reduce the number of tie votes.

Justices of the Supreme Court, as well as other federal judges, are appointed for life by the president. Judicial appointments at all levels are subject to the advice and consent of the Senate. The high court's present structure — eight associate justices and one chief justice — was codified into law in 1869, in the aftermath of the Civil War.

The Judiciary Act of 1789 also established a system to handle civil and criminal trials, as well as federal law enforcement. The act set up thirteen judicial districts, one for each state, in which there would be a lower court, a marshal, and a federal prosecutor. The act called that prosecutor the "district attorney," which gave rise to the popular term for local prosecutors today. Those district attorneys were eventually placed under the administration of the attorney general of the United States. Today, federal prosecutors are called U.S. attorneys and are appointed by the president with the advice and consent of the Senate.

The judicial system set up in those early days of the republic was made up of only two levels. Under the 1789 act, the appellate process allowed direct appeals from the district courts to the Supreme Court.

By the late 1800s, the two-tiered federal court system was proving unwieldy and burdensome. Originally the idea was to add a new judicial district every time a new state entered the union, but Congress quickly moved to limit the number of district courts. Long before the Civil War, Congress concluded that there were simply too many states for each state to be a judicial district of its own.

Consolidation of judicial districts did not address the fact that the increase in national population was producing more court cases and more appeals than the system could handle. So Congress found itself confronted with the issue of limiting the number of cases going to the Supreme Court. To ease the Supreme Court's caseload, Congress devised a middle level of appellate courts. In the Judiciary Act of 1891, Congress created the U.S. Court of Appeals, three-judge panels that hear appeals from the lower courts. The act also placed limitations on the automatic right of appeal to the Supreme Court.

The 1891 changes helped, but the Supreme Court docket continued to be overloaded. In 1925 Congress further restricted cases reaching the nation's highest court, and in 1988 Congress gave the Supreme Court virtually unlimited discretion regarding what cases it will hear and what petitions will be rejected.

In addition to the evolution of the three-tiered federal judiciary, Congress has occasionally established courts of special jurisdiction. The only two which are currently in existence are the U.S. Court of International Trade and the U.S. Tax Court. (See section 4.8.)

Key Points

- The Supreme Court is the only federal court established in the Constitution, Article III Section 1.
- Article I Section 8 says Congress may establish such other inferior tribunals as deemed necessary.
- Today there are three tiers of the federal judiciary: the Supreme Court at the top, the Court of Appeals in the middle, and U.S. District Courts.
- Federal prosecutors are called U.S. attorneys and are appointed by the president.
- The Courts of Appeals did not come into existence until the late 1800s.
- District courts are both criminal and civil trial courts.
- Congress did not act to make nine the number of Supreme Court justices until 1869.

4.2 The Rise of the Supreme Court

The separation of powers embodied in the U.S. Constitution set up a government of three theoretically coequal branches. But in the early years of the new country, the federal judiciary was the least equal of the three. The Supreme Court didn't sit for nearly two and a half years after the Constitution was ratified, until after Congress set the number of justices at six.

For a decade after that the federal judiciary limped along, impeded by the ambiguous language of the Constitution itself. Aside from local criminal and civil trials heard in the 13 District Courts and a few appeals from those lower courts to the Supreme Court, there was considerable legal debate about what the court should, in fact, be doing.

In 1801, John Marshall, who had been President John Adams' secretary of state, was named chief justice. That one appointment was a catalyst for profound changes in the nature, direction, and scope of the Supreme Court. The first three chief justices — John Jay, John

Rutledge, and Oliver Ellsworth — were reluctant to let the court do very much at all. They were highly cautious if not timid. But Chief Justice John Marshall was an activist who believed the court had to assume a more direct and definitive role as a coequal partner in the government.

Marshall's appointment came near the end of the Adams administration and the beginning of the Jefferson administration. There was a deep-rooted philosophical disagreement between Adams' Federalist party and Jefferson's Democratic-Republican party over the authority of Congress, the prerogatives of the executive, and the authority of the Supreme Court to judge whether the other branches of government acted within the Constitution.

In a series of last minute appointments to the federal bench, "midnight judges" according to the Jeffersonians, President Adams tried to pack the federal judiciary with his Federalist Party supporters. One of those appointees was William Marbury. He was given the position of justice of the peace in the District of Columbia. Adams' appointment of Marbury won the approval of the Senate. But the action came so late that formal commissions of office were not delivered during the last days of Adams' presidency. James Madison, Jefferson's new secretary of state, chose to ignore the judicial appointments of Marbury and several others, and withheld the commissions of office.

Marbury and the others appealed to the Supreme Court, seeking the congressionally authorized commissions that Madison withheld. The court ruled that the Senate acted legally and within the Constitution by granting commissions to Marbury and the others and Madison was required to deliver them. Marshall wrote, "It is emphatically the province and duty of the judicial department to say what the law is." The decision relied, at least in part on earlier writings in the Federalist Papers, notably *Federalist No. 78*, authored by Alexander Hamilton, who used strikingly similar language in saying interpretation of the law "is the proper and peculiar province of the courts."

From this case the bedrock principle of judicial review was born, and lives today.

Many legal scholars and historians also believe that it was *Marbury v. Madison* that signaled the ascendency of the judicial branch into full coequal status with the other two branches, as envisioned by the framers of the Constitution.

The coequal status of the Supreme Court and the principle of judicial review was further solidified thirteen years later, also by the Marshall court, in the case *Martin v. Hunter's Lessee*. That 1816 case established the authority of the Supreme Court to review the decisions of state courts and the constitutionality of state statutes.

Some journalists and many students presume that these two decisions give the Supreme Court the power to tell the other branches and the states what to do. Not so. It is important to note that the authority of the Supreme Court to exercise judicial review of the actions of the other branches of the federal government, as well as to review the actions of state courts and legislatures, turns on whether or not the action of those other bodies was within the limits placed on them by the U.S. Constitution.

Key Points

- The Constitution sought to create three coequal branches of government but in the early days of the nation the judiciary was not coequal.
- The assertion of power of the Supreme Court in the principle known as judicial review grew out of a political dispute between the outgoing Adams administration and the incoming Jefferson administration.
- The Supreme Court established its authority to exercise judicial review of the constitutionality of the actions of the other two branches of government in the 1803 case *Marbury v. Madison*.
- In 1816 the Supreme Court codified its authority to exercise judicial review of the constitutionality of state statutes.

4.3 The Lower Courts

It was obvious to the first Congress that every legal case in the new country could not be handled by the Supreme Court alone. As a result, the Judiciary Act of 1789 set up a series of District Courts (originally one for each state) to be courts of original jurisdiction. But as the young country grew, it quickly became obvious to the lawmakers that adding a new judicial district for each new state was not workable. Without change the court system would become too cumbersome.

What has evolved through a series of congressional actions, starting in 1789 and going through the 1990s, is a three-tiered system with a layer of U.S. District Courts making up a dense bottom tier. There are District Courts all over the country — including the territories of Guam, the U.S. Virgin Islands, and the commonwealth of Puerto Rico. Today there are 91 District Courts with congressional authorization for 663 district judges. At almost any given moment there are vacancies due to death, illness, retirement, and/or the inability of the president and the Senate to agree on new judicial nominees.

District Court judges are paid the same in every location, the result of an 1891 act of Congress to make judicial salaries uniform. Originally district judges were paid based on how much business Congress estimated would be conducted in each court. Like Supreme Court justices, federal judges serve for life, although they may retire at age seventy with ten years on the federal bench and at sixty-five with fifteen years on the bench.

In the federal court system, District Courts are the trial courts, hearing both civil and criminal cases. The majority of cases are civil. Criminal cases are tried before a jury; civil cases may be tried with or without a jury.

The Courts of Appeals form the middle tier of the federal judiciary pyramid. They are three-judge panels. The Courts of Appeals did not come into existence until 1891 and their jurisdiction was expanded through the first half of the Twentieth Century. Today there are thirteen circuits — eleven of them are numbered, responsible for distinct geographic areas, and the other two are the D.C. Circuit and the Federal Circuit. (For example, the Tenth Circuit Court of Appeals is responsible for cases originating in Colorado, Wyoming, Utah, Kansas, Oklahoma, and New Mexico.)

Each Supreme Court justice is responsible for at least one circuit, acting, in effect, as the senior appellate judge. They are called circuit justices in this capacity. Among other things the circuit justices do is to consider emergency petitions, such as death row appeals. The current chief justice, William Rehnquist, carries the heaviest load and is the circuit justice in the Fourth Circuit, the D.C. Circuit, and the Federal Circuit.

In addition to hearing appeals from the U.S. District Courts, the circuit courts also hear administrative law appeals challenging the regulatory decisions of executive departments and agencies.

Key Points

- U.S. District Courts are federal trial courts, in existence since 1789.
- Today, there are District Courts in every state, as well as in Puerto Rico, Guam and the U.S. Virgin Islands.
- District Courts try criminal and civil cases.
- The Courts of Appeals are intermediate level courts.
- Courts of Appeals sit with three judges.
- There are 13 circuits covering all jurisdictions where there are U.S. District Courts.
- Each circuit is overseen by a Supreme Court justice, known as the circuit justice.

4.4 Federal Criminal Law

Despite high profile criminal cases, such as the trial of Oklahoma City bomber Timothy McVeigh or the terrorists who tried to blow up New York City's World Trade Center in 1993, the majority of cases that come before U.S. District Courts are civil, not criminal. (Most criminal cases arise in the various state courts.)

Nonetheless the scope of federal criminal jurisdiction is extensive. There are three broad categories that can result in a criminal case being filed in federal court: 1. Any person committing a crime on federal property faces federal prosecution; 2. A non-Indian or someone who is not a member of the affected tribe committing a crime on an Indian reservation faces federal prosecution; and 3. Anyone charged with violating a federal criminal statute faces federal prosecution.

There are more than 120 separate categories that constitute federal criminal conduct. The crimes that tend to generate the most media attention include terrorism, treason, espionage, kidnapping, or assassinating or attempting to assassinate the president. There are other notable federal crimes, even if they are less likely to garner massive amounts of news coverage. These include drug or controlled substance violations, racketeering, immigration violations, mail fraud, wire fraud, bank robbery, counterfeiting, child pornography, interstate prostitution, income tax evasion, civil rights violations, hate crimes, and interstate flight to avoid prosecution.

Anything that would normally constitute a state crime — such as rape, robbery, murder, mayhem, arson, and the like — would also be a federal crime if committed on federal property or on an Indian reservations. (Federal property includes all government-owned land, military installations, public buildings owned by the federal government, national parks, and national monuments.)

Title 18 of the U.S. Code deals with federal criminal procedure. Under the code, each criminal case goes through a series of steps:

1. Arrest and interrogation — a suspect is taken into custody and questioned. It is at this point that the suspect is told he/she is not required to talk to law enforcement authorities and that he/she is entitled to legal counsel.
2. Arraignment — an initial court appearance, often before a U.S. magistrate judge, in which preliminary charges are entered and the accused enters a plea of guilty or not guilty.
3. Bail hearing — also an initial court procedure frequently performed in a U.S. Magistrate Judge's Court, at which bail is set.
4. Grand jury proceedings — a panel of citizens (usually fourteen to twenty-four) is presented evidence by the prosecution. The grand jury determines if there is probable cause, (a grand jury consensus that there is sufficient evidence to convince a reasonable person that a crime was committed and the accused did it.) If the grand jury determines that probable cause exists the prosecution will then decide whether to take the case to trial. It takes only a simple majority of a federal grand jury to determine probable cause and return an indictment. Grand jury proceedings are one-sided. Only the prosecution, the U.S. attorney, presents evidence and calls for testimony. There is no defense presentation or exculpatory evidence; thus, it is more common for a grand jury to indict when asked to do so than to reject the case for lack of probable cause.
5. Pre-trial proceedings — includes setting a trial date, preliminary motions, and officially binding the defendant over for trial.
6. Discovery — trial preparation on the part of the prosecution and defense involving pre-trial interviews with witnesses, experts, victims, and so forth. The discovery process also involves each side sharing what it has uncovered with the other. Real trials are not like Perry Mason in which "surprise" witnesses or "surprise" evidence shows up to cement the case. In virtually all federal criminal trials, both sides have fairly complete knowledge of what the other will

present because the rules require the sides to disclose their evidence. Failure to disclose evidence can result in delay of the trial and/or a contempt of court citation.

7. Trial — involves several steps. It usually starts with impaneling the jury, (see section 4.5), followed by opening statements by both sides. The prosecution's case comes first (including direct testimony by the witnesses, cross-examination by defense counsel, re-direct, and re-cross); the defense case follows (including witness testimony, etc.) When both sides have rested or concluded their presentations and rebuttals, there is summation by both sides. Finally the judge instructs the jury with regard to the law and what the jury is charged with deciding. The jury retires to a jury room for deliberations and rendering of the verdict. The jury, the defense, and the prosecution all return to the courtroom to hear the jury's verdict.

8. Sentencing — the punishment phase of the trial, done in federal court by the judge.

9. Appeals — reporters must be aware that appeals are allowed only on matters of law, those decisions rendered by the judge. Findings of fact, such as guilt or innocence, are not subject to appeal unless there is evidence of impropriety involving the jury, such as jury tampering. Appellate motions are filed with the appropriate Court of Appeals.

In criminal cases, there are often overlapping state and federal issues involved. The federal case usually takes precedence in the order of process, but it is not unusual for a defendant to face trial in state court, in addition to a federal trial, with regard to the same criminal act. There are numerous examples of defendants being acquitted on one set of state criminal charges, only to be tried in federal court on a different set of charges for the same acts. The classic example was the gangster Al Capone, who was acquitted by state courts on a laundry list of charges, only to be tried and convicted in federal court for income tax evasion.

Journalists ought to know that while the rules governing such things as jury selection, evidence, admissibility, and courtroom procedure vary greatly from state to state, the rules are uniform throughout the federal courts. Thus covering a trial in District Court in San Francisco is virtually identical to covering a trial in District Court in

St. Louis, but it likely will look substantially different in state trial court in the two jurisdictions.

Key Points

- While most criminal cases arise in the states, there are more than 120 categories of federal crimes.
- One of three general criteria usually must be met to warrant a federal case being filed: the alleged crime was committed on federal property, the alleged crime was committed by a non-Indian or non-tribal member on an Indian reservation, or the alleged criminal conduct violated a federal criminal statute.
- Federal criminal procedure usually includes arrest and interrogation, arraignment, bail hearing, grand jury proceedings, pre-trial proceedings, discovery, trial, sentencing, and appeal.
- State and federal laws frequently overlap and a federal criminal case does not preclude a state case related to the same activity from being filed.
- Federal procedure does not vary from court to court or jurisdiction to jurisdiction; there is great variation among state procedures.

4.5 Juries and Jury Trials

Grand juries and juries are different legal entities and have different functions in the legal process. Grand juries hear evidence from prosecutors and determine whether the case is sufficient to indict a defendant. Juries sit in judgment at trials. Grand juries conduct their business entirely in secret. Juries hear cases in open court. A single grand jury may rule on several different cases during the period of its term. A jury is impaneled for only one trial. Grand juries hear only criminal charges. A jury may be impaneled to sit on either a criminal or civil trial.

The right to a trial by jury is as old as the republic. It is enshrined in the Sixth Amendment, which requires a "speedy and public trial, by an impartial jury." The systems of calling, selecting, impaneling, and trying a case before a jury are similar in all states and the federal courts.

In federal criminal cases the standard jury is made up of twelve men and women. Most states also require twelve-member juries for cases involving serious crimes. Depending on the case, one or more alternate jurors may be seated to hear the case. If one of the regular jurors becomes incapacitated because of illness or other special circumstance, or is disqualified because of misconduct, such as talking to a reporter outside of court, the alternate will take the regular juror's place. If the alternate jurors' services are not needed, the alternates are dismissed prior to jury deliberations.

The right to a jury trial is extended to many, but not all, federal civil cases. Parties to civil actions can waive their right to a jury trial. It is not uncommon for a federal civil case to be heard by a judge, alone. There are numerous high profile cases, including the government's anti-trust action against software giant Microsoft, in which the trial was conducted before a judge without a jury.

The number of jurors in civil trials also varies. In some cases a civil jury may be as few as six people.

In all jury trials, the jury is the legal entity that decides matters of fact, such as whether a crime was actually committed and whether enough evidence has been presented to prove the person charged is guilty. In criminal cases the standard, or burden of proof, a jury must determine has been met in order to convict a defendant is that the proof of guilt is "beyond a reasonable doubt." Other terms bandied about, such as beyond a shadow of a doubt, simply do not exist legally.

Guilt beyond a reasonable doubt means that in light of the evidence presented, a reasonable man or woman would be satisfied that the person accused acted as charged. Reasonable doubt does not mean beyond any doubt nor does it mean fanciful doubt. In federal criminal trials the jury vote must be unanimous that the burden of proof has been met.

The burden of proof in a civil trial is substantially lower. In most civil cases — both state and federal — the jury will render its decision based on a "preponderance of the evidence." That means that the scales of justice merely need to tilt toward one side or the other, based on evidence presented. This is in contrast to criminal cases in which the scales must be overwhelmingly tipped toward guilt. Also unlike criminal cases, the jury vote in civil cases does not always have to unanimous.

In the federal courts, a group of citizens known as the jury pool are called to serve for a specified period of time. From the jury pool the clerk of the court impanels a group — usually selected by a random drawing of names from the entire jury pool — that might serve in a particular case. Once those jurors enter the courtroom, the judge and the lawyers for both sides begin the process known as jury selection.

The judge and the lawyers will ask questions of the jurors. This is known as *voir dire*. Common questions include whether the prospective juror knows any of the trial participants, has a particular interest in the case, has read or heard anything about the case in the news media, and whether the person has any biases, prejudices, or preconceived notions that would render it impossible for him/her to be fair.

During *voir dire*, the attorneys for either side may seek to dismiss a juror through a procedure known as a challenge. There are two types of challenges in the federal courts and in virtually all state courts: challenges for cause and peremptory challenges.

A challenge for cause requires one side or the other to present reasons to the court for dismissing a juror from the case. The most common reasons are familiarity with the case, personal acquaintance with one or more of the trial participants, a stated prejudice, or a declaration that the potential juror, for any reason, is unable to render a fair and impartial verdict. In some capital, or death penalty, cases, a declaration from a potential juror that he/she has moral objections to the death penalty may result in a challenge for cause.

In most criminal trials both sides are given a certain number of peremptory challenges. Peremptory challenges allow either side to dismiss a potential juror for no reason at all. The exact number of peremptory challenges is not specified in law, but is usually decided as a matter considered in pre-trial proceedings.

Once the jury is seated, the trial may begin.

Occasionally, a case is so volatile, likely to generate so much publicity, or likely to generate inappropriate contacts with the jury (such as in organized crime and/or terrorist cases) that the jury is sequestered. A sequestered jury is housed in a hotel and fed at public expense for the duration of the trial. Occasionally in extremely long trials, sequestered jurors are allowed supervised visits with immediate family members. And some jurisdictions provide for conjugal visits for married jurors.

The jury hears the evidence in the case. When both sides have presented their cases and rested, the judge instructs the jury on matters of law, including the definition of the crime and what the jury must decide. The jury then retires to deliberate. Inside the jury room the first order of business is usually to elect a foreman or forewoman, and to take an initial poll on the question of guilt or innocence on each of the counts in the case.

Criminal conviction requires a unanimous vote of the jury. If one person believes the burden of proof has not been met, the jury cannot return a conviction. When jurors determine that they have reached an impasse and cannot come to a unanimous agreement, they return to court and report that to the judge. Such a split jury is known as a hung jury. In the case of a hung jury the case is dismissed.

Reporters covering trials in both federal and state courts should be aware that in virtually every jurisdiction it is a crime for a reporter to attempt to talk to a juror while the case is being heard or deliberations are in progress. The courts have held that reporters may contact jurors after the verdict has been rendered, although jurors are under no obligation to talk to the news media.

Key Points

- The Sixth Amendment provides for a "speedy and public" trial by an impartial jury.
- In the federal courts the process of jury selections begins with a jury pool, called for a number of months to be available for trial duty.
- In criminal cases the burden of proof is on the prosecution to show the defendant is guilty beyond a reasonable doubt.
- In civil cases the burden of proof is based on a preponderance of the evidence.
- Most federal criminal trials are heard by twelve-person juries.
- Civil cases are often heard by smaller jury panels, frequently six people.
- The questioning of potential jurors in court is *voir dire.*
- Jurors may be challenged and dismissed for cause, such as bias or familiarity with the case.
- Each side is allowed a certain number of peremptory challenges in which a juror may be dismissed for no reason at all.
- In criminal cases the jury vote must be unanimous to convict.
- Failure of a jury to reach unanimity is called a hung jury and results in dismissal of the case.
- It is a crime for newspeople try to contact members of a sitting jury while the trial is in progress.

4.6 Federal Civil Law

Federal civil cases may be heard in District Court before a jury or, if the parties agree, in front of a judge without a jury. Civil juries are often reduced in size from twelve to six in federal District Courts. There is no constitutional language that requires juries to consist of a specific number of jurors.

Civil cases involve claims by individual entities (including corporations and individuals). The scope of civil litigation includes lawsuits against the federal government, suits against individuals under federal law, requests for injunctive relief (asking the court to stop or enjoin a particular action or conduct), suits alleging torts (civil wrongs such as libel or trespass), suits alleging contract violations, and prisoner appeals.

Federal civil actions may be initiated by departments and agencies of the federal government against non-governmental entities — such as the Justice Department's case against AT&T. Federal civil actions may be brought by private individuals against other private individuals — such as professional golfer Casey Martin's suit against the PGA Tour claiming violation of the Americans with Disabilities Act in denying him the right to ride a golf cart in pro tour events.

In criminal cases, the punishment can be as severe as death and often involves imprisonment and/or fines. In civil cases individuals, corporations, or governments are usually seeking some other form of judicial action, including:

1. Actual monetary damages (compensation for something lost)
2. Punitive monetary damages (money over and above what was lost as a form of punishment)
3. Injunctive relief (a court order prohibiting or enjoining a particular action or activity sometimes in the form of an injunction)
4. Specific performance (a court order requiring a particular action such as fulfilling a contractual obligation)

A usage note for reporters covering civil cases in either federal or state court: "damage" is what is alleged to have been done and often what brought about a lawsuit in the first place; "damages" (with the "s") is the monetary compensation — either actual or punitive. Damages are sought to compensate for damage.

The rules governing federal civil procedure are contained in Title 28 of the U.S. Code.

Key Points

- Civil law involves non-criminal legal actions involving two or more parties.
- Federal civil cases may be heard by a judge sitting without a jury, only if all parties to the action agree.
- Federal civil juries are frequently made up of fewer than twelve jurors, six being the common number.
- The burden of proof in a civil action is preponderance of the evidence, a lower standard than the criminal burden of proof which is guilt beyond a reasonable doubt.
- Civil actions usually seek some legal remedy other than incarceration, including actual monetary damages, punitive damages (money awarded as punishment), injunctive relief (in which the court stops somebody from doing something), and specific performance.

TABLE 4.1.   **Categories of federal civil actions**

Contract actions (including)	**Actions Under Specific Statutes**
Government contracts	Anti-trust
Interstate contracts	Bankruptcy
Employee relations	Banks and banking
Stockholder suits	Civil rights
Voting rights	Americans with Disabilities Act
Real property actions (including)	Interstate commerce
Sales and acquisition claims	RICO (anti-racketeering)
Land condemnation	Public accommodations
Foreclosure	Welfare fraud and abuse
Rent and lease	Liquor laws
Deportation	Food and drug rules
Personal property actions (including)	USDA acts
Truth in lending	Occupational safety and health
Fraud	**Other civil actions**
Physical damage	Selective Service violations
Tort actions (including)	Copyright
Product liability	Patent and trademark
Workers' compensation	Tax suits
Personal injury	Freedom of information
Medical malpractice	Constitutionality of state statutes
Securities and Exchange	State reapportionment
Labor law actions (including)	Prisoner petitions
Fair Labor Standards Act	
Railway Labor Act	
Labor/Management Relations Act	
ERISA (pension protection)	

Note: There are literally hundreds of categories and sub-categories of civil actions that are tried in federal court. This is a partial list of some of the most notable and common ones.

4.7 How Cases Get to the Supreme Court

Most cases that get to the U.S. Supreme Court are appeals from lower federal or state courts. The most common method for taking a case to the high court is through a petition for a writ of certiorari. Such a writ may be sought if a Court of Appeals in one circuit has rendered a decision that is in conflict with the decision of a Court of Appeals in another circuit, if a state court of last resort (usually but not always called the state supreme court (see Chapter 10, section 10.1) has decided a major federal question that conflicts with the decision or decisions of other courts, or if a federal or state appeals court has decided an important issue that the appellant seeks to be reviewed.

While appeals to the Supreme Court usually result from decisions of federal Courts of Appeals and from the highest courts in the states, there are provisions for certain other petitions and appeals. In rare instances cases may be appealed directly from U.S. District Courts. In even rarer instances the Supreme Court will consider petitions for extraordinary writs, such as death penalty appeals. In all cases appeals are only considered at the discretion of the justices.

The Judiciary Act of 1789 established an appellate procedure through which cases could be appealed directly from District Courts to the Supreme Court. The volume of cases reaching the high court quickly spiraled out of control and over the years Congress took steps to limit the number of Supreme Court cases. Today, the justices have total discretion over which cases they will hear and which they won't. Reporters often hear lawyers declare, "We'll appeal this all the way to the Supreme Court." That's more often bombast than reality.

The Supreme Court receives an average of eight thousand petitions for review every year. In lawyers' shorthand the petitions for writs of certiorari are often referred to simply as "cert." Of the appeals submitted, the justices usually agree to decide between 100 and 120 cases in an average year. That number has occasionally been higher, but public comments by several justices indicate the workload generated by 100 to 120 cases is about as much as the justices themselves want.

The petitions for writs of certiorari go through an internal screening process that usually starts with each justice's clerks going through the stack of petitions. The clerks make the initial determination of the cases that are most significant. Among other things they are looking for unique cases that deal with constitutional issues not considered before by the court. They look for cases that deal with deeper or broader social issues than the narrow action of the parties involved in the original action. They also look for cases that have been decided differently by two or more Courts of Appeals, or by state and federal courts, and cases that seek clarification or expansion of previous high court rulings.

Once a case has been heard and decided by the Supreme Court, it is unusual for the justices to revisit the issues and legal precedents established, unless there has been a profound change in the makeup of the court or the passage of time has dictated a deep social change in the country. In rare instances, however, the court will determine to reconsider issues previously decided. This happened in 1954, when the high court agreed to reconsider the issue of school segregation first decided in 1896 in the case *Plessy v. Ferguson*. In that case the Supreme Court ruled that "separate but equal" facilities for blacks and whites was constitutional. Fifty-eight years after approving "separate but equal," the court delivered its ruling in *Brown v. Board of Education*, reversing *Plessy* and declaring "separate but equal" is not constitutional.

Once each clerk has presented his/her recommendations, the individual justices determine the cases they wish to hear. All nine justices then meet in a closed conference (which can take several days) and discuss each case they might consider. Every case is voted on in a process that's steeped in the history and tradition of the court. The vote is oral and starts with the chief justice and works down the bench in order of seniority. The most junior justice is charged with taking hand-written notes of the conference. The clerk of the court will turn those notes into a public announcement of the disposition of each petition considered. Four justices must vote to hear a case for it to be placed on the Supreme Court docket.

Once a petition has been accepted and put on the docket, it is scheduled for oral arguments. By court tradition and practice, the attorney for each side is usually given thirty minutes to present his/her case. While each lawyer invariably walks in with a well-rehearsed presentation, modern Supreme Courts have rarely just listened. Often an attorney doesn't get more than a few sentences out before he/she is peppered with questions from the bench.

Oral arguments are open to the public, but the Supreme Court does not allow camera coverage of its proceedings. In 2000, the court allowed the audiotape of oral arguments (long used by transcribers to make the verbatim transcript of the proceedings) to be made available to news organizations. So for the first time, people who did not personally sit in the Supreme Court chamber were able to hear the sound of the justices' voices and the way their questions were answered by the attorneys presenting the case.

The court sits for oral arguments on Monday, Tuesday, and Wednesday, usually hearing three or more cases each day. Within days — Wednesday afternoon for cases heard Monday, and Friday afternoon for those heard Tuesday and Wednesday — the justices meet to vote. Frequently they vote more than once, with so-called swing votes or swing justices changing sides as the issues are weighed and considered. When a consensus is reached, the most senior justice in the majority is charged with deciding who will write the majority opinion.

Those justices who disagree may submit dissenting opinions. They may either write their own dissent or join in the dissent of another justice. If a justice agrees with the conclusion of the majority but disagrees with the legal underpinnings of the majority opinion, that justice may write a concurring opinion, outlining the differences in interpretation of law.

Justice Clarence Thomas provided a glimpse of what goes on in the justices' inner sanctum in a Savannah, Georgia, speech aired in August 2001 by C-SPAN. He said that justices frequently voice strong opinions and argue them with passion regarding various cases. He observed that there is no shortage of passionate and intense persuasion among the justices. But he added that the tone is always civil, cordial, and collegial.

Most decisions are handed down on Mondays. They are first announced by the court in chamber, sometimes with justices reading all or part of their opinion or their dissent. For journalists, a ritual that looks bizarre to an outsider unfolds a floor below the Supreme Court chamber in the pressroom. There's a crowd every decision day, but when a decision is expected in a case of major national significance, it takes on the look of a combination rugby scrum and the Tokyo subway at rush hour.

Reporters and TV producers jam into the office of the court's press officer and his/her assistants. When a decision has been announced in the chamber, the clerk of the court telephones the press office and tells the press officer the docket number. Copies of the printed opinion are handed to the waiting journalists, starting with the wire services.

Since nobody knows what decisions will be handed down on a given day, reporters occasionally stand there all morning to receive only relatively minor opinions. If it is the case the reporters have been waiting for, the journalists explode out of the press office. Print and wire service reporters race to their computers to put out "bulletins." Radio reporters go running to their broadcast booths, located in a dark anteroom under the staircase that leads to the court chamber. And TV producers go at full tilt out the side door to the front plaza where TV correspondents are standing under their lights with their microphones and telexes waiting to deliver word of the decision to the nation.

The Supreme Court term begins each fall on the first Monday in October. The last of the year's decisions is usually handed down just before the justices go on their summer recess, generally in June. Even when the court is not sitting, the justices will consider emergency appeals, such as death row inmates seeking last minute stays of execution. As with other cases, four justices must vote in favor of reviewing the case or it is rejected.

Key Points

- Most petitions to the Supreme Court come from decisions of the Courts of Appeals or the highest courts of the states.
- Every term the Supreme Court gets thousands of petitions, but usually decides fewer than 150 cases per term.
- The most common petition to the Supreme Court is for a writ of certiorari.
- The court may also consider petitions to hear cases directly from District Courts or entertain extraordinary writs such as death row appeals.
- The court has total discretion regarding which cases it will hear.
- Four of the nine justices must vote to hear a case.
- After certiorari is granted, the case is put on the docket and moves to oral arguments.
- Each lawyer presenting oral arguments to the court gets a half hour, almost always interrupted by questions from the justices.
- The justices vote on the case within days of oral arguments.
- The majority opinion delivers the decision of the court.
- Justices write concurring opinions when they agree with the result but disagree with the interpretation of law.

- Dissenting opinions explain why justices disagree with the majority opinion.
- Supreme Court proceedings are not televised, but an audiotape of oral arguments is occasionally made available after the session and may be broadcast.

4.8 Courts of Special Jurisdiction

In accordance with the constitutional authority enumerated in Article I Section 8, to "constitute tribunals inferior to the Supreme Court," the Congress has occasionally seen fit to create courts of special jurisdiction to deal with areas of specialized litigation. Only two such courts are currently in existence.

Congress set up the Court of Claims in 1855 to relieve its own workload. Until 1789, any monetary claim based on a federal statute, a regulation promulgated by executive branch departments and agencies, or resulting from a contract with the U.S. government, was decided by a petition directly to Congress. The Court of Claims was established to decide those particular matters. (It was the same act of Congress that created the office of solicitor general of the United States, the attorney who represents the U.S. government in such monetary disputes.)

In 1982, Congress sought to make the federal court system more efficient. A law was passed that abolished the old Court of Claims and gave its jurisdiction to the newly-created U.S. Court of Appeals for the Federal Circuit. In the same law, Congress created a new, lower-level Court of Federal Claims, whose judges are appointed for fifteen-year terms, rather than life, and whose final decisions are appealable to the Court of Appeals for the Federal Circuit.

In 1890, Congress established a judicial body known as the Board of General Appraisers, which shortly thereafter became the Customs Court, with a charter to resolve customs disputes. For the most part these disputes resulted from the appraised value of goods imported into the United States and the tariffs imposed on them. Twenty years after the board and then the Customs Court were established, Congress changed the jurisdiction and the name again, creating first the Court of Customs Appeals, then finally changing the jurisdiction again and renaming the body the Court of Customs and Patent Appeals.

In 1980, Congress consolidated that special court's jurisdiction, and established the U.S. Court of International Trade, which is still in existence. The Court of International Trade was designed to be equal

Reading a Supreme Court Opinion

Brown v. Board of Education of Topeka
347 U.S. 483, 74 S. Ct. 689
Mr. Chief Justice Warren delivered the opinion of the Court.
[Body of the decision.]
It is so ordered.

1. Title of case — The first name in the title tells who is the appellant, the person or institution bringing the appeal. The second name is the defendant in the appeal. The name as it appears in the Supreme Court case may not be the same as it appeared in the trial court or in the Court of Appeals. For example, in a federal criminal case the title might read *United States v. Smith*. That tells you the entity bringing the charges is the U.S. government and the defendant, the accused, is Smith. If Smith appeals, the case would be *Smith v. United States*. In cases where the Supreme Court has agreed to decide an extraordinary writ, the case is usually entitled *In re [petitioner's name]*, such as *In re Oliver* or *In re Quarles*.

2. Citation — In this example the numbers tell where the case can be found in a law library. The first number is the volume, the initials are for what law book series, and the second number is the page. (74 S.Ct. 686 means the case is in Volume 74 of the Supreme Court Reporter, at page 686.) A decision that has just been handed down by the Supreme Court will generally not have been assigned pages and volumes yet. The only number on those cases will be the Supreme Court docket number.

3. Author — The next line says which justice wrote the opinion.

4. Body — Court opinions usually start with a recitation of the facts of the case, followed by the legal issues of the case, the resolution of the legal (constitutional) issues, and the Court's remedy.

5. Concurring opinions(s) — If there are concurring opinions, they will follow the majority decision, with the author and those justices joining the concurrence listed in the first line.

6. Dissenting opinions(s) — If there are dissenting opinions, they will follow the concurrences and will state the author and those justices joining the dissent. (Reporters should note that dissenting opinions often present excellent counterpoint quotes in stories about controversial Supreme Court decisions.)

to the District Courts in resolving disputes involving such trade issues as enforcement of trade agreements. The court was to have the power to authorize monetary judgments and grant injunctive relief, with appeals going to the Court of Customs and Patent Appeals. When the new, broader Court of Appeals for the Federal Circuit was created in 1982, the Customs and Patent Appeals Court was dissolved, with its duties and jurisdiction going to the new Circuit Court, where it is today.

Finally, taxation has long generated legal controversy. In 1924, Congress created an early version of what is today called the U.S. Tax Court. The jurisdiction of the Tax Court was codified in the Tax Reform Act of 1969 and is specifically designed as a judicial forum in which people charged with tax deficiencies by the Internal Revenue Service may have their cases heard. The court is based in Washington, D.C., but judges travel to designated cities in each state to hear cases. Appeals of Tax Court decisions go to the Courts of Appeals.

Key Points

- Since 1855, Congress has established courts of special jurisdiction to deal with narrow but specialized jurisdictions.
- Several of these courts were abolished in 1982 when the new Court of Appeals for the Federal Circuit came into existence and was assigned to take over the specialized functions.
- The U.S. Court of International Trade still exists to deal with trade disputes.
- The U.S. Tax Court hears cases involving tax disputes in which taxpayers can challenge IRS allegations of tax deficiencies.

4.9 U.S. Magistrate Judges

The caseload of District Courts grew rapidly in the years after World War II. Judges were forced to deal with more and more matters, often procedural and ancillary to the actual work of trying cases. As a result, the federal court system operated more and more slowly. To some, the delays verged on infringement on the Sixth Amendment right to a "speedy and public trial."

In 1968, Congress sought to ease the burden on the District Courts and speed up the system by passing the Federal Magistrates Act, creating a subordinate level of federal judges to deal with many of those procedural and ancillary matters. These judges, appointed to eight-year terms, were known originally as U.S. magistrates. Their title was changed in 1990 to U.S. magistrate judges.

The jurisdiction of U.S. magistrate judges includes issuing search warrants, conducting criminal arraignments and other pre-trial proceedings such as bail hearings, conducting some civil trials (if all parties consent to such a trial), and accepting the findings of federal grand juries. In addition, U.S. magistrate judges hear misdemeanor cases and other minor offenses that may be punished with no more than one year imprisonment and/or a fine of no more than $1,000.

District Courts, under a provision known as local rules, may from time to time require U.S. magistrate judges to perform other functions such as reviewing prisoner petitions or acting as special master in civil cases. (Special masters are representatives of the court appointed for a specific legal purpose in relation to a particular case. A common example is the oversight of disposal of property in accordance with an order of the court.)

Key Points

- U.S. magistrate judges are subordinate to District Courts and perform some of the procedural duties once performed by district judges.
- Magistrate judges are appointed for eight-year terms.
- Magistrate judges issue search warrants and perform such pre-trial functions as arraignments and bond hearings.
- Magistrate judges receive reports of federal grand juries.
- Magistrate judges can conduct civil trials if all parties to the case agree.
- Magistrate judges conduct trials for misdemeanors and other minor offenses that are punishable by no more than a year in prison and/or a fine of not more than $1,000.

4.10   Notes for Reporters Covering Federal Courts

Cameras are not permitted in the federal courts. In 2000, the Supreme Court took its most dramatic step in history toward allowing limited broadcast coverage of its proceedings by releasing the recording of oral arguments from which the written transcription is made. While release of audiotapes has been rare, for the first time it allows the general public to hear the voices of the justices as they ask their questions of the lawyers presenting oral arguments. Several sitting justices are on the record as saying they oppose allowing camera coverage of Supreme Court proceedings. Others predict it is only a matter of time.

Some federal courthouses have pressrooms, where reporters may broadcast or conduct interviews, but they are the exception rather than the rule. In most federal courthouses, reporters (as well as trial participants and the public) must pass through metal detectors and be subjected to other security screening. Reporters carrying tape recorders, cameras, microphones, and the like are either denied access or are required to check their electronic equipment with the U.S. marshals.

Cellular phones and laptop computers are allowed in courthouses. U.S. marshals will usually check cellular phones to see that they are off before they are allowed into courtrooms.

In addition, courtroom sketch artists are permitted into all federal courts, including the U.S. Supreme Court. Occasionally, judges will waive the usual rules and allow the media sketch artists to sit in the jury box, if there is no jury impaneled.

Trials are open to the public and the news media in U.S. District Courts. In most cases, there are ample seats to accommodate the news media and the public. Reporters can expect trials to start around nine-thirty or ten in the morning, with a break around eleven. Lunch is usually an hour, although occasionally judges use the lunch period to see lawyers in their chambers and as a result the break can often be longer. The afternoon session is usually about three hours, one to four or one-thirty to four-thirty, with a break about midway through. Judges usually allow reporters to come and go as they want or need to, as long as they do not disrupt the proceedings.

Appellate proceedings are open to both the news media and the public in the Courts of Appeals and the Supreme Court. Reporters wishing to cover the U.S. Supreme Court can gain access with a Capitol Hill press credential or by contacting the court's press office and arranging for admission to the oral arguments. Most of the workspaces in the Supreme Court pressroom are assigned, although there is a first-come-first-served table in the middle of the room from which visiting journalists may work. Bring your own cellular phone, as the phones in the pressroom are the property of the news organizations which installed them, and public payphones are about a block away.

Key Points

- Cameras are not allowed in any federal courts.
- The U.S. Supreme Court occasionally releases an audiotape of oral arguments after the proceeding is complete.
- U.S. District Court trials are open to the news media and the public.
- Oral arguments before the Courts of Appeals and the Supreme Court are open to the media and the public. News media sketch artists are permitted into all federal courtrooms.

Extraordinary Circumstances:
War, Impeachment, and
Amending the Constitution

Part of the brilliance of the U.S. Constitution is the way in which the framers made it flexible and adaptable. What follows are some of the extraordinary circumstances the framers provided for. Time and technology have required some modifications. The issue of war, for example, bears little resemblance to what it was in 1787. Impeachment, on the other hand, has followed the constitutional model scrupulously in the rare cases in which it has been used. And while the amendments to the Constitution reflect their own historical time, such as those that were a direct result of the Civil War, the process of amending the Constitution has been unchanged since Madison put quill to parchment.

5.1 War

The whole concept of war, when the Constitution was adopted, was a far cry from what it is today or might be in the future. War in the late Eighteenth Century consisted of colorfully dressed opposing armies marching in formation and firing at each other with ball-and-powder weapons or approaching so close that they would do battle with swords and sabers. Nobody among the founding fathers, not even the genius Thomas Jefferson or the scientifically prescient Benjamin Franklin, could have contemplated the weapons of mass destruction, delivery systems using lasers and computers, satellite guidance, or the sophisticated killing machines we have at hand today.

In the late Eighteenth Century, war was viewed as relatively routine and commonplace. Article I Section 8 vests Congress with the exclusive power to declare war. But that power follows mundanely upon a lengthy list of other actions exclusive to Congress, including raising taxes, paying debts, borrowing money, regulating commerce, writing rules for immigration and bankruptcy, coining money, setting up the post office, promoting science, and setting up courts.

In giving Congress the power to declare war, the framers made it abundantly clear that they did not want the power to plunge the country into armed conflict in the hands of one man. The framers agreed that there had to be a military chain of command and the president should be at the top of the chain. But, in keeping with the concept of separation of powers, they opted to place the command structure and the ability to inaugurate a war in the hands of two different branches of government.

Throughout history, there has been a struggle between the president, in his role as commander-in-chief, and the Congress, with its power of the purse and the sole authority to declare war. From the time Jefferson sent the U.S. Navy against the Barbary pirates in 1801 to Bill Clinton's actions in what was once Yugoslavia as the sun set on the Twentieth Century, presidents have been far more inclined to send U.S. troops into conflict on their own initiative than to seek a congressional declaration of war.

U.S. military forces have been sent into action without a formal war declaration more than two hundred times since 1800 — a little less than once a year. Yet since the adoption of the Constitution, Congress has formally declared war only five times — the War of 1812, the Mexican-American War, the Spanish-American War, World War I, and World War II. Even those conflicts popularly called the Korean War and the Vietnam War were not "wars" declared by Congress.

Until the Lyndon Johnson administration, U.S. military forces, and the actions in which they engaged, enjoyed a reasonable measure of popular support. That changed in the 1960s and '70s. Some historians argue that the main reason public sentiment toward the military action in Vietnam changed was that it was the first American war fought on television. Night after night the battles and the blood were brought into peoples' living rooms. Journalists who did not live through the period should be aware that even the Vietnam conflict had a solid measure of public support in the early years.

On August 7, 1964, Congress approved a measure that came to be known as the "Gulf of Tonkin Resolution." It was passed only three days after North Vietnamese naval vessels allegedly attacked U.S. intelligence ships in the Gulf of Tonkin and it authorized U.S. military action in North and South Vietnam, Laos, and Cambodia.

Over the next six years, public skepticism about the Vietnam War increased and anti-war unrest on the nation's college campuses erupted. The pivotal year was 1970. On May 4, 1970, there was an anti-war demonstration on the campus of Kent State University in Ohio. National guardsmen fired on the student demonstrators and when the gunfire stopped, four students lay dead. Public outrage was intense. Less than two months later Congress repealed the Gulf of Tonkin Resolution. But President Nixon ignored the action and the war in Vietnam raged on.

On June 19, 1973, Congress passed the Case-Church Amendment which forbade any further U.S. military action in Southeast Asia. The Nixon administration was furious, but the votes in both the House and Senate were well in excess of the number needed to override a presidential veto. The passage of that amendment set the stage for one of the most controversial congressional actions in modern history, passage of The War Powers Act of 1973, Public Law 93-148. President Nixon vetoed it. The veto was easily overridden.

The War Powers Act of 1973 or War Powers Resolution (both are correct) stated that under the law, the president of the United States "in every possible instance shall consult with Congress before introducing U.S. armed forces into hostilities" or into areas where hostilities are imminent. If troops are sent into a hostile situation the president must notify Congress within forty-eight hours. The president must then hold consultations with the Congress regularly until the troops are withdrawn from action. The resolution limits the president to using troops for sixty days without specific congressional approval. After that he's either got to get a congressional declaration of war, some other form of congressional approval, an extension of the deadline, or be able to show that the deadline cannot be met because of an attack on the United States.

Every president since the War Powers Resolution was passed — Nixon, Ford, Carter, Reagan, Bush, Clinton, and Bush — has actively opposed it, most declaring it unconstitutional. Every administration has contended that the War Powers Act inhibits the president's constitutional authority as commander-in-chief. All presidents have been willing to challenge or even ignore the War Powers Resolution when they felt it necessary. President George H. W. Bush, for example, made it clear that he intended to go to war to drive Iraqi forces from Kuwait in 1991 with or without the approval of Congress. In the end, after a tempestuous debate, the president won congressional approval for Operation Desert Storm.

But journalists involved in coverage of military affairs, foreign policy, Congress, and/or the White House must know that more than three decades after passage of the War Powers Resolution there are many unanswered questions and unresolved issues.

It is not enough for presidents to simply declare the law unconstitutional. The federal courts — and in all likelihood the Supreme Court — must do that, and so far the courts have been reluctant to weigh in. The Supreme Court has refused to decide the issue, despite a significant number of opportunities. Administration after administration has argued that the War Powers Resolution places unconstitutional limits on presidential authority. They have said that the War Powers Act is at best a cumbersome intrusion by Congress and at worst a potential danger to national security and a threat to the safety of our men and women in uniform.

What can Congress do if a president ignores the War Powers Resolution and sends troops into conflict anyway? Obviously, Congress could cut off funding for such operations. In 1993, Congress gave President Clinton a deadline to remove U.S. forces from Somalia or face a cut-off of funding, but the troops were out before the deadline passed so the issue became moot.

When terrorists attacked the United States on Tuesday, September 11, 2001, Congress moved almost immediately to give President Bush all the authorization he might need to root out those responsible and (in unusually broad language) those who harbor them, help them, and/or provide them safe haven. The congressional resolution did not name a particular terrorist target, nor did it specify which countries were believed to shelter terrorists. During consideration of the measure, the grotesque images of terror on U.S. soil were fresh in the minds of everyone. For the first time in history, an attack on the United States was witnessed live on national television.

Using hijacked jetliners as their missiles, the terrorists knocked down New York's World Trade Center and blew a gaping hole in the

Pentagon. On Friday, September 14, Congress approved the sweeping resolution unanimously in the Senate and with only one dissenting vote in the House. Nobody wanted to resurrect the debate about the legality of the War Powers Act while the rubble in lower Manhattan was still smoking. Nor did anybody want to draw any comparisons to the action of Congress in 1964 when it approved the Gulf of Tonkin Resolution.

The extraordinary resolution of September 14, 2001, addressed the provisions of the 1973 War Powers Act, but it neither named the controversial act nor delivered a formal declaration of war. There was no doubt that war had been declared on the United States. There is little doubt Congress would have given the president a formal declaration of war had he sought one. But members pointed out that to declare war it is implicit that there must be a tangible, identifiable enemy. Once again the conditions surrounding war had changed from what it was in 1787.

The last time Congress formally declared war, after the Japanese attack on Pearl Harbor in 1941, there was no question who the enemy was. In September 2001, the issue of war, the president's role as commander-in-chief, the 1973 War Powers Resolution, and the role of Congress were as murky and indistinct as ever.

Key Points

- Congress has the sole power to declare war.
- The president is the commander-in-chief of U.S. military forces.
- The above two constitutional authorities have created a long-standing tension between the legislative and executive branches.
- During the Vietnam War Congress moved to restrict presidential authority in an undeclared war.
- The War Powers Act of 1973 (also called the War Powers Resolution) is still the law of the land.
- Every president since Nixon has said the law is unconstitutional.
- Without a formal declaration of war, the resolution requires the president to consult with Congress prior to sending troops into conflict.
- The resolution gives the president sixty days to withdraw the troops, obtain a declaration of war or other congressional authorization, or an extension of the time limit.

- No court has ruled on the constitutionality of the War Powers Resolution.
- In September 2001, after the terrorist attacks on New York and Washington, Congress plowed new ground by giving the president authority to use the military well beyond the scope of the War Powers Act, but short of a declaration of war.

5.2 Impeachment

There is a deep public misconception about impeachment. Impeachment does not mean "to remove an official from office." Impeachment is the first step in a two-step formal process of charging an official accused of misconduct. Removal from office is one possible outcome of impeachment and trial. The official accused cannot be removed from office or otherwise sanctioned without being convicted by the Senate. The process of impeaching and trying a government official — either an elected official such as the president, or an appointed official such as a federal judge — was designed to be cumbersome.

The founding fathers were keenly aware of human frailty and weakness, that at some point it might become necessary to discipline an official or even remove that person from office. Historians note that by splitting the impeachment process between the House and Senate, the authors of the Constitution took into consideration the highly political nature of the House of Representatives and the more somber and deliberative nature of the Senate. Even the standard for congressional sanctions is deliberately vague and broad, defined as the commission of "high crimes or misdemeanors."

In its final clause, Article I Section 7 gives the power of impeachment to the House of Representatives, where the process begins. Some legal scholars liken impeachment in the House to an indictment by a grand jury. To impeach an official requires only a simple majority vote in the House. Impeachment starts in the House Judiciary Committee. As with other legislation, the committee holds hearings and votes on whether to send the question to the full House.

Article I Section 3 of the Constitution makes the Senate the body that tries the official charged with "high crimes and misdemeanors" once impeachment is voted by the house. In the case of the impeachment trial of the president, the Constitution requires that the chief justice of the United States preside over the Senate. (In impeachment cases against lower officials, the vice president or the president pro tempore may preside.) Unlike the House, the Senate must vote by a two-thirds majority to remove an official from office or to impose any other lesser sanction.

Only two U.S. presidents — Andrew Johnson and Bill Clinton — have been impeached by the House and in both cases the Senate vote fell short of the two-thirds majority needed to remove either man from office. The harshest sanction that the Senate may impose, under Article I Section 3, is removal from office, with a prohibition against holding public office again or receiving any other public benefits from having held the office.

Nonetheless, Article I Section 3 also provides that imposition of a penalty by the Senate does not immunize the person against further prosecution and punishment by the legal authorities and the courts after he/she is out of office. This specifically supercedes any claim of double jeopardy under the Fifth Amendment.

Key Points

- Impeachment originates in the House of Representatives, starting with the Judiciary Committee.
- The House impeachment vote is a simple majority.
- The Senate tries impeachment cases.
- The condition for impeachment is the commission of "high crimes or misdemeanors."
- The Senate must vote to impose a sanction (or punishment) by a two-thirds majority.
- In the case of the Senate impeachment trial of a president, the chief justice of the United States must preside.

5.3 Amending the Constitution

The framers of the Constitution knew that to keep it a living, vibrant document the U.S. Constitution would have to be changed from time to time. Since it was ratified in 1787, it has only been amended twenty-seven times. While acknowledging the need for a mechanism to change the document, the framers deliberately made the process so difficult that the Constitution would not be changed frivolously.

Article V of the Constitution is devoted to the amendment process and provides two ways in which amendments may be proposed and adopted. Constitutional amendments can be the result of congressional initiative or the initiative of the state legislatures, although the latter method has never been used. Legal scholars and historians have debated and written lengthy treatises on how such a process would actually work, without reaching a consensus.

So far, all constitutional amendments have been initiated, debated, and voted on in the U.S. House of Representatives and the Senate. Either chamber may originate a constitutional amendment. And both chambers must approve the proposed amendment by two-thirds majority votes. Only then may the proposed amendment be sent along to the states for ratification.

Unlike other legislation, the president's signature is not necessary for an amendment to become part of the Constitution or to send it to the states. The president has no veto power over a constitutional amendment. In fact, the executive branch has no role in amending the constitution.

After congressional action, three-quarters of the state legislatures (both houses in all but unicameral Nebraska) must then approve the amendment for it to become a part of the Constitution. Two methods of state ratification are possible and both have been used. In all but one case, constitutional amendments have been ratified by three-quarters of the state legislatures by simple up or down votes.

However, the Twenty-first Amendment, the repeal of prohibition, became the historic exception. The condition imposed by Congress in drawing the language of the amendment required state ratification conventions for approval. In demanding a convention, some members of the U.S. Congress felt it would limit the role of the state legislatures by allowing average citizens to take part in the ratification convention and to act on the amendment.

But deciding on the exact process of selecting convention delegates fell to the various states and the result was a methodological hodgepodge. At least one state allowed the governor to name the members of the state legislature as the delegates to the ratification convention. Some states provided processes allowing average citizens to stand for election as delegates. Some required candidates to announce in advance whether they supported the proposed Amendment or not. Despite the procedural confusion, the Twenty-first Amendment was finally approved. The convention process for ratification has never again been used.

Most, but not all, recent constitutional amendments, starting with the Eighteenth enacting prohibition, have given the state legislatures a time limit, usually seven years, in which to ratify a proposed amendment. In 1972, the so-called "Equal Rights Amendment" was sent to the states for ratification with a seven-year time limit. Congress extended that to a ten-year time limit but the amendment still failed to become a part of the Constitution. It needed ratification by one more state legislature before the deadline expired in 1982. Ratification deadlines are not a part of Article V.

Journalists covering stories connected with proposed constitutional amendments should be aware that scores of amendments are drafted and put forward every session of Congress. Many of them are perennials, showing up session after session in various forms. Reporters should be cautious in reporting the mere introduction of a constitutional amendment as a major news story and check to see if the proposed amendment is actually new at all.

Journalists should also be mindful of the deliberate difficulty imposed by the founding fathers on the process. Few proposed amendments ever make it to committee hearings; fewer still ever get out of committee to the floor of either the full House or Senate; and only a scant number ever come up for votes in both chambers. Even then obtaining the two-thirds majorities required to send the amendment to the states is an extreme rarity.

Key Points

- A proposed amendment can originate in Congress or in the states but state origination has never happened.
- All twenty-seven amendments have started with a two-thirds vote of both the U.S. House and Senate.
- The president's signature is not necessary to ratify a constitutional amendment.
- Three-quarters of the state legislatures (both houses, with the exception of Nebraska, which has only one chamber in its legislature) must ratify an amendment for it to become part of the Constitution.
- All of the amendments but one (the Twenty-first which was approved by state ratification conventions) have been ratified by votes of the state legislatures.

The Amendments — Thumbnail Sketches and Annotation for Journalists

Amendment I

Prohibits legislative infringement on freedom of speech, religion or the press; protects right of assembly and to petition the government.

This amendment does not confer the enumerated rights. The presumption of the authors of the Bill of Rights was that Americans had freedom of speech, religion, and press and had a right to assemble and petition the government. The purpose of the amendment — as eloquently noted by Justice Ruth Bader Ginsburg during her confirmation hearing before the Senate Judiciary Committee — was to prohibit any legislative action that would diminish or revoke the enumerated rights. Congress has run afoul of the First Amendment in several recent cases where lawmakers have undertaken to prohibit flag burning and Internet pornography, the laws struck down as abridgements of the "free speech" clause.

Amendment II

Provides for a militia and establishes the right to "keep and bear arms."

The Second Amendment is a political hot-button issue. In covering stories involving the Second Amendment, and that includes virtually every gun control, gun registration, gun crime, or gun ownership story, there are two very distinctly drawn sides. One (exemplified by organizations that want stricter gun controls) argues that the amendment relates to the necessity of a well-regulated militia and that the right to bear arms is only within the context of militias. They posit that unlimited gun ownership by average citizens was not the intent of the authors of the Bill of Rights. The other side (exemplified by the National Rifle Association) believes gun ownership is a fundamental American right enshrined in this amendment and extends to everyone whether in the militia or not. Reporters should not get snookered into reporting just one side.

Amendment III

Proscribes quartering of troops.

Amendment IV

Prohibits "unreasonable searches and seizures."

The founding fathers never envisioned the technology of the Twenty-first Century. As a result, "search and seizure" issues have made their way to the Supreme Court several times in recent years. In 2001, the court said searching somebody's home using heat-sensing scanners is a violation of the Fourth Amendment. The September 11, 2001, terrorist attack on the United States resulted in a Justice Department request for Congress to broaden federal wiretap laws. Civil liberties groups pledge to keep watch over congressional action in that area to preserve the rights enshrined in the amendment.

Amendment V

Prohibits being tried twice for the same crime (double jeopardy); prohibits self-incrimination; requires due process of law.

Journalists have occasionally fallen into the trap of presuming guilt when a person undertakes the right not to incriminate him/herself. At no time in U.S. history was the use of that right more flagrantly abused than during the dark period known as the McCarthy Era. Republican Sen. Joseph McCarthy of Wisconsin used the power of his office to pursue Communists both within and outside of government. One of his tactics was to summon a person accused of being a Communist or a Communist sympathizer before his Senate committee and interrogate the person. If the person refused to testify citing his/her right against self-incrimination, McCarthy thought nothing of convicting the person without trial by publicly labeling him/her a "Fifth Amendment Communist." To McCarthy, using the right was akin to a confession of guilt. It is not and reporters must guard against making it so.

Amendment VI

Provides for a speedy and public jury trial in criminal cases; requires the ability to confront witnesses.

The issue of confronting witnesses has been in the news with regularity in the last several years, particularly with regard to child molestation and/or abuse cases. Because of the fact that adults in positions of authority and occasionally parents or stepparents are the accused, courts have occasionally attempted to create conditions in which the child-victim will testify without fear or intimidation. The techniques the courts have used include video cameras with the child in another room and screens set up as a physical barrier between the child and the accused. In several cases adults convicted with the use of such techniques have appealed, claiming a violation of their Sixth Amendment right to confront witnesses.

Amendment VII

Provides for a jury trial in civil cases.

Amendment VIII

Prohibits "cruel and unusual punishments."

The courts continue to hear appeals of the death penalty on the grounds that it violates the Eighth Amendment. In 2001 the Georgia state supreme court declared the state's electric chair as cruel and unusual punishment, causing the state to switch to lethal injection as its method of execution.

Amendment IX

Rights enumerated by the Constitution don't deny other rights retained by the people.

Amendment X

Often called the state's rights amendment. It says those powers which are not within the federal sphere are retained by the states.

This amendment arises in political discourse from time to time. It is often cited by conservatives and neo-federalists as a limitation on the rights of the federal government to reach into the business of the states. It is sometimes cited as well as the constitutional underpinning for the elevation of private property rights, largely the domain of the states, to a position co-equal with the other provisions of the Bill of Rights. Journalists must take pains to clarify exactly what news sources are saying when they cite the Tenth Amendment.

Amendment XI

Federal courts can't intervene in suits against any one state by citizens of another or by foreign nationals.

Amendment XII

Delineates the function of the Electoral College and certification of presidential elections. (Repeals part of Article II Section 2.)

Amendment XIII

Abolishes slavery and involuntary servitude. (Repeals part of Article IV Section 2.)

Amendment XIV

Applies the other amendments to the states and says the states may not deprive any person of "life, liberty, or property, without due process of law." (Repeals part of Article I Section 2.)

Amendment XV

Gives former slaves and African Americans the right to vote.

The Thirteenth, Fourteenth and Fifteenth Amendments are a direct result of the Civil War and have been surrounded by a highly charged political atmosphere well into the late Twentieth Century, especially during the civil rights movement of the 1960s and '70s. Many southerners believed that the three were imposed on them as punishment and without representation because their state legislatures were made up of Yankee carpetbaggers.

Amendment XVI

Congress can impose and collect income taxes.

Amendment XVII

Provides for popular election of senators. (Repeals part of Article I Section 3)

Amendment XVIII

Establishes prohibition.

This Amendment, which entered the Constitution in 1919, marks the only time in U.S. history when the Constitution was frivolously amended in response to a volatile social issue of the day. To this time, and since, the procedural difficulties in changing the Constitution have served as a firewall between temporal political issues and those that are likely to have a lasting legal and social significance. It took fourteen years to undo the damage done by this amendment. The unintended consequences of prohibition included public disregard for the amendment itself which allowed otherwise law-abiding, patriotic people casually to break the law, trivialize the Constitution, and disrespect the law enforcement authority of the federal government.

Amendment XIX

Gives women the right to vote.

Amendment XX

Sets the inauguration of the president for noon on January 20 and requires Congress to meet on January 3. (Repeals part of Article I Section 4.)

Amendment XXI

Repeals prohibition.

Amendment XXII

Sets a two-term limit for the president.

Amendment XXIII

Gives the District of Columbia representation in the Electoral College.

Amendment XXIV

Outlaws poll taxes.

It took nearly a century to resolve one of the systemic failings left by the Civil War. One key issue for the civil rights movement was a form of taxation that effectively denied African Americans their right to vote. While the right to vote was the law of the land, a number of states imposed legal obstacles restricting full enfranchisement. Some states required people to pay for the right to vote in the form of a voting or poll tax. Until this amendment was ratified there was no federal mechanism for changing those state laws.

Amendment XXV

Establishes the procedure for selecting a new vice president when the vice president replaces the president.

Amendment XXVI

Gives 18-year-olds the right to vote.

This amendment was a direct result of the social upheaval of the late 1960s caused by the war in Vietnam. All over the country, students (and a lot of their parents) argued that sending young men off to war without giving them the right to vote was a profound injustice. In 1971 the amendment was ratified, just in time for young Americans to vote in the 1972 presidential election. Some analysts speculated that the youth vote might turn the tide in favor of Democrat George McGovern, but the incumbent Republican Richard Nixon won in a landslide and the impact of the youth vote was negligible.

Amendment XXVII

Prohibits members of Congress from receiving a pay raise until after the next congressional election.

Where Normal Rules Don't Apply

The presumption of this book is that citizens of the United States have a right to know what their government and their public officials are doing and that journalists, as the primary conduit of that information, have a duty and an obligation to pursue the people's right to know. It presumes a journalist's right of access to public places and public officials. The First Amendment clearly prohibits legislative infringement on the right of a free press.

But the right is not absolute. There are exceptions where the normal rules don't apply. For example, reporters do not have the right to disclose details of military operations, especially in a time of conflict. Reporters do not have the right to cover anything they want on military bases, even though bases are public property. The news media do not have a right to disclose material that might be of aid to this country's enemies.

American reporters usually have limited access when foreign officials and leaders visit the U.S.; the level of access is often determined by what kind of coverage the foreign leader or official will permit. Some foreign leaders go out of their way to allow greater access to American reporters than they allow to the news media of their own country.

Reporters have no right of access to foreign embassies on U.S. soil. Access can be extended and withdrawn by the country that occupies the embassy.

Even within the states, there are exceptions to normal newsgathering and reporting practices, specifically on the country's Indian reservations. The relationship between the U.S. government and the nation's Indian tribes is based on treaties — like those with foreign governments — and such issues as open meetings, sunshine laws (see

Chapter 8, section 8.10), and general news coverage are not the same on Indian reservations as elsewhere.

Finally, newsworthy people occasionally find themselves behind prison bars. Access to prisons and prisoners has been the subject of a great deal of litigation, but the bottom line is that when it comes to prisons and prisoners, the usual rules don't apply.

6.1 U.S. Military Operations

The U.S. Army, Navy, Air Force, and Marines make up the largest military organization controlled by a democratic, civilian government in the world. The commander-in-chief of the U.S. military is a civilian — the president. The top executive at the nation's supreme military headquarters, the Pentagon, is a civilian — the secretary of defense. The dissemination of news to journalists is coordinated through the office of a civilian — the assistant secretary of defense for information.

The military has a dual command structure — civilian and uniformed. Below the secretary of defense are a deputy secretary and several assistant secretaries. There is an individual civilian secretary in charge of each uniformed service — secretary of the Army, etc. — but these secretaries are subordinate to the secretary of defense within the civilian ranks.

The top of the uniformed command structure is made up of general officers, in the Army, Air Force, and Marines, and flag officers in the Navy. The four most senior military officers comprise the Joint Chiefs of Staff. The chairman of the Joint Chiefs is considered the highest-ranking uniformed military officer in the country and can be from any branch of the service.

For a journalist who covers military affairs, the Pentagon is similar to covering any other beat most of the time. It involves getting to know principal players and making the same kind of personal contacts reporters make in any other sector. Getting military information, however, becomes much more difficult when the United States is engaged in a military conflict. As a practical matter, when U.S. military forces are preparing for, or are actively engaged in, foreign operations the normal flow of information available to news reporters becomes limited. Sometimes it dries up completely.

It is the job of the journalist to try to obtain as much information as possible. And it is the job of the nation's military commanders to protect their forces and not provide valuable information to the enemy, which has instant access to the American news media via satellite and the Internet. While journalists complain when military information is withheld from them, there is very little they can do about it. Most newspeople are keenly aware that there are things that should not be reported even if they do become known.

In 1917 and 1918 Congress enacted and modified the Espionage and Sedition Act. That law provided criminal penalties for disclosing military information that might help the enemy or encourage disloyalty or mutiny among U.S. troops. It remains illegal to disclose secret information that might harm national security or endanger U.S. forces.

Many reporters thought that the U.S. Supreme Court opened the door for greater media freedom in obtaining and disclosing military information in 1971, when the justices ruled that *The New York Times* and *The Washington Post* could not be prohibited from publishing a document known as "The Pentagon Papers." The case *New York Times v. United States* applied the doctrine against prior restraint detailed in *Near v. Minnesota* forty years earlier.

In *Near*, the Supreme Court struck down a Minnesota law that allowed courts to grant injunctions against publication of a newspaper that was deemed "malicious, scandalous, or defamatory" before it was actually published. Chief Justice Charles Evans Hughes wrote without equivocation that "the constitutional guarantee of the liberty of the press gives immunity from previous restraints."

But as if to remind reporters that the doctrine against prior restraint is not absolute, in 1979 the Supreme Court upheld an order restraining publication of an article in *The Progressive* magazine about how to make a nuclear bomb. Justice Potter Stewart, in *United States v. Progressive, Inc.*, wrote that the doctrine against prior restraint does not apply when there is "the likelihood of direct, immediate and irreparable injury to our nation and its people."

While information during a time of military conflict is seldom complete, the civilian authorities are generally responsive to a public demand for news, even if the uniformed command would like to keep everything secret. In military conflicts of the late Twentieth Century, the Pentagon usually took pains to provide at least a minimal amount of public information regarding ground and sea engagements, air sorties, battle damage assessment, personnel movement, and tactics.

Historically in times of conflict, the news media have had fairly open access to the troops in the field, so long as the journalists accepted the risks and conditions connected with working in a war zone and didn't get in the way of the troops doing the fighting. During the Civil War, photographer Matthew Brady roamed freely among the troops of both sides at will.

For the most part, journalists who seek to enter combat zones agree to certain conditions, such as not disclosing their exact location or reporting on a mission while it is in progress.

In World War II there was an Office of Military Censorship. General Douglas MacArthur, for example, required reporters to submit their stories to multiple censors before they could be released. The practice of official military censorship continued in the Korean conflict, but was disorganized and often ineffective.

In Vietnam, the news media generally followed a list of conditions for news coverage that amounted to voluntary censorship. Yet because of the volume of war news and the often-critical way it was reported, relations between the military (at all levels) and the news media became strained. Without oversimplifying, there was a feeling by the end of the war among the military that journalists were generally opposed to the war, opposed to what was caustically referred to as the military-industrial complex, and opposed to soldiers, sailors, airmen, and Marines as individuals. That set the stage for a period of distrust that occasionally verged on hostility between reporters and the military. The Pentagon suffered the press, but only the most trusted, most well-known reporters had much of a chance of getting anything beyond the information contained in banal news releases.

In the 1980s, the Pentagon information machine adopted a policy of releasing information in a form known as "response to query." In short, an information officer would provide a minimum amount of information to a reporter inquiring about a specific story. If the reporter had questions the information officer would answer them. The theory was that only those reporters with a background in military affairs would have sufficient knowledge to ask the precisely correct "silver bullet" questions to elicit anything but superficial information.

In 1982, when President Reagan sent U.S. troops to invade the island-nation of Grenada, the news media weren't told until after the fact. Despite howls of outrage from reporters, the Pentagon and the administration did not retreat from the decision to circumvent journalists.

After Grenada, the Pentagon created a Defense Department media pool. Membership in the pool rotated among the various national news organizations. The theory was that it would be activated whenever there was a military operation and members of the pool would accompany the first military units into the field. The media agreed to a condition of secrecy, which occasionally proved ineffective. The pool accompanied troops on maneuvers and exercises, but has never been activated for an actual conflict.

By 1990, when war loomed in the Persian Gulf, the Pentagon had devised a strategy designed to keep a tight rein on the news media. The strategy was two-pronged. First, virtually all information would come out of one central location, the command center in Dhahran, Saudi Arabia. And second, most coverage of military activities in the field would be limited to "pools" of reporters and photographers. (Pools involve selection of a limited number of video and still photographers and reporters — print, radio, TV — who go into the field and report back to the entire press corps, providing detailed accounts, pictures, video, and audio to all.)

A review by the Freedom Forum, published in June 1991, of the Persian Gulf War revealed mixed reactions among the news media. While some participating journalists acknowledged the need for a pool system in order to avoid chaos in the field — given the huge number of journalists (some 1,400) who covered the war — others bristled that it was nothing more than a way to control reporters and manage the flow of information.

Finally, despite Pentagon efforts, enterprising reporters did an end-run around the U.S. military and hitchhiked into the war zone, and ultimately into Kuwait City, with foreign military units that were part of the international coalition arrayed against Iraq.

When the United States engaged in a military operation against terrorism, starting in October 2001, reporters raced to Afghanistan, Pakistan, Uzbekistan, and Tajikistan without waiting for the Pentagon for transport or assistance. They could go where they wanted and report what they wanted. Many joined the fighters of the so-called Northern Alliance, who were eager to display their military prowess in opposition to Afghanistan's repressive Taliban rulers. Some U.S. reporters made it into the war zone by linking up with local forces that supported the U.S. military mission or by organizing media convoys from Pakistan through the Khyber Pass into Afghanistan. Nonetheless there were dangers inherent in going into combat areas. By January 1, 2002, eight journalists had been killed trying to reach the front, more than the number of U.S. troops killed in combat to that time.

The Pentagon ultimately did assist reporters seeking to accompany troops into places where access was difficult, setting up pools to report from ships anchored off Pakistan and from remote and highly secure staging areas such as Camp Rhino in the Afghan mountains. In return for Pentagon assistance and access, journalists agreed to conditions established for news coverage such as a request that reporters not use the last names of men and women involved in the operations for fear of terrorist reprisals against their families at home. Reporters were also asked not to disclose the exact location of bases, camps, and operations and not to disclose the nature and goals of missions while they were in progress.

U.S. military information came primarily from the Pentagon, with Defense Secretary Donald Rumsfeld and Joint Chiefs Chairman Richard Myers briefing reporters almost daily. Early in the war Rumsfeld made it clear that he did not intend to lie to the news media, but neither did he intend to disclose everything he knew.

There is an inevitable tension between reporters and the Pentagon information machine during a military conflict. The news media are in the business of getting and reporting as much information as possible; the military has a vested interest — in terms of security, strategic planning, operational secrecy, and command and control — in not divulging anything that might be of help to the enemy. In one instance early in the war in Afghanistan, newspeople were prevented from getting to the scene of a friendly fire incident in which U.S. troops were killed. Subsequently the Pentagon conceded that journalists should have been granted quicker access to medics, rescue personnel, and survivors and promised to take corrective steps.

Even in peacetime, the Pentagon is a clubby place. Those who work there, both civilian and military personnel, and the journalists who cover military affairs, think of themselves as a community. Outsiders aren't exactly shunned, but visiting reporters should know that membership in the club is not automatic with acquisition of a press credential. Special credentials are required to cover the Pentagon, and even then there is a pecking order. Those people who cover the Pentagon occasionally get one type of credential; those who cover it daily get another. Since the terrorist attack September 11, 2001, that left permanent scars on the Pentagon building itself, access and security have been tightened.

The reality is the Pentagon regulars get the most information. It used to be that reporters with a military background were more readily accepted into the club than those without military backgrounds, but that discrimination has largely disappeared.

The clubby atmosphere is also evident in covering military bases. The local reporters who cover their base(s) as a regular news beat naturally will have better relations with the base commanders and the ranks below them than newspeople who only cover base affairs occasionally.

Reporters should be aware that the U.S. Coast Guard is often mistakenly considered one of the armed services. It has the same ranks as the Navy, but it is not a part of the Department of Defense. The Coast Guard is part of the Department of Transportation, and has a different mission than that of the uniformed military forces. Coast Guard personnel are occasionally armed and serve in a law enforcement capacity, arresting drug smugglers, pirates, and illegal aliens in U.S.-controlled waters. The Coast Guard also occasionally acts in a defensive capacity, notably guarding ports, commercial shipping lanes, and coastal nuclear power plants after the September 11, 2001, terrorist attack on the U.S.

Key Points

- There are multiple exceptions to the First Amendment prohibition against legislative restrictions on freedom of the press.
- The general prohibition against prior restraint, especially when the United States is engaged in military conflict, is not absolute.
- The top commanders of the U.S. military are civilians.
- The most senior military officers comprise the Joint Chiefs of Staff, with the chairman of the Joint Chiefs effectively the country's top military officer.
- In peacetime, covering the Pentagon is very much like covering any other news beat.
- When U.S. forces are engaged in operations, the flow of information from the Pentagon is tightly controlled.
- While a free press is protected in the First Amendment, news organizations do not enjoy an unlimited right to broadcast or publish if it might threaten national security or the safety of U.S. forces.

- Official military censorship was in place in World War II and Korea.
- In Vietnam journalists accepted conditions of coverage that amounted to voluntary censorship but by the end of the war relations between the military and the media were strained.
- In recent foreign conflicts the Pentagon has engaged in deliberate and calculated strategies designed to restrict news media access to field operations and information.

6.2 Military Bases

There is no absolute right for news reporters to have access to U.S. military installations. In fact, there are times — in the interest of national security — when bases are off limits to newspeople completely. In those cases news organizations can appeal to the Pentagon's office of public information, but for the most part when the military wants to clamp a lid on news coverage, at the base, post, fort, armory, or air station level, it can.

When U.S. forces are placed on the highest level of threat alert, bases are generally sealed. Journalists may stand on public sidewalks outside the bases and even interview any soldiers, sailors, airmen, or Marines who choose to talk. But in the face of a national security

TABLE 6.1. **United States Military Ranks**

Commissioned Officers	
Army, Air Force, Marines	**Navy**
General of the Army (Army only) (5 stars)	Fleet Admiral
General (4 stars)	Admiral
Lieutenant general (3 stars)	Vice admiral
Major general (2 stars)	Rear admiral
Brigadier general (1 star)	Commodore
Colonel	Captain
Lieutenant colonel	Commander
Major	Lieutenant commander
Captain	Lieutenant
First lieutenant	Lieutenant, junior grade
Second lieutenant	Ensign
Non-commissioned Officers	
Sergeants	Petty officers
Enlisted Personnel	
Privates and corporals	Seamen

threat most military commanders clamp a lid on what their troops can say and whom they can talk to.

For the most part the policy of the military is to maintain good relations with the communities near their facilities and with the media that serve those communities. Generating favorable and positive news coverage is a part of the role of most base commanders. Local news organizations often have excellent relations with the local bases. It is in their mutual interest.

When the military wants media attention or expects favorable publicity, gaining access to bases and base personnel is made easy. Tensions arise when the media want information that may be unfavorable to the military, such as accidents involving U.S. forces, operations that did not go as planned, incidents involving civilian casualties or damage, or misconduct on the part of individuals or groups of military personnel. For reporters who regularly cover their local military base, times of crisis are when carefully cultivated sources will pay huge dividends.

When one of the heavy guns blew up aboard the battleship *U.S.S. Iowa* in 1990, information from the ship's home port, Norfolk Naval Base, dried up like the Sahara. "All information is to come out of the Pentagon," was the response to repeated phone calls. The base remained open to reporters although much of it was restricted, with military police stopping journalists who strayed from authorized areas without passes. Reporters were allowed to cover the memorial service for those killed in the explosion and the docking of the ship itself, but news media contact with base commanders and the families of U.S.S. Iowa crew members was tightly controlled and extremely limited. The base made available a few family members who agreed to talk to the media, but they were selected by the Navy and presumably rehearsed by Navy information officers about what kinds of questions they might be asked.

Occasionally, the military has extended news media restrictions beyond the physical borders of a military base. In 1997, an Air Force fighter jet crashed in a Baltimore neighborhood. The Pentagon declared the entire area a "national defense zone," ordered residents to evacuate their homes, and set up a security perimeter complete with armed troops keeping everyone away. Residents were not allowed to return home for three days. Despite media appeals, the Pentagon insisted the security was necessary in order to investigate the cause of the crash and to prevent any classified materials from falling into unauthorized hands.

Few military bases are completely isolated from the surrounding civilian world. As a result it is difficult to hide or mask large troop or equipment movements. People will see the fleet sailing or an abnormally large number of takeoffs without an equally large number of landings. But knowing that something's going on is easier for reporters to ascertain than finding out where the troops and/or equipment are going, especially in a time of international friction or pending conflict.

Key Points

- Journalists do not have an absolute right to cover stories on military bases.
- When national security is threatened, military bases are often shut to the media.
- Most military bases have a policy of encouraging good relations with the local news media.
- Except for local activities, the Pentagon public information office is the primary source for reporters seeking military information.

6.3 Embassies and Foreign Dignitaries on U.S. Soil

The United States maintains diplomatic relations with about 180 countries, according to the State Department, and nearly 160 of them have embassies or diplomatic missions in Washington, D.C. Some countries, such as Canada, Mexico, and the United Kingdom, also maintain consulates, a diplomatic post subordinate to an embassy, in major cities around the country.

The organizational chart is similar for most nations' embassies. The chief official at most embassies is called the ambassador; sometimes that person is called chief of mission. There is usually a second in command with one of several titles: assistant ambassador, deputy chief of mission, or first secretary among them. Many, but not all, have public relations officers, often called secretary for information or press officer.

Occasionally foreign embassies will invite the U.S. media to news conferences or briefings, generally with the ambassador in his or her capacity as the highest-ranking official of that particular country in the United States. Within hours of the assassination of Israeli Prime Minister Yitzhak Rabin in 1995, the Israeli Embassy in Washington held a news conference for American reporters.

A significant number of countries take pains to try to accommodate newsgathering and interview requests from American journalists. Notable for their accessibility and cooperation with the American media are the embassies of the United Kingdom, Canada, Israel, Australia, Ireland, and Japan. Most European embassies, along with those of Mexico, Brazil, Russia, India, and South Africa, are relatively user-friendly for reporters seeking information.

Others are not. Some, in fact, are downright hostile to American reporters and will make it deliberately difficult to navigate through their organization. Occasionally you won't get past the first person that picks up the phone. In general, countries with a tradition of a vigorous, free press tend to be more cooperative with the U.S. media than countries that do not have a free press at home.

Sometimes the problem is language. Most diplomatic and embassy personnel stationed in the U.S. speak some measure of English, although occasionally it's convenient for them to pretend they don't. The embassy of the former Soviet Union was notorious for feigning an inability to speak English, and then when a reporter switched to Russian, the embassy would usually just hang up. Selective answers, diplomatic obfuscation, or deliberately ignoring the question are techniques reporters encounter in trying to obtain information from a foreign embassy.

Occasionally the problem is cultural. For example, female American reporters sometimes find barriers when dealing with governments whose official policy relegates women to second class citizenship in their own country. Sometimes the problem is that the foreign embassy finds no benefit and, therefore, feels no obligation to help an American reporter. For the reporter, there is no recourse, save for reporting the lack of cooperation in the news story.

A few countries that do not have diplomatic relations with the United States have an embassy, consulate, or mission in New York City that is diplomatically linked with the United Nations. Occasionally, reporters pursuing stories involving such nations as Iran, Cuba, and North Korea, with which the U.S. does not have diplomatic relations, can obtain information by contacting those United Nations posts.

In accordance with the specific language of treaties between the U.S. and various countries and pursuant to international law, foreign embassies in the United States (like U.S. embassies and consulates in foreign countries) are considered the sovereign territory of the nation that owns the embassy. For example, the Egyptian Embassy in Washington is sovereign Egyptian territory. So the rules that govern news coverage of the U.S. government — including the right of public access, open meetings, and the presumption of a public right to know — rarely, if ever, apply with regard to foreign embassies.

At some point, almost every reporter will have to find information regarding some kind of foreign story. A local resident has an accident or is lost, kidnapped, or killed in a foreign country. A foreign national is accused of a crime in the area where you work. A foreign dignitary is planning to visit your city or town. The local high school or college is sending a class to a foreign country. The possibilities go on and on.

Reporters who cover the United Nations have the most frequent access to foreign diplomats in the United States. News conferences are commonplace. Reporters in other locations have far less occasion to cover foreign diplomats or leaders. Once in a rare while a foreign head of state will participate in a joint news conference with the U.S. president, allowing for questions from the White House press corps. On even rarer occasions a foreign leader will meet with American reporters on Capitol Hill. Occasionally foreign politicians will make themselves available for questions. Before he ran for prime minister of Israel, Benjamin Netanyahu would frequently meet with Washington reporters.

More often than not, a visiting head of state is likely to meet exclusively with the reporters from his/her own country that are covering the official visit for consumption back home. While American reporters bristle at this, the visitor is under no obligation to invite the American media to such sessions. Frustrating as it is for U.S. newspeople, there's no avenue of appeal if a request for an invitation is denied.

The lead U.S. government department that deals with foreign policy and foreign governments is the Department of State. When a foreign head of state, political leader, or dignitary makes an official visit to the United States, the State Department Office of Protocol moves center stage. Working with the department's public affairs office, State Department officials will coordinate news media coverage of the foreign official's visit. If you, as a reporter covering the visit of a foreign official, feel like you are being manipulated, maneuvered, and corralled into covering only the best, most positive, least controversial, and most tightly controlled aspects of the event, it's because you probably are. The State Department is involved in only official visits.

When a foreign celebrity, sports star, author, actor, or musician makes a trip to the United States, they are private citizens and their travel is not coordinated by the U.S. State Department. In many cases, information about such private visits can be obtained from the embassy of the country from which the celebrity hails. But foreign celebrities are subject to the same general parameters of news coverage as U.S. celebrities. Most who want or expect news interest hire U.S. public relations and security firms to deal with the news media.

Key Points

- There are about 160 foreign embassies in Washington, D.C.
- Each embassy in the United States (like all U.S. embassies in foreign countries) is considered the sovereign territory of the nation whose embassy it is.
- Many embassies have public information officers and/or public information offices but they frequently provide little more than newspeople could get from the tourist office.
- A reporter seeking information from the embassy of a country that does not honor a free press at home should not expect the kind of help a reporter might anticipate from embassies of countries with a tradition of a free press.
- When a foreign leader or politician makes an official visit to the United States, the State Department's Office of Protocol is usually in charge of coordination, including coverage by U.S. news media.
- The State Department does not coordinate visits by foreign celebrities.

6.4 American Reporters Working Abroad

There has always been a mystique about foreign correspondents. Movies and television have portrayed them as glamorous ink-stained swashbucklers crusading for truth and justice in far-off, hostile places. The hostility is often very real; the glamour is more often than not the product of a fiction writer's imagination. Nonetheless, it occasionally falls to American journalists to cover news stories in foreign countries. Do not presume it will be like what you see in the movies. Be well advised before you go that the rules outside the United States for journalists are often very different than they are at home.

A few basics: With the exceptions of Canada and Mexico, the first thing you'll need is a passport. Some countries require visas, which are routinely denied to journalists. Even if the story you are covering is benign or positive about the country you are visiting, be prepared to answer questions if you are allowed to enter. Some nations, such as Syria, Libya, and Burma, do not welcome western journalists at all.

Once you have your passport and visa, check with the State Department or your physician to see what, if any, immunization you should have. See if there are any other health warnings posted for the country to which you intend to travel. For example, reporters going to Belarus are warned about high levels of radiation outside major cities as a result of the country's proximity to the Chernobyl nuclear accident. Don't take these warnings lightly. One of the worst things that can happen to a reporter is to get sick while on a foreign assignment.

In some cases journalists end up in places that are dangerous, either because of the nature of the story being covered (such as conflicts, riots, social strife, or war) or because of the attitude of the government. Reporters and photographers were killed in the war against terrorism in Afghanistan. In one case a convoy of journalists was ambushed and four journalists were beaten with stones and rifle butts before they were shot to death. Journalists have been arrested recently in such places as Turkey and Indonesia.

The State Department regularly issues advisories and warnings to Americans traveling abroad about areas of hostility or danger. Reporters routinely ignore those warnings. But journalists must be aware that they are assuming the risk of going into hostile or dangerous places.

Kidnapping, torture, and murder are all possible and have all happened to American reporters working in danger zones. On Tuesday, January 22, 2002, Daniel Pearl, a reporter for the *Wall Street Journal,* went to meet a source in Islamabad, Pakistan, and was not heard from again. A few days later his kidnappers released a photo of Pearl with a gun to his head. About a month later, it was confirmed that he had been brutally murdered.

Associated Press reporter Terry Anderson was abducted in Beirut,

Lebanon on March 16, 1985, and did not see freedom again until December 4, 1991. Sometimes, when Americans get into trouble overseas, U.S. embassies can help. On occasion other government officials or agencies can be of assistance. But for the most part reporters who get into trouble abroad are on their own.

That is especially true if the reporter has chosen to go to such places as Cuba, Iran, or North Korea where the United States has no diplomatic relations. In addition reporters who cover hostilities in places like Afghanistan, the former Yugoslavia, Angola, or the Middle East, are assuming the risk connected with getting the story. Still other countries don't like Americans as a rule and afford no special treatment to American reporters regardless of how sympathetic, educative, informative, or positive their stories might be.

Key Points

- American journalists covering stories in foreign countries other than Canada and Mexico will need a passport.
- Many countries require visas and routinely refuse to issue them to American newspeople.
- Reporters working abroad should check with the State Department or their own physician regarding immunization.
- Many foreign nations are hostile to American reporters.
- U.S. embassies can occasionally help or intervene if an American reporter gets in trouble working outside the U.S., but journalists cannot count on help if they are arrested, detained, or kidnapped.

6.5 Indian Reservations

Reporters are occasionally called upon to cover stories involving Native Americans, especially those reporters who live in states with large Indian populations — including Alaska, Washington, Oregon, California, Arizona, New Mexico, Montana, South Dakota, Oklahoma, and Wisconsin. Unfortunately, few reporters know anything about the customs and cultures of Native Americans and about the unusual relationship between the tribes and the U.S. government. Reporters who work in an area where there is an Indian reservation would be well advised to do a little research about the history and culture of the tribe that lives there.

The relationship between Washington and the nation's Indian tribes is based on government-to-government treaties, in the same manner that treaties establish the framework for relations between the U.S. and foreign governments. As with all treaties they are negotiated by the executive branch and approved by a two-thirds majority vote of the U.S. Senate. While Native Americans are citizens and enjoy the constitutional rights to vote, to travel, to relocate, and to associate, those who live on reservations occupy a unique position.

Indian reservations are lands set aside, with their boundaries defined in the treaty documents, specifically for the use of a particular tribe or group of tribes. The title to the land is held by the United States in trust for the particular tribe that negotiated the treaty. The tribes have legally enforceable interests in the land. Most treaties prohibit tribes from selling reservation land. In some instances they may lease it, as some of the Sioux tribes do in South Dakota, to neighboring non-Indian ranchers for grazing purposes.

There are myriad examples of treaty violations over the last two centuries, almost exclusively by non-Indians and/or the U.S. government itself. White settlers pushing west frequently ignored existing treaties and settled on, annexed, usurped, and stole Indian lands, often with the tacit — if not overt — cooperation of the government. Appeals to the Bureau of Indian Affairs, the agency charged as caretaker of Indian interests in Washington, were regularly rejected, if they were ever considered at all.

In the late 1960s the American Indian Movement began. It was a loosely organized, sometimes militant organization dedicated to returning Native Americans to their social, cultural, and religious roots. AIM, as it is known, viewed the government in Washington and the non-Indian news media in general as partners in a deliberate campaign to perpetuate the myth that Native Americans are ignorant and lazy savages, steeped in alcohol and perpetual poverty. Among AIM's stated goals were greater tribal autonomy, enhanced tribal control of the reservations and reservation life, and removal of the federal presence — including law enforcement and schools — from all reservations.

This was in conflict with the mission of the Bureau of Indian Affairs, established by the Indian Reorganization Act of 1934. This act declared that the policy of the U.S. government was assimilation of Native Americans into the mainstream of American life. AIM supporters viewed the Indian Reorganization Act as the tool the federal government would use to deny the tribes their languages and religion, destroy their culture and heritage, and ultimately to get rid of Indians and Indian tribes altogether. The most militant AIM supporters considered assimilation nothing less than a method of genocide.

In the winter of 1973, AIM took over the village of Wounded Knee on the Pine Ridge Reservation in South Dakota. An armed, month-long standoff ensued, pitting AIM against U.S. marshals dispatched by the Nixon administration. For Native Americans the symbolism of AIM's actions was intensified by the fact that Wounded Knee was the site of the 1890 massacre in which as many as 300 Lakota Sioux men, women, and children were killed by the U.S. Army. The 1973 takeover of Wounded Knee catapulted Native American issues onto the nation's front pages. Many Native Americans felt the news media sided with the U.S. government, which prompted varying degrees of hostility against the non-Indian news media around the country and especially near reservations.

It prompted a cycle that continues. Journalists, seeking to report Indian stories, often received a chilly, if not openly hostile, reception on reservations, especially from people who aligned themselves with the views of the American Indian Movement. As a result of the anti-media hostility, many of the stories have had a negative edge reflecting what the reporters encountered. That prompted even more hostility and reluctance to cooperate, which generated more negative stories. And on and on. Reporters should be aware that the residue of the 1970s exists today on many Indian reservations.

The treaties with the various tribes allow those tribes to make and enforce their own laws. If a non-Indian commits a crime on an Indian reservation, the case is tried in federal District Court. If an Indian from one tribe commits a crime on another tribe's reservation, the case is tried in federal District Court. But if a tribal member commits a crime on his/her own reservation the case is tried in tribal court under tribal law. Most reservations have tribal police forces, tribal judges, and even tribal jails.

Indian tribes have governments. On most, but not all reservations, the main legislative body is the tribal council. The head of the executive department is the tribal chairman or chairwoman, the president, or the chief. The structure of tribal law is codified in a constitution that deals with many of the same kinds of issues we see in state constitutions: land use, law enforcement, emergency preparedness, schools, health care, and telecommunications. But tribal constitutions also deal with issues seldom seen anywhere but in Indian America, such as who is entitled to be a member of the tribe, who is entitled to fish or hunt on reservation land, and what steps must be taken as a matter of law to protect and preserve tribal culture, religion, society, and heritage.

Many, but not all, tribal constitutions have clauses protecting press freedom. Non-Indian reporters need to know that getting news on Indian reservations is often a challenge. Among many Native Americans there is a deep distrust of the non-Indian news media. There is a presumption that the non-Indian media are profoundly prejudiced against Native Americans, that virtually every story written about Native Americans is negative and stereotypical, and that past cooperation with non-Indian reporters has not brought good results.

Some tribes, such as the huge, sprawling Navajo Nation in Arizona and New Mexico, are very sophisticated in their dealings with the news media. The Navajo government has a press office and exerts control the same way as congressional press secretaries act as gatekeepers for their bosses. In other cases, such as on the Pine Ridge Reservation of the Lakota Sioux in South Dakota, it is possible to walk up to the tribal chair's office and get an interview almost instantly.

As with Americans everywhere, Native Americans are under no obligation to grant news interviews, answer reporters' questions, or cooperate with the media. Some Native Americans are sensitive or reluctant, based on their traditional religions, to having their photographs taken. Unlike other public places in the United States, news reporters, other than those from the tribe's own newspaper or broadcast outlets, do not have any particular right to be on Indian reservations or to attend public meetings or hearings. Tribal documents are generally not covered under freedom of information laws, unless the documents sought have been turned over to a federal or state government authority, such as a court.

A significant number of Indian tribes have turned to the active pursuit of non-Indian visitors. Gambling on some Indian reservations has proved to be a boon to tribal economies and a lure for non-Indian customers. A few tribes have established other travel and tourism ventures, such as the Warm Springs Confederation in Oregon, which operates a golf resort.

For reporters covering stories on Indian reservations, advance preparation will pay dividends in access, cooperation, and production of accurate, factual, and fair stories.

Key Points

- The unique relationship between Indian tribes and the U.S. government is contained in a series of government-to-government treaties.
- Indian reservation lands are owned by the United States but for the exclusive use of a particular tribe of Indians, as enumerated in the various treaties.
- There is a general distrust of non-Indian news media on the part of many Native Americans.
- Indian reservations have their own government, police force, court system, and schools.
- Tribes have constitutions, similar to many state constitutions, but not all contain a "freedom of the press" clause.
- Reporters should not assume that the rules and practices of news coverage on Indian reservations is the same as it is off the reservations.

6.6   Prisons

News organizations have long argued that prisons are public buildings and when newsworthy events go on behind prison walls, the news media have a right to cover those events. The courts have generally been reluctant to uphold that view. The U.S. Supreme Court has routinely ruled that newspeople have no greater right of access to prisons than that afforded to the general public.

State and federal courts have cited security, the stability of prison administration, and the notion that some inmates achieve a disproportionate level of notoriety as the result of media attention as the underpinning of their rulings. Some courts have suggested that it is a valid public policy interest not to allow certain inmates to attain celebrity status as a result of media attention. Some prisons adopted new rules regarding media access to prisoners after sensational prisoner interviews, such as talk show host Geraldo Rivera's chat with mass murderer Charles Manson.

Media access to other notorious criminals — including terrorist Ramze Yussef and "Son of Sam" serial killer David Berkowitz — has been denied by prison officials and the courts have upheld those denials. Media claims and prisoner appeals on First Amendment grounds have largely been rejected. Federal prisons occasionally allow highly restricted access to inmates. Oklahoma City bomber Timothy McVeigh could have given a limited number of telephone interviews to the media in his final days, but he elected to communicate with the news media only through letters.

When a person is convicted of a criminal offense, in state or federal court, that person is automatically deprived of some constitutional rights. The courts have held that it is not unconstitutional for prison authorities to refuse media requests for in person or broadcast interviews with prisoners. The media may be able to contact inmates by mail, and in some cases by phone. In some cases prisoners can add media representatives to their lists of approved visitors, although this varies widely from state to state.

In virtually all cases, media contacts with prisoners will be monitored by prison officials, including phone calls, mail, and the totality of any personal interviews.

Reporters seeking access to prisons or interviews with prisoners usually must make their request to the prison warden or the information office of the state prison authority. In the case of the federal penitentiaries, journalists must direct their requests for access to the Bureau of Prisons. In reviewing such requests, some states specifically limit them to credentialed representatives of legitimate news organizations, denying access to freelancers, independent filmmakers, independent documentarians, or independent radio producers or reporters.

In 2001, Oklahoma City bomber Timothy McVeigh requested that his execution be televised. The request was rejected, but it sparked a lively debate — both in academic and journalistic arenas — about whether executions should be televised. None of the thirty-eight states that have the death penalty, nor the federal government, allow broadcast coverage of executions, although all have some kind of provision for public and/or media witnesses to attend executions. While media representatives who witness an inmate's death routinely report about it to other members of the media who were not present, there are no moves afoot anywhere to allow televised executions.

Key Points

- While news occasionally happens behind prison walls, state and federal courts have not seen fit to grant the news media any exceptional right of access.
- Media and prisoner appeals on First Amendment grounds have routinely been denied.
- Prisons have been held to have a legitimate right to deny media access, based on security, routine prison administration, and the impropriety of giving some prisoners celebrity status.
- Despite a request from Oklahoma City bomber Timothy McVeigh to have his execution televised, no state or the federal government allows broadcast coverage of executions.
- Journalists seeking access to prisoners usually need to make their interview requests through the agencies that run the individual state or federal prison housing the inmate.

Section II
State and Local Government

7

State Government Overview

There are wide variations in how state governments are structured and function. Some of the differences are subtle, such as differing minimum ages for certain state offices and differences in state fiscal years. Some are quite striking, such as whether a state allows citizens directly to enact new laws or reject the actions of the state legislature at the polls.

All states follow the federal model insofar as each has executive, legislative, and judicial branches. All have law enforcement authority, courts, and penitentiaries. All have some mechanism for generating revenues. All have departments and/or agencies to deal with local emergencies. And every state considers public education a primary function and concern. That said, every reporter covering state government needs to make it his or her business to know the particular function of that state. The constitution of the state is a great place to start. (All are available on-line. See Appendix B.)

These chapters are not intended to supply one-size-fits-all answers, but to highlight some of the questions journalists need to ask.

The way the fifty states work today is rooted in our national history going all the way back to pre-revolutionary times. It is useful in examining the current makeup of the state governments to take a brief look backward at the original thirteen colonies and how they made the transition from offshoots of the British crown to independent states. Only two of the original colonies were self-governing from their beginning — Rhode Island and Connecticut. Their independent governments, chartered by the English monarch, were largely unchanged from the time they were founded until 1776.

The other eleven colonies had disparate forms of government, but with similarities, notably a proprietary connection with England. This proprietary relationship was designed for a single purpose, to assure the English monarch's control over his far-flung holdings. All eleven non-independent colonies were effectively ruled by an autocrat called the royal governor, appointed by the king as the direct representative of the crown. Royal governors were authoritarian powers unto themselves, with the ability to convene and dissolve the legislatures at will. They were empowered to appoint and remove judges and law enforcement officials, veto laws without the possibility of legislative override, and command the colony's militia.

Royal governors ran the gamut from honorable men concerned with those they governed to venal and petty tyrants who lusted for the trappings of power. The average colonial citizen had very little representation in the colonial government.

With the exceptions of Pennsylvania and Georgia, the colonies had bicameral, or two-chamber, legislatures modeled after the British Parliament. Most called the upper house "the council" whose members were appointed by the governor, served at his pleasure, and almost always sided with him in disputes. In rare cases where the council did not side with the governor, he could simply dissolve the council and appoint new members more in tune with his views. Throughout the colonies, the councils reflected the temperament and values of the governor. In many colonies, the council also served as the highest court in the territory.

Only the lower chamber, known as "the assembly," was popularly elected, and then generally only by white, male landholders. Women, Indians, non-landed workers, indentured servants, and slaves were not people when it came to voting or citizenship. The colonial assemblies ostensibly had the power to enact laws, but either the governor or the king could veto them, ignore them, or set them aside without any recourse for the lawmakers or the citizens of the colony.

While the system was effective in giving the monarchy an iron grip over the government of the colonies, popular discontent — over an array of issues, most notably taxation without representation, quartering of troops, and widespread trampling of citizens' rights — started to undermine the real authority of the crown over colonial citizens.

One of the actions of the Continental Congress immediately after adoption of the Declaration of Independence in 1776 was to encourage the establishment of independent state governments. Central to all thirteen early state constitutions was some sort of statement that their source of authority came from those governed and that the state should have an independent tripartite system of government.

The constitution of Maryland, adopted in November 1776, declares that the "legislative, executive and judicial powers of government ought to be forever separate and distinct from each other." The language is strikingly similar in the Georgia constitution, adopted in February 1777. It cites the people "from whom all power originates" and sets up "separate and distinct" legislative, executive and judicial departments so that none "exercise the powers properly belonging to the other." The New York constitution, adopted in April 1777, specifically states that no authority shall be exercised over the people other than that "derived from and granted by them."

The new states took differing approaches to the selection of judges, sheriffs, coroners, militia commandants, and the like, along with such issues as compensation, length of term and qualifications for various offices, rules and regulations for government entities, and taxation. As Shakespeare observed, "What's past is prologue," and much of what was established at the time of the American Revolution endures today.

All states today, for example, have a governor, who acts as the chief executive. As with the president in the federal model, governors appoint key state officials and have the authority to activate the National Guard in times of emergency. Governors also act as their state's top law enforcement official and must sign bills into law or veto them. Governors preside over state executive departments and oversee the implementation of administrative rules and regulations.

With the exception of Nebraska, all states have bicameral legislatures. In a quirk of history, Nebraska had a bicameral legislature until 1937, when it switched to a unicameral, or one-house, system. Since then more than a dozen states, including California, Illinois, New York, and Texas, have studied the possibility of shifting to the Nebraska model. So far none has made the change.

The greatest variation among the states is in their judicial branches. All states have a supreme court, although that name is not used uniformly. Most states have one intermediate level of appellate courts. Some have two appellate divisions — civil and criminal. Many states have a range of lower level courts, delegating authority to counties and/or major municipalities over civil and criminal trials, traffic courts, and justices of the peace. In some cases there are both local and state trial court jurisdictions. Some states have a separate probate court specifically to dispose of wills and estates.Rules regarding the practice of law and qualifications for admission to the bar fall within the administration of the various state court systems, and admission to the federal court and U.S. Supreme Court bars requires prior membership in the bar of one of the states. For example, former President Bill Clinton was disbarred in Arkansas in 2001 and thus was subsequently disbarred from practice before the U.S. Supreme Court.

Key Points

- All fifty states follow the federal model insofar as they have executive, legislative, and judicial branches.
- The modern structure of state government is linked directly to the systems developed by the thirteen original states around the time of the American Revolution.
- All states have state constitutions.
- All states have a chief executive called governor.
- All but Nebraska have bicameral, or two-chamber, legislatures.
- All have some form of supreme court, not necessarily called that.
- State court systems vary widely at the appellate and trial court levels.

Variations and Differences — Questions for Reporters

- When did my state enter the union?
- What did its first constitution say with regard to the three branches of state government and how much has it changed?
- What is the makeup of the three branches of state government?

State Legislatures

Forty-nine of the fifty states base their legislative structure on the federal model. The names for the legislative branches vary in the constitutions of the states. Some call it the general assembly; others call it the state legislature. Every state calls its upper chamber the senate; the lower chambers are mostly called the house of representatives, although Virginia calls its lower chamber the house of delegates and New York's is the state assembly. Only Nebraska has a unicameral, or one-chamber, legislature called the senate and whose members are senators.

8.1 Makeup of the State Legislatures

As with the federal model, the states have enshrined the makeup, organization, qualifications, and powers of their legislatures in their constitutions. While a substantial number of large state legislatures, such as New York, Ohio, Michigan, and California, meet all year, most state legislatures are part-time with the length of sessions spelled out in the various constitutions. A few state legislatures, including Texas, Montana, and Oregon, meet only every two years, unless there is an emergency requiring a special session.

Every state provides for special or emergency sessions to be convened while the legislature is in recess in the case of extraordinary circumstances. Many states vest the power of calling special sessions with the governor, although a substantial number of state constitutions also allow top legislative leaders to reconvene their legislatures.

For the most part, the men and women elected to the lower houses serve two-year terms. To qualify for election the minimum age ranges from twenty-one to twenty-five, with all states requiring a minimum length of state and district residency. Many states have limits on the number of terms a legislator may serve. Term limits range from two up to five terms. Several states have limits on consecutive terms. In Arizona, for example, a state representative may serve no more than four consecutive terms, but if he or she sits out one full term then that person may be elected again for another four consecutive terms.

State senators generally serve four-year terms. The minimum age for election to the state senates ranges from twenty-one to twenty-five. There are also minimum state and district residency requirements. Many, but not all, states stagger their senate terms, as with the U.S. Senate, so that a portion of the state senate is up for election every two years.

The state legislatures have presiding officers in the upper and lower chambers. Most states call the presiding officer of the senate the president of the senate; most call the presiding officer in the lower chamber the speaker. As with the federal structure, the majority political party wields enormous power in selecting the officers of the legislature, appointing support officials, and naming committee chairs.

Key Points

- All states except Nebraska have state legislatures modeled on the U.S. Congress.
- Nebraska has a unicameral, or one-chamber, legislature.
- Only a few large-state legislatures meet full-time; most are part-time and some only meet every two years.
- All states have minimum age and residency requirements for election to the state legislature.
- Some, but not all, states have enacted limits on how many terms legislators may serve.

Variations and Differences — Questions for Reporters

- What is the name of the lower chamber?
- What is the minimum age for legislators?
- Does the state have term limits for legislators?
- Who are the key legislative players: speaker, senate president, majority and minority leaders in both chambers?
- Is the legislature full-time and is the length of the legislative session limited?

8.2 Following the Federal Model

In most cases, reporters covering any of the fifty state legislatures, with the obvious exception of Nebraska, can turn to the U.S. Congress as a general example of how the institution works and then inquire about the differences in that particular state. (See Chapter 2, sections 2.1, 2.2, 2.3, and 2.4.)

All state constitutions, to one degree or another, allow each chamber of the legislature to make its own rules, including floor procedures, movement of legislation, oversight, investigations, conduct of members, support offices and staff, and ethics. State courts have been as reluctant to involve themselves in the internal rule-making and enforcement of those rules by the state legislatures as have the federal courts with the U.S. Congress making its own rules. The only time such legal actions have occurred is when a legislature overstepped the limitations placed on it by the state constitution.

All state legislatures are involved in some degree of oversight. The level of oversight varies from state to state, but generally includes oversight of revenue collection, transportation safety, education, insurance, public health, environment, business and commercial regulation, law enforcement, and prisons. Committees of the state legislature, as with those in Congress, are charged with holding oversight hearings and gathering testimony from witnesses. Most of those hearings are open to the press and the public and most are covered under open meeting statutes. (See section 8.10.)

Most state constitutions provide for some form of investigative function by the legislatures, although the legislatures and their committees in many states do not pursue independent investigations as rigorously or as regularly as does the U.S. Congress and its committees.

Every state legislature has an advice and consent function, usually reserved to the state senate. Members of the governor's cabinet, other top state executive branch officials, and state supreme court judges (in states where they are appointed and not elected) usually must make some kind of appearance before the state senate for confirmation of their appointments.

All states have constitutional provisions for impeachment, sanction, and removal of elected state officials for criminal misconduct, treason, or ethical impropriety. The power of impeachment is vested in the state legislatures. As with the federal model, the process usually begins in the lower chamber, with the trial and punishment phase reserved to the state senate. (See Chapter 5, section 5.2.)

Key Points

- Most states follow the federal model fairly closely for delineating the structure and functions of the state legislature.
- Every state allows its lower chamber and senate, separately, to make and enforce their own rules regarding such things as procedure and member conduct.
- Every state legislature exercises some measure of oversight with regard to executive departments and agencies.
- State legislatures pursue independent investigations, but some states do not permit legislative investigations to the extent the U.S. Congress exercises its investigative authority.
- Most states provide for their state senates to advise and consent in the case of top state government appointments.
- All states have provisions for impeachment and removal of elected state officials in the case of criminal misconduct, treason, and ethical improprieties.

Variations and Differences — Questions for Reporters

- What are the rules of procedure in the state house and senate?
- What are the ethics rules for state legislators?
- What are the specific oversight functions of the legislature?
- To what extent does the state legislature exercise an investigative function?
- What state officials' appointments require the advice and consent of the state senate?
- What are the state rules regarding impeachment and removal from office of elected officials?
- What are the ethics rules for state legislators?

8.3 How Bills Become State Laws

Despite differences among the states, the process of moving legislation is similar to the way the U.S. Congress operates. (See Chapter 2, section 2.4.) For the most part a bill can be introduced by any member of either chamber and there are always more bills introduced than will make their way into law.

Many states follow the U.S. constitutional requirement that revenue, or tax, bills originate in the lower chamber. The framers included that provision because originally the U.S. House of Representatives was the only popularly elected body in the national government. Only a few states began their legislative histories that way, and as a result the requirement in state law was more traditional than born of resentment over the English monarch taxing the colonies without representation. A significant number of state constitutions also require appropriation and budget bills to originate in the lower chamber.

In most states, as in Congress, once a bill is introduced it is referred to the proper committee of jurisdiction and then to a subcommittee for hearings, debate, amendments, and votes. The majority political party controls the committee structure. State legislative committee and subcommittee chairs are every bit as powerful in their realms as the chairs in the U.S. Congress. Without the support of a committee or subcommittee chair, a bill has scant chance of becoming law.

Those bills that get through the subcommittee and committee hearing process are marked up into legislative form and are voted out of committee. They then go to the floor of the originating chamber. If the bill is approved on the floor it goes to the other chamber where it is assigned to a committee (and often a subcommittee) and the process starts anew with hearings, debate, amendments, and votes.

As with the U.S. Congress, when the versions of a bill are not identical when they emerge from the two legislative chambers, the measure goes to a conference committee, where the differences are ironed out. The conference report then goes back to both chambers for floor votes. (See Chapter 2, section 2.4.)

When an identical measure is approved by a majority in both chambers, it goes to the governor for his/her signature.

The states differ on such procedural points as how much time must elapse between agreement on the language of the bill, its written presentation to members, and a final vote. For example, Michigan's constitution stipulates that a bill cannot become law "until it has been printed or reproduced and in the possession of each house for at least five days." In the overall picture this is relatively minor; it is major if you are a reporter covering a state legislature.

In the case of a gubernatorial veto, the bill is returned to the originating chamber of the state legislature with a message containing the governor's objection, a process that is identical to the federal government. State procedures vary in the length of time the governor has to veto and return a bill and in the number of votes needed to override a governor's veto. Most states follow the federal ten-day model. Most require a two-thirds majority of both chambers of the legislature to override a governor's veto, but a significant minority, including Illinois and Nebraska, only require three-fifths. If the requisite majorities are obtained the veto is overridden and the bill becomes law without the governor's signature. (See Chapter 2, section 2.5.)

In many states a governor may exercise a pocket veto (as with the president) by ignoring a bill until the legislature adjourns. In other states, including Colorado, the opposite is true. If the governor does not act on the bill it automatically becomes law. In a significant number of states the adjournment date for the state legislature is enshrined in the state constitution and thus the prospects of a pocket veto increase if a bill is passed within ten days of the adjournment date. This often becomes high political drama and grist for the journalist's mill especially in instances where the governor and the majority in the legislature are of different political parties.

Even when the governor and the legislative majority are of the same party, hardball politics frequently ensues. Consider a bill that enjoys enough bipartisan support from legislators to win passage. If that same bill, however, is opposed by the legislative majority leaders and the governor, the majority leadership — those powerful people who control the movement of bills — may opt to hold the legislation until very late in the session. Then even if it is passed the governor can pocket veto it and not have to worry about the prospect of having his/her veto overridden.

When bills becomes laws, many states have specific constitutional waiting periods before the laws take effect. This varies widely from state to state. Some state legislatures specify an effective date for legislation, usually at the start of the next fiscal year.

Nebraska's unicameral legislative process is roughly the same as moving a bill through one chamber in any other state — committee (and often subcommittee) hearings, amendments, votes, floor debate and final vote. With passage the bill goes to the governor for signature.

Key Points

- Despite minor differences, the movement of a bill through the various state legislatures is similar to the way it works in the U.S. Congress.

- A bill (with the exception of tax and spending bills) can be introduced by any member of the state legislature.
- Most states follow the federal model and require tax (and often spending) bills to originate in the lower chamber.
- Once a bill is introduced it goes to a committee of jurisdiction and is often then assigned to a subcommittee.
- In state legislatures the majority party controls the committee system just as in the U.S. Congress.
- If a bill is voted out of committee, it goes to the floor for debate, amendments, and votes.
- If it passes the originating chamber, it goes to the other chamber and if an identical version is passed by both, it goes to the governor for his/her signature.
- If the measure is not identical in both chambers, it goes to a house-senate conference committee to resolve any differences in the two versions of the bill.
- The conference committee sends an identical version of the bill back to both chambers, starting with the originating chamber, and if both chambers pass it, it goes to the governor.
- If the governor signs the bill it becomes law.
- If the governor vetoes a bill it goes back to the legislature where both chambers must approve it, usually but not always, by two-thirds majorities in order to override the veto.
- In a majority of states, if the legislature adjourns within ten days and the governor does not sign the bill it dies as the result of a pocket veto.

Variations and Differences — Questions for Reporters

- Which party is in the majority in the upper and lower chamber of the legislature?
- What is the exact procedure for final passage of a bill, including how many readings are required and how long must the printed version be in members' hands before a vote can be taken?
- How long does the governor have between final passage of a bill and when it must be vetoed and returned?
- What size majority is needed to override the governor's veto?
- What does the state constitution say about a waiting period before laws take effect?
- Does my state's governor have a pocket veto?

8.4 Initiatives and Referenda

The U.S. Constitution expressly gives the authority to enact statutory laws to Congress. As a result, there is no mechanism, on a national level, by which citizens have any direct lawmaking involvement. States, however, are not limited by this constitutional restriction, and 24 state constitutions provide for direct citizen participation in lawmaking and veto. There are two primary forms of citizen involvement — ballot initiative and popular referendum.

Ballot initiatives, sometimes called "propositions," are a method by which citizens may directly propose and enact laws. Popular referenda give citizens the authority to reject laws passed by the legislature and signed by the governor. The process for getting both before the voters is similar in all states where initiatives and referenda exist.

Once a ballot initiative is drafted, its promoters and supporters go out among their fellow citizens and gather signatures on petitions. Signatures are also gathered for referenda. When a specific number of signatures is collected, the number being delineated in the state constitution or established by the legislature as a matter of state law, the petitions are delivered for certification. (As an example, in Arizona the state constitution requires signatures from 10 percent of "qualified electors" to put proposed laws on the ballot. If the initiative is an amendment to the state constitution, 15 percent of qualified electors must sign petitions to place it on a ballot.)

Certification is usually done by the secretary of state's office, a painstaking procedure in which every signature on every petition is examined. Each name is checked against voter registration rolls to make certain only those eligible to sign have done so. Once the signatures are verified and counted, the citizen-generated measure is ready to be placed on the ballot. Usually ballot measures go before the voters only in general elections, although some states permit initiatives and referenda to be placed on primary election ballots as well.

In some states, the legislature can refer bills that have passed to the voters for approval. These legislatively referred measures do not require signatures to be gathered and certified. Most of the states that provide for legislative referral also provide for citizens to force bills not referred onto the ballot by gathering enough signatures to qualify for a referendum.

All states that allow initiatives and referenda place limits on how

long proponents have to gather signatures and file petitions for certification.

In the case of initiatives, many states restrict how often the same issue may be placed before the voters, even if enough signatures are collected. (A common limit restricts the same or similar proposed laws
from being placed on ballots more than once every five years.) Most
state constitutions establish either specific dates or waiting periods following passage of any initiative for it to take effect. These vary widely
and reporters must check the law wherever they happen to be working.

Notable citizen-generated laws enacted through the ballot initiative process include California's Proposition 209, approved in 1996,
which abolished that state's affirmative action system by banning
racial preferences in hiring and promotion. When a ballot initiative is
passed by the voters, neither the state legislature nor the governor is
empowered to change, modify, or veto it in most states. A few states
provide for legislative review of citizen generated laws.

If there is a challenge to the constitutionality of a ballot initiative,
as with any statutory law, the only appeal is to the courts. For example
in 1998 four ballot initiatives — in Alaska, Nevada, Oregon, and
Washington — approved the medical use of marijuana, only to have
those citizen-generated laws declared unconstitutional by the U.S.
Supreme Court.

Unlike a ballot initiative that proposes a new law, a popular referendum places a law enacted by the state legislature before the voters
for approval or disapproval. Some scholars liken it to a citizen veto or
a vote of confidence in the actions of the legislature. In 1998 the voters of Arizona used this method to reject a law passed by the legislature
banning the use of medical marijuana — a converse approach to the
four states that enacted medical marijuana laws through ballot initiatives.

Reporters should be aware of the geography of initiatives and referenda. They are very popular in the west, the newer states in the
chronological history of the United States. Most states west of the
Mississippi River provide for either ballot initiatives or popular referenda or both. The exceptions are Minnesota, Iowa, Kansas, Louisiana,
Texas, and Hawaii. Most of the states in the east and south, which
comprise the older states in the union, do not have provisions for initiatives and referenda, except in the case of state constitutional

amendments. Notable exceptions to this generality are Maine, Massachusetts, Maryland, Ohio, Michigan, Illinois, Kentucky, Missouri, Arkansas, Mississippi, and Florida.

While the concept looks like fundamental, grass-roots representative democracy at work, it is important to underscore the fact that very often ballot initiatives and popular referenda are the work-product of well financed interest groups. Rarely does a ballot initiative win enough support for passage without expensive advertising and a public relations campaign to promote the idea behind the ballot proposal. Organized opposition can also be expected to raise money and use the same tools — advertising and public relations — in an effort to defeat the measure. Reporters will often find as much of a story in this aspect of the ballot initiative and popular referendum process as in the ballot measures themselves.

Key Points

- Twenty-four states provide for direct citizen participation in the lawmaking process.
- The two mechanisms of citizen participation in lawmaking are ballot initiatives and popular referenda.
- A ballot initiative is the proposal of a law by citizens.
- A referendum may be likened to a citizen veto or vote of confidence in a specific legislative action, in which voters can reject a law that was passed by the state legislature.
- Both initiatives and referenda require backers to gather a specific number of signatures from qualified voters on petitions, unless the state provides for referral of bills directly from the legislature to the voters.
- To be placed on a ballot, the petition signatures must be certified, usually by the secretary of state's office.
- If voters approve an initiative, most states have no provision for legislative repeal or gubernatorial veto.
- People wishing to challenge an initiative, like any other law, must take the issue to the courts.

Variations and Differences — Questions for Reporters

- Does my state constitution allow for ballot initiatives?
- Does my state constitution allow for popular referenda?

- What percentage of the population must sign petitions to place either on the ballot?
- Is there a difference in the signature threshold for laws as opposed to constitutional amendments?
- What is the length of time between filing the initiative and/or referendum petitions and the election in which they will be considered?
- How long is the waiting period between passage of an initiative and the effective date of the law?
- Can the legislature refer a bill it passes to the citizens for a vote?
- Is there a mechanism for legislative review of an initiative or referendum?

8.5 Taxation

Every state, like the federal government, must be able to raise enough money in the form of taxation to provide state services, pay state employees, run state agencies, enforce the state's laws, and deal with emergencies that threaten the health and safety of the state's citizens.

Specific budget areas supported by state revenues include public health, road building and maintenance, highway safety, waterways, ports and airports (which are frequently under local jurisdiction), business regulation, environment, licensing (including motor vehicle, business, liquor, pharmacy, medical, and legal), building and construction regulation, law enforcement, courts, prisons, emergency preparedness, and higher education. This list is far from complete, but these areas are common to most states. The names for the various agencies and departments vary widely. For example what may be the department of transportation in one state may be the highway department in another; what is the department of corrections in one state may be the bureau of prisons in another.

Every state has a department of education, and most devote a significant portion of the state budget to schools. In most states, colleges and universities are run at the state level, while primary and secondary education is generally the province of the cities and/or counties. Most of these local jurisdictions use revenues generated from property taxes to cover some of the expenses connected with primary and secondary public schools.

States generate their revenues in a variety of ways. Forty-one states have some form of state income tax. The nine that do not are Alaska, Florida, Nevada, New Hampshire, South Dakota, Tennessee, Texas, Washington, and Wyoming. A vast majority of states have excise taxes on certain commodities, most commonly tobacco and alcohol. Many states have some form of state sales tax. Many states generate additional revenues through usage fees — a charge for using toll roads, bridges, and tunnels, requiring the purchase of passes to state parks, monuments, and museums, and charges for business licenses. (Property taxes are almost exclusively the domain of cities and/or counties, although many states have state-level oversight agencies to prevent local abuse of the taxing authority.)

The process for enactment of tax bills in the states is similar, in most cases, to that of the U.S. Congress. (See Chapter 2, section 2.8.) Most states follow the federal model and require tax bills to originate in the lower chamber of the state legislature, even though the genesis of the federal model was rooted in the colonial objection to taxation without representation and the fact that only the U.S. House of Representatives was directly elected when the Constitution was adopted in 1787. That was not the case in the states.

Most states have a version of the House Ways and Means Committee. In the states the name of that particular committee varies although "ways and means" is common.

Tax bills move through the state legislatures like other bills. Hearings are held and the bills are debated, amended, and voted on. When a tax bill is approved it goes to the state senate where the same process occurs — committee hearings, debate, amendments, and vote. A house-senate conference committee is convened to iron out any differences and a conference report is returned first to the lower chamber and then, if approved, to the state senate. When an identical version of the tax bill has cleared both chambers, it goes to the governor for his/her signature or veto. If the governor signs the bill or both chambers of the legislature vote to override the veto, the revenue measure is then law in twenty-six states, usually after a waiting period or on a specific date established in the state constitution.

In the other twenty-four states, however, the tax law may become the object of a popular referendum, and it can be rejected by the voters. Such referenda have grown in popularity over the last quarter century. The process of generating a popular referendum regarding a tax measure is the same as for citizen challenges of other legislation. (See section 8.4.) It involves gathering petition signatures, certifying those signatures, and having the issue placed on the ballot.

In one state there's no option. When the Colorado legislature approves a tax increase, it must be placed on the ballot for voter approval or rejection. In two other states, Missouri and Washington, anything other than certain small percentage increase in taxes must go before the voters.

Ever since the English Stamp Act that spawned the American Revolution, taxation has been a hot-button political and social issue. In recent years, taxation has been one of the most volatile issues in the country. Voters have taken various actions to demonstrate their anger over what they view as an unreasonable tax burden, including rejecting the re-election bids of politicians seen as too eager to raise taxes, popular referenda striking down specific tax increases, and ballot initiatives to restrict state taxing authority.

Perhaps the most famous tax revolt at state polls was in June 1978. Californians who were fed up with skyrocketing property taxes voted overwhelmingly (65 percent) to adopt a ballot initiative called Proposition 13. That measure, as now incorporated in Section 2 Article XIIIA of the California constitution, limits any increase in property taxes to "no more than the rate of inflation or 2 percent, whichever is less." Proposition 13 was upheld by the California Supreme Court in September 1978 and by the U.S. Supreme Court in 1992.

Most politicians are as reluctant to tell voters that they want to raise taxes as they are to touch a high voltage wire. Reporters need to be on the lookout for smoke screens, buzz words, and euphemisms, such as "revenue readjustment," that politicians use to avoid saying the poisonous words "tax increase."

Key Points

- States, like the federal government, need money from citizens in the form of taxes to provide a host of state services.
- Most states require tax bills to originate in the lower chamber of the state legislature.
- Tax bills move through state legislatures very much like they do through the U.S. Congress.
- Tax bills start in variously-named legislative committees that function very similarly to the Ways and Means Committee in the U.S. House.

- If the identical bill is approved by both chambers, it goes to the governor for his/her signature.
- In twenty-four states, tax bills can be challenged and rejected by citizens through popular referenda.
- Colorado is the only state that requires tax increases to be submitted to the voters, and two other states require voter approval for all but very small tax increases.

Variations and Differences — Questions for Reporters

- Does my state require tax legislation to start in the lower chamber of the legislature?
- What's the name of the legislature's equivalent of the House Ways and Means Committee?
- When a tax bill is passed, what's the length of time from the governor's signature until the bill takes effect?
- Does my state allow for popular referenda on tax legislation?
- Is there any law or amendment to the state constitution in place, like California's Proposition 13, that limits the state's taxing or tax-raising authority?
- Are there active anti-tax organizations and/or lobbying groups with which I should be familiar?

8.6 State Budgets and Spending

One of the primary functions of every state legislature is to develop a state budget, appropriating money to the various state programs, agencies and departments, and making sure that the state is raising enough revenue to cover its expenditures. There is no area in which the states and the federal government function more differently than in the area of budget and appropriation.

One of the most striking differences is that Congress may elect to spend more than the federal government earns in revenue, thus creating a deficit. States do not have that option and are required to balance their budgets.

The federal approach involves a lengthy three-part process: The budget formulation, authorization, and appropriation. (See Chapter 2, section 2.7.) In most states the approach is two-pronged: Revenue estimates and forecasts are folded into a proposed budget which is turned into a package of appropriation bills in the legislature. Where the U.S. Congress distinguishes between authorization (earmarking where money should be spent) and appropriation (actually spending the money), the states tend to lump it into one single step.

The states are split among those that prepare annual budgets and those that work from biennial budgets. Some of the states with biennial budgets, such as Virginia, provide for extensive amendments to the budget in the second year of the two-year cycle.

Not every state has the same fiscal year, and states are not required to have the same fiscal year as the federal government. A majority of states begin their fiscal years in July, but there are notable exceptions, including Texas which begins its fiscal year in September, New York which begins its fiscal year in April, and Michigan which follows the federal model and begins its fiscal year in October.

States tend toward similarity in the way they start the budget process. Virtually every state develops some kind of revenue estimate and forecast — how much money the state is making and how much it's expected to make. How the revenue estimate and forecast is developed varies widely. The majority of states estimate and forecast their revenues through entities with names such as Revenue Estimating Conference and Revenue Forecasting Consensus Board. These entities are made up of members of both the legislative and executive branches of state government. Some, but not all, specify that members of both the majority and minority parties in the state legislature be represented. A handful, including Louisiana, Kentucky, Iowa, and Kansas, require someone or several people from outside state government to be included among the revenue estimators. Kentucky, for example, requires four university economists to participate.

A significant minority of states place the revenue estimates and forecasts exclusively in the hands of the executive branch. They specify a variety of agencies and individuals to prepare and submit the revenue estimate, including the governor and his/her executive staff, the state treasury department, the state department of revenue, and the comptroller of public accounts.

These various methods of calculating revenue estimates and forecasts all result in the data from which the state's budget legislation is drawn. Most states allow for some deviation in the form of amendments during the legislative process.

In a few cases state law requires the revenue estimates and forecasts, regardless of the method used to compute them, to bind the budget, which means there is little discretion left to the drafters of the budget bill with regard to spending levels and income projections.

As with revenue estimates and forecasts, the states present an enormous array of variation in the processes of enacting a state budget. A few work from one, huge omnibus budget bill encompassing everything. California's budget bill looks like a stack of phone books. Some break out education and then develop an omnibus bill for everything else. Some adopt three separate bills — one each for the executive, legislative, and judicial branches of the state's government. A few have multiple budget bills. The New York legislature considers between ten and thirty, Iowa has twenty, Montana has seventy, and Oregon has one hundred.

Most states separate appropriation bills (bills that spend money) and tax bills (bills that increase revenues), although a few state constitutions require both to be considered at the same time as part of the overall budget process. In most cases the state legislatures are permitted to change, modify, amend, or adjust budget bills either in committee or on the floor of either chamber of the state legislature, provided the result is a balanced budget.

Every state has some provision for budget hearings and public testimony once the spending bills are drafted. Some states, such as Virginia, have laws requiring regional hearings — in which legislators go to the voters rather than requiring voters who want to be heard to travel to the state capitol — in order to take public testimony on the budget.

Passage of the budget requires a majority in both houses of the state legislature (with the unicameral exception of Nebraska). At that point the practices and processes of the fifty states diverge even more sharply from the federal model.

All state governors have the power to veto individual items from budget bills, without vetoing the entire bill. This is called a line-item veto, and it gives the state governors extraordinary discretion over how state money is spent. The state constitutions provide for legislative override of line items singled out and vetoed by the governor but, as with other vetoed legislation, to override requires a super-majority, usually two-thirds of both houses. And most states require a separate override vote on each line item vetoed, which can run to the hundreds.

In 1996, the U.S. Congress voted to give the president a limited version of the line-item veto, only to have the law overturned in 1998 by the U.S. Supreme Court. The high court said the line-item veto infringes on the exclusive congressional power to legislate and the presidential veto process delineated in the Constitution.

Finally, many states, especially those with biennial budgets, require a midterm or other interim review of whether the revenue estimates and forecasts on which the budget was based are on track. Some state legislatures may be called into special session to adjust or amend the budget/appropriation law if the forecast of how much money the state will take in is not keeping up with the level of spending approved in the legislation.

Key Points

- There is no area in which the federal process and the state processes vary more than in budgeting, authorization, and appropriation.
- Some states prepare budgets annually and others do it every two years, known as biennial budgeting.
- All states start the budget process with an estimate of state revenues, how much money the state is projected to take in.
- The budget bills are written from the revenue estimates and forecasts.
- While the federal budget may run a deficit, state budgets must balance.
- Most states separate appropriation (spending) bills and tax bills, but a few lump them together as part of the same process.
- All states provide for public hearings before legislative committees prior to enactment of the budget and/or appropriation bill(s).
- Both chambers of the state legislature must pass the budget bill.
- Using a mechanism called the line-item veto, state governors can remove individual items or lines from a budget bill.
- The state legislature may override a governor's line-item veto in the same manner as other veto overrides.

Variations and Differences — Questions for Reporters

- Does my state have an annual or biennial budget?
- What constitutes the state's fiscal year?

- Who is responsible for the revenue estimates and forecasts and what is the formal name of that revenue estimating and/or forecasting entity?
- How many appropriation/budget bills does my state legislature act on each year?
- When and where are public hearings on the budget held?
- What, if any, are the limits of the line-item veto authority of the governor?
- What is the process by which the legislature may override a line-item veto?

8.7 Reapportionment

Every ten years, states confront the task of reapportionment, redrawing congressional and state legislative districts. There are separate districts for seats in the lower chamber of the state legislature, the state senate, and the U.S. House of Representatives. Candidates for the U.S. Senate run statewide as do candidates for governor and other state offices.

Most state constitutions authorize the legislature to play the key role in redistricting, although a substantial number of states provide for a commission on reapportionment. In some cases the commissions act in an advisory capacity; in others the commission is activated only if the legislature fails to act on reapportionment by a specific date. These reapportionment commissions always include members from the legislature. Some also include representatives of the executive branch. A few add citizens and/or academic experts.

United States congressional representation is determined by the U.S. census. Every ten years some states end up with more U.S. representatives and others lose representatives as a result of an increase or decrease in state population. The influx or outflow of people within various parts of a state will provide the raw data for reapportionment, both at the state and federal level.

Reapportionment has long been a political hot potato, going back to the earliest days of the nation. In 1812, Massachusetts Governor Elbridge Gerry approved a redistricting plan designed to protect the seats of members of his own party. In pursuit of the political goal, one legislative district was said to look like a salamander when its boundaries were redrawn. The critter was dubbed a gerrymander, and the practice, which lives today, is known as gerrymandering.

Many state constitutions prescribe specific time-lines for legislative action on reapportionment. The Illinois constitution, for example says, "In the year following each federal decennial census year, the General Assembly by law shall redistrict the legislative districts and the representative districts [for the U.S. Congress]." The provision goes on to say that if the legislature does not act by July 10, the function falls to an eight-member legislative commission made up of members of the state house and senate and four people who are not members of the legislature. If that commission fails to act by August 10, the state supreme court appoints two people, not of the same political party, and the state's secretary of state draws one name at random to fill a ninth seat on the commission and resolve any ties.

The Illinois model is not universal, but most states have a similar mechanism, or series of steps to reapportion the state's legislative and congressional districts.

Key Points

- Every ten years every state must reapportion its state legislative districts and U.S. congressional districts, based on results of the U.S. census.
- Going back to the early days of the 1800s, reapportionment has been a highly political process.
- In most states the legislature is the principal redistricting body.
- Many states provide for reapportionment commissions to be part of the process either before or after legislative action or to end a legislative stalemate.

Variations and Differences — Questions for Reporters

- When is the state legislature required to start work on reapportionment?
- What is the specific process within the legislature?
- Is there a provision for an outside reapportionment commission to advise the legislature before reapportionment or to act if the legislature is deadlocked by a specific date?
- If there is a reapportionment commission, what is its makeup?
- Is there a requirement in the state constitution regarding a specific date by which a reapportionment plan must be adopted?

8.8 Specific Prohibitions on State Legislatures

State legislatures enjoy a broad range of powers, but as with the U.S. Congress, the powers of the legislatures are restricted. Those restrictions have a certain universality, along with some individual differences. States usually give their legislatures broad lawmaking authority but restrict enforcement, application, and implementation of those broad laws to either the executive branch or to local jurisdictions.

In general, almost every state has codified in its constitution a provision that state laws may address only one subject. Sweeping, omnibus, or multifaceted laws are generally prohibited.

Most states do not allow their legislatures to grant bonuses or additional compensation to people doing business with the state once a contract has been approved for products and services. In addition most states prohibit their legislatures from changing or increasing compensation, after those products and services have been delivered.

While state legislatures enact the general laws governing the requirements and qualifications for corporate status, most states do not allow their legislatures to grant individual corporate status. Under most state laws of incorporation, approval of individual corporations on a case-by-case basis is usually the province of the executive branch, most often the state's secretary of state.

A great majority of states prohibit their legislatures from taking control of local schools, local courts, or arbitrarily moving or changing county seats. Many states prohibit their legislatures from granting name changes to individual citizens, although as a matter of general law they may set the legal standards and overall policy for name changes for all people within the state. And many states prohibit the legislature from arbitrarily changing or fixing interest rates.

In many states that permit ballot initiatives and/or popular referenda, the state legislatures are prohibited from changing, amending, or vetoing those citizen-generated laws without first submitting those changes to the voters. In virtually all initiative and/or referendum states, amendments to the state constitution may not be changed or vetoed by the legislatures.

Various states have incorporated other prohibitions into their state constitutions. Without attempting to deliver a comprehensive list, some of those specific prohibitions include: The Iowa general assembly may not grant divorces; the Louisiana legislature may not legalize the unauthorized or invalid acts of state employees; the Colorado constitution prohibits the legislature from imposing state tax increases without voter approval; the Utah legislature is prohibited from enacting laws on the taking of wildlife or establishing hunting seasons without a two-thirds majority vote; and the South Dakota legislature is prohibited from passing any law granting individuals or corporations squatter's rights, or a right of occupation, use, and/or improvement, on any public land.

Key Points

- State legislatures do not have unlimited power, and restrictions on the authority of the legislative branch are enshrined in every state constitution.
- Nearly every state legislature is prohibited from passing laws that deal with more than one subject.
- Most states do not allow their legislatures to provide bonuses or additional compensation after a contract has been signed or goods and services have been provided to the state.
- In many states that provide for ballot initiatives and/or popular referenda, the legislature is prohibited from amending or altering those laws without returning the amendments or alterations to the voters for approval.
- In virtually all initiative and/or referendum states the legislature may not change or veto constitutional amendments approved by the voters.

Variations and Differences — Questions for Reporters

- What specific prohibitions on the legislature are contained in the state constitution?
- Are there any prohibitions that are unique to my state?
- Are ballot initiatives and popular referenda permitted in the state and what limits are placed on the legislature regarding the action of voters?

8.9 Extraordinary Circumstances and State Emergencies

Responding to natural and man-made disasters, catastrophes, and emergencies are matters of public policy. Most states delegate the authority to provide and administer emergency services and to seek federal disaster assistance and money to the governor or the executive branch of state government. Those services include law enforcement, protection of public health and safety, and activation of the state militia and/or National Guard. The state governors are the commanders-in-chief of their National Guard components, except when those units have been called up and activated for national service.

Many state constitutions specifically address the subject of special legislative sessions to provide emergency appropriations for disaster relief but, in general, the policy decisions and actions belong to the executive. Some states have special funds set aside to deal with emergencies.

Every state constitution provides for what the Wisconsin constitution (along with those of several other states) calls "continuity of civil government" in the face of war or enemy action. It is anticipated that such enemy action may kill top state or local officials and/or render them missing or unable to fulfill their public duties. The Wisconsin constitution requires the legislature to provide for prompt, temporary succession to state and local offices by appointment or special elections.

California's constitution contains similar language to "meet the needs resulting from war-caused or enemy-caused disaster." The California constitution specifically provides a process for filling the offices of state legislators and governor until such time as successors can be elected. In addition the California constitution addresses contingency plans for convening the legislature and temporarily changing the seat of state or county government if it should be necessary.

In the wake of the September 11, 2001, attack on the World Trade Center in New York City, measures have been discussed in several states to revise emergency and/or disaster legislation, including temporary suspension of term limits and rescheduling elections because of enemy attack or terrorism. As this book goes to press, no such actions have been approved by any state legislature.

Key Points

- Emergency action in dealing with natural or man-made disasters is usually left to the executive branch and/or the governor of the states.
- Governors are the commanders-in-chief of their state militias and/or National Guard units (unless those National Guard forces have been called up for national service.)
- In the case of war or enemy action that kills or incapacitates top state or local officials, most state constitutions give their legislatures the authority to fill vacancies temporarily.

Variations and Differences — Questions for Reporters

- What does the state constitution say with regard to continuity of civil government in time of war or enemy attack on the state?
- What specific emergency powers are given to the governor?
- What specific emergency powers are given to the state legislature?
- What, if any, are the limitations on the legislature to act in such an emergency?
- What specific offices is the legislature allowed to fill in the case of war or enemy attack?
- Is there any legislation pending or being considered that would change the state's term limit laws in times of enemy or terrorist attack?

8.10 Freedom of Information and Sunshine Laws

The original federal Freedom of Information Act (commonly cited with the acronym FOIA) was enacted in 1966. The U.S. Congress strengthened it in 1974, after Watergate, and since then every state has adopted some form of FOI (or freedom of information) law. There are variations, but most have substantial areas of commonality.

The federal FOIA was designed to facilitate easy access to government documents for the public and the news media. Some states opted to streamline and combine their open document laws with measures aimed at easing public and media access to government meetings, hearings, and legislative proceedings. These open meeting laws (whether enacted separately or incorporated into a general FOI law) have become knows as sunshine laws. All states and the federal government have some form of sunshine law.

In the case of government documents, most FOI laws presume that everything is in the public domain unless it is specifically excluded. Common exemptions from freedom of information requests in both state and federal law include: Documents connected to ethics, personnel, and labor relations matters; documents concerning ongoing criminal investigations or individuals connected with those investigations; documents revealing internal legislative, agency, or executive discussions of alternatives prior to the public announcement of a new policy or action, changed policy or action, or repealed policy or action; and documents provided by private business interests to government that might reveal internal business, trade, financial, or corporate secrets.

States commonly make FOI exceptions in the case of student records, documents addressing the purchase and sale of government property, library circulation records, medical records, and records concerning employee disciplinary actions. The federal FOIA specifically allows documents to be kept secret that involve national security, nuclear facilities, oil and gas wells, or information relating to banking and financial institutions.

Most FOI requests for documents must be made through the agency, department, legislative committee, or government bureau that generated the documents; a few states and the federal government require FOI requests to be in writing. A majority of states allow people to ask for records during the regular business hours of an agency. A few government entities accept FOI requests on-line. A few states are exploring the idea of a central document clearinghouse, largely accessible on the Internet, for FOI requests.

If a request for documents is denied, journalists should first seek to know which particular exception is cited for denying the request. If a journalist wishes to appeal a denial, all states have a series of appellate steps that must be followed.

Documents provided under FOI laws are not necessarily free. Reporters should be aware that many states and federal agencies charge fees for duplication, handling, and processing of documents sought under FOI laws. Lengthy documents can result in hefty charges.

In the case of meetings, hearings, and legislative sessions, the federal government and all fifty states have some kind of sunshine, or open meeting, laws that require certain government meetings to be held in public. There are significant differences among the states regarding the threshold at which a meeting must be deemed open to the public. Until it was clarified, Florida's sunshine law, for example, said any time two or more public officials discussed state business it was to be considered a public meeting. As a result, some state officials were fearful of having lunch together lest they run afoul of the sunshine law.

Generally states exempt social gatherings, religious activities, ceremonial functions, and sporting events from their sunshine laws. Other conditions under which state and federal government meetings may be held in private include personnel matters, ethics hearings, collective bargaining sessions, discussions about the sale or purchase of public real estate, and meetings with lawyers about ongoing or pending legal actions against the government entity.

Most state sunshine laws specifically say that meetings must be public when public policy decisions are being made or when a quorum of a multi-member organization or agency is conducting public business. Generally the laws require some form of notice of such meetings, including a printed and publicly available agenda. After such meetings, many states require a record, minutes, or journal of the proceeding be made available to the public and the media in a timely manner.

Key Points

- All states and the federal government have some kind of FOI (freedom of information) law.
- These laws are designed to facilitate easy public and media access to government documents.
- Many states incorporate sunshine (or open meeting) laws into their FOI statutes, although some have separate laws involving open meetings.
- All states and the federal government have a list of documents that may be excluded from FOI requests, including personnel documents, documents about on-going criminal investigations, and private corporate documents provided to government that might disclose business secrets.
- Sunshine, or open meeting, laws usually require government meetings to be open if they involve policy decisions.

- The states' and the federal sunshine laws set out specific exemptions to meetings that must be open, including labor negotiations, ethics hearings, personnel matters, and government real estate transactions.

Variations and Differences — Questions for Reporters

- Where can I obtain a copy of my state's FOI and sunshine laws?
- What are the specific exemptions with regard to government documents and open meetings?
- What is the appellate process if my FOI request is denied?
- How much do agencies charge for duplication fees when I make an FOI request?

8.11 Notes for Reporters Covering State Legislatures

Covering state legislatures is not unlike covering the U.S. Congress. (See Chapter 2, section 2.13.) The key for reporters is to have a thorough understanding of the legislative process in their individual state. Knowing the federal model will provide a substantial level of understanding with regard to the role of the political parties, the committee process, movement of legislation, taxation, and appropriation. (See Chapter 2, sections 2.3, 2.4, 2.7, and 2.8.) The principal document for journalists working in any state capitol is a copy of the state's constitution. Reporters covering state legislatures have much greater access to the key players on a daily basis than those covering Congress; getting firsthand information is much easier than it is in the nation's Capitol.

As with any beat, successful legislative reporters make it their business to know the members of the state senate and the lower chamber on a personal level. The top political leadership is crucial to a reporter. Key committee chairs and top legislative aides are also high on the list of people reporters should know. Nothing beats being in the state capitol building on a daily basis when the legislature is in session.

Rules governing news coverage in state capitol buildings and the U.S. Capitol building are similar (see Chapter 2, section 2.13); legislative rules committees usually have jurisdiction. Reporters must obtain proper credentials. Reporters need to know where newspeople may and may not go, where cameras and microphones are permitted and prohibited, what the rules are for radio, TV, and photo coverage on the floors of the senate and the lower chamber, and what the rules are on the state capitol grounds.

Key Points

- Understanding the federal model of how Congress works will provide the basics for how state legislatures work. The state constitution is the key document for understanding how the state legislature, and state government in general, functions.
- Each state has its own rules regarding the credentialing of the news media.
- Each state has its own rules regarding news coverage inside the capitol building or on the capitol grounds.

Variations and Differences — Questions for Reporters

- Where can I obtain a copy of my state's constitution?
- How does the legislative practice of my state differ from that of the U.S. Congress?
- What are the rules regarding credentials for the news media?
- What are the rules regarding covering the news inside the capitol building or on the capitol grounds?
- How do I get pictures and/or sound from the floors of the legislative chambers and/or hearings rooms?
- Is there an archive containing audio, video, and/or printed records of legislative sessions?

Governors and State Executive Branches

The office of governor predates the Constitution and goes back to colonial times, when governors were the handpicked representatives of the English king. With the Declaration of Independence and the subsequent development of thirteen independent state governments, the office remained, but became subordinate to the will of the voters of each state.

Today, every state has a governor as its top executive. Qualifications in virtually all states include U.S. citizenship and state residency for a minimum period that varies from two to eight years. A few states simply restrict eligibility to people of voting age, but most states have a minimum age for a person to be elected governor or lieutenant governor. The majority of states set thirty as the minimum age; a substantial minority set it at twenty-five.

Only the commonwealth of Massachusetts, in the state constitution, states specifically that the governor "shall be called His Excellency."

A substantial majority of states have a lieutenant governor, although the function varies from being the second ranking executive in the state to a largely ceremonial position. A half dozen states — Arizona, Maine, New Hampshire, Oregon, West Virginia, and Wyoming — have no office of lieutenant governor.

9.1 Executive Officers

The U.S. Constitution is largely silent on the manner in which states govern themselves, other than that they all be democratic and representative. All states follow the federal model insofar as each has an executive branch with the governor as chief executive. Governors are elected for four-year terms. There the uniformity ends.

Some states have term limits for their governors, following the example of the Twenty-second Amendment limiting presidents to two terms. Some states restrict governors to two consecutive terms, but place no limits on the total number of terms he/she may serve. Occasionally the system has been politically manipulated. In Alabama, for example, in 1965 the governor was limited to one term. Democrat George C. Wallace wanted to succeed himself as governor. After failing to get the state legislature to change the law, Wallace circumvented it. He had his wife Lurleen run for governor in his place. She won and he was elected again after her term.

State executive branches encompass a wide variety of organizational divisions. All states have a core group of executive officers. While the exact titles may vary, virtually every state has a state treasurer, secretary of state, and attorney general. Many states also have an insurance commissioner, education commissioner, and/or transportation commissioner. States also vary widely in which of these positions are filled by election and which are filled by gubernatorial appointment.

Top state executive officials comprise the governor's cabinet. Cabinet departments and agencies can number as few as eight and as many as twenty or more. Commonly state executive agencies and departments have authority and jurisdiction over one or more of the following areas: roads and highways; ports and airports; primary and secondary schools; colleges and universities; taxation and revenue; budget and appropriation; public health; social services; emergency management; agriculture; public lands and land use; labor, industrial relations, and fair labor practices; insurance; gaming, gambling, and lotteries; and economic development and tourism.

Every state provides for succession in the case of the death, disability, or disqualification of the governor. The lieutenant governor is first in the line of succession in states that have that office; those states without the office of lieutenant governor are split — in Arizona, Oregon, and Wyoming the secretary of state succeeds the governor, and in Maine, New Hampshire, and West Virginia the president of the senate succeeds the governor. Some states require a special election to fill a vacancy in the governor's office permanently; others provide for the next in line to serve out the remainder of the governor's term.

Key Points

- Every state has a governor as its chief executive officer elected for four-year terms.
- Many states have term limits for governors.
- Most states have a lieutenant governor, although the role varies from the second ranking state executive to purely ceremonial.
- Six states have no office of lieutenant governor.
- All states have either elected or appointed executive offices of state treasurer, secretary of state, and attorney general.
- Many also have an education commissioner, insurance commissioner, and/or transportation commissioner
- The number of additional executive departments and agencies varies widely from state to state.
- The lieutenant governor is first in the line of succession if the governor should die in office, or become disabled or disqualified in states that have the office.
- States without a lieutenant governor are split between the secretary of state and president of the senate as first in line of succession.

Variations and Differences — Questions for Reporters

- What are the qualifications for election as governor or lieutenant governor?
- Is the governor limited to a set number of terms?
- What are the top state executive offices?
- Which are elective positions and which are appointed?
- What are the executive departments and agencies of the state?
- What is the line of succession if the governor should die, be disabled or disqualified from service?

9.2 Powers of the Governor

All state constitutions state similar primary gubernatorial powers, although the language used differs greatly. Nevada's, for example, says that the governor "shall see that the laws are faithfully executed." Iowa's constitution says, "The governor shall have the responsibility to see that the state's business is well administered and that its laws are faithfully executed."

In addition, governors are the commanders-in-chief of the state's National Guard and/or militia forces. The governor's role as commander-in-chief is superceded when the National Guard is federalized in the case of a national emergency. Most state constitutions detail the circumstances under which a governor may activate the National Guard or the militia, such as to quell public disturbances, maintain law and order, or prevent lawlessness in a time of state emergency or disaster. On this subject the constitutions vary from one terse sentence to an entire paragraph. Minnesota's language is about as plain as it gets: "He [the governor] is commander-in-chief of the military and naval forces and may call them out to execute the laws, suppress insurrection and repel invasion."

All governors are authorized to appoint certain key state executive officials and, in those states where judges are appointed, the governor usually makes judicial appointments as well. (Some states have a separate judicial appointment committee or commission that either sends nominations directly to the legislature or passes them to the governor who sends them to the legislature for confirmation.) The states differ in which specific offices are filled by gubernatorial appointments and the degree to which the governor is required to seek the advice and consent of the state legislature.

Every governor has some sort of veto power over bills passed by the state legislature. State laws vary with regard to the process for overriding a governor's veto. Most follow the federal model and require a two-thirds majority vote in both chambers of the state legislature. (See Chapter 2, section 2.5.) Some require only a three-fifths majority in both chambers to override.

Most, but not all, state constitutions require the governor to communicate with the state legislature, usually near the beginning of the legislative session, about the condition of the state. Many governors, following the presidential tradition, deliver a state of the state address to the legislature that is carried to the citizens of the state via television and radio. Most states authorize the governor to grant pardons to persons convicted of crimes, as well as to commute sentences (reducing their severity). Hawaii's provision is typical: "The governor may grant reprieves, commutations and pardons, after conviction, for all offenses . . ." However, some states restrict the governor's authority in particular cases. South Carolina only allows the governor to commute a capital sentence to life in prison; the South Carolina state legislature must act in order to grant clemency in capital cases.

A substantial number of states authorize the governor (or his/her designee within the executive branch) to prepare and submit a proposed budget and appropriation package. Those states whose legislatures meet only biennially or that operate on biennial or two-year budgets, usually require the governor to oversee the process of assuring that projected revenues are, in fact, going to be sufficient to support the spending appropriated by the legislature.

In addition to the powers enumerated in the state constitutions, governors are the chief policy-makers of each state. This unenumerated role means the governor sets the tone and direction a state will take during his/her term. In some cases the policies of the governor were a part of his/her campaign for election and reflect the popular sentiment of the state by virtue of the fact that the governor won. In other cases state policies grow out of changed circumstances, such as natural disasters, economic upticks or downturns, local emergencies, war, terrorism, or a shift in the social and political sentiment of the state's citizens.

Governors' policy-making powers include setting the agenda with regard to primary, secondary, and/or higher education, environmental policy, public health, fiscal policy, labor relations, highways and transportation, crime and prisons, real estate development, utilities, and insurance regulations. Governors have a direct impact on budget priorities and tax policy. Governors also frame the public and legislative debate on such volatile political and social issues as abortion, guns and gun control, capital punishment, drugs, growth, and land use policy.

A governor's policy-making influence is buttressed by the executive officials he/she chooses to fill key state positions. On the other hand, when the top state executive positions are filled by the electorate at the ballot box, the voters can exert significant limitations on the governor's policy clout by electing individuals from more than one political party.

Key Points

- The governor of each state is required to see that the state's laws are faithfully executed, with language to that effect in every state constitution.
- Governors are also the commanders-in-chief of the state militia and/or the National Guard, except when the National Guard has been federalized.

- Governors have the power to appoint key state executive officials, including judges in states where judges are not elected.
- Most states require the governor to deliver a message to the state legislatures about the state of the state.
- All governors have the power to veto bills passed by their state legislatures, although the number of votes needed to override a governor's veto varies.
- Most governors can pardon convicted criminals, grant clemency, and commute or reduce sentences for prisoners.
- Some states require the governor's office to submit a budget and appropriation package to the state legislature.
- Some states require the governor to monitor revenue projections to see that they will be sufficient to meet state spending goals, especially when the legislature is not in session.
- In addition to the powers specifically stated in the constitutions of the states, governors are the states' chief policy-making officials.

Variations and Differences — Questions for Reporters

- Under what conditions may the governor activate the National Guard or the state militia?
- What state executive officers does the governor appoint?
- Does the governor deliver a state of the state address and if so when?
- Are there any restrictions on the governor's ability to grant clemency, commute prison sentences, or pardon convicts?
- What, if any, is the role of the governor in preparing the state budget and monitoring revenue projections?
- What is the governor's policy agenda?
- Are the governor and the majority of the state legislators in the same or opposing political parties?

9.3 Governors and the Presidency

The majority of U.S. presidents have not been governors, but a substantial minority did serve as a state's chief executive before attaining the White House. Thomas Jefferson and James Monroe were the only governors among the earliest presidents. Both had been governors of

Virginia, as was John Tyler. James Polk and Andrew Johnson were governors of Tennessee. William McKinley and Rutherford B. Hayes were governors of Ohio. Calvin Coolidge was governor of Massachusetts. More New York governors became president than from any other state: Martin Van Buren, Grover Cleveland, Theodore Roosevelt, and Franklin D. Roosevelt all served as governor of the Empire State.

Many governors have unsuccessfully sought the presidency. Since World War II the list includes Adlai Stevenson, George Wallace, Nelson Rockefeller, Michael Dukakis, Jerry Brown, Lamar Alexander, and Bob Kerrey.

The level of public respect and the corresponding electoral clout connected with being a governor has ebbed and flowed during the last half of the Twentieth Century. From the end of World War II through the Ford administration, not a single governor became president. Eisenhower had been an Army general; Kennedy had been a U.S. senator; Johnson, Nixon, and Ford had been vice presidents; Johnson and Nixon also had been senators and Nixon and Ford also had been U.S. representatives.

Not until Jimmy Carter, the governor of Georgia, came along did the era of the governor arrive. Of the last five presidents in the century, only George Bush the elder did not hold the office of governor. Presidents Carter, Reagan, Clinton, and Bush the younger had all served as the chief executive of a state before assuming the presidency.

Key Points

- A majority of U.S. presidents never served as governor of a state.
- New York has produced the most presidents from the ranks of its governors.
- Four of the last five presidents of the Twentieth Century had previously served as governors.

Variations and Differences — Questions for Reporters

- How is my state's governor viewed in the context of national politics?
- Does my state's governor have presidential aspirations?

10

State Judiciary Branches

The framers of the U.S. Constitution were largely silent on the structure of the federal court system. Article III consists of only three sections, a total of six paragraphs. Section 1 provides for one Supreme Court and "such other inferior courts" as Congress shall create. It was not until two years after the Constitution was adopted that the modern federal judiciary started its two centuries of evolution. It began with the enactment of the Judiciary Act of 1789. (See Chapter 4, sections 4.1, 4.2, and 4.3.)

At that time all states had their own judiciary systems, a residue of the government structures that were adopted immediately following the signing of the Declaration of Independence in 1776. As with the federal judiciary, the development of modern state courts has been the product of evolution.

Today, all states have an appellate court of last resort, most calling it the supreme court. Most states also have a secondary level of state appellate courts. And all have at least one level of trial courts.

Nowhere in the structure of the state governments is there an area of greater divergence from the national model than in the state judicial systems. A look at the state constitutions underscores the variety: North Dakota, Vermont and Hawaii cover the judiciary in less than two pages; Colorado and New Mexico each devote eight pages to state courts; and the judiciary section of the New York constitution runs to twenty-two pages in minuscule type.

To provide anything other than a broad outline and to indicate some of the questions journalists must ask in each state would be to risk serious error and confusion.

10.1 State Supreme Courts

All states have some form of supreme court. Not all states call it that. Maryland and New York, for example, call their highest state court "the court of appeals." In New York the Supreme Court is the lowest, or trial, level of state courts. The state Appellate Division occupies the middle tier with the New York Court of Appeals at the top of the judicial pyramid. In West Virginia the highest state court is called the "supreme court of appeals."

All states require that one of the high court justices (or judges) be designated chief justice (or chief judge), although the selection process for the chief is far from uniform.

Most state constitutions specifically authorize the supreme court to be the administrator of the other courts in the state. That administrative authority is generally not challengeable. In several cases, even the U.S. Supreme Court has specifically refused to involve itself in state court administration. In *Chandler et al. v. Florida*, Chief Justice Warren Burger wrote simply, "[T]his court has no supervisory authority over state courts."

The number of state supreme court justices (called judges in some states) varies from three to nine. The states are split among those that elect supreme court justices and those that appoint them. There is no uniformity about the length of judicial terms — four to ten years for state supreme court justices is the common range.

Some states, like Colorado, have created their own hybrid systems. The Colorado constitution provides for appointment of supreme court justices selected by a judicial nominating commission. The judges serve provisional two-year terms and then must stand for a "yes" or "no" retention election. Subsequently the judge may run for as many terms as he/she desires, but the election is always "yes" or "no" and not against an opponent. The Colorado example is unusually convoluted.

In addition, supreme court justices and lower court judges are required to be qualified electors in the states where they sit. Most states specify a minimum period of time during which the justice or judge has practiced law, usually with the requirement that the practice be in the state where he/she sits. (The U.S. Constitution is silent on the issue of whether a U.S. Supreme Court justice must be an attorney.) Some states, such as Delaware, require justices to be "learned in the law." Maryland's constitution mandates selection of judges "who are most distinguished for integrity, wisdom and sound legal knowledge."

There is no uniformity among the states with regard to whether cases may be appealed directly from trial courts to the state supreme court or whether petitions for review must stop first at a mid-level appellate court. Those thirty-eight states that have capital punishment provide for automatic appeal of a death sentence to the highest court in the state. If the state decision involves a U.S. constitutional issue, the decision of the state supreme court may be appealed to the U.S. Supreme Court.

All state constitutions provide for removal of supreme court justices for misconduct and provide for succession in the case of death, resignation, or incapacity. These processes are not consistent among the various states.

Key Points

- All states have a court system with a supreme court as the highest state court, although not all states (such as New York) call their highest court by that name.
- By whatever name, state high courts are the ultimate appellate court in each state.
- Each state requires any high court justice (or judge) to be a resident of the state and a member of the state bar.
- States with the death penalty provide for automatic appeal to the state's highest court.
- All states provide some mechanism for removal of high court justices in the case of misconduct.

Variations and Differences — Questions for Reporters

- What is the name of the highest court in the state?
- How many justices (or judges) are there on the highest court?
- Are the justices elected or appointed?
- If they are appointed, is the appointment by the governor or by judicial nomination commission or similar body?
- How long is the term of supreme court justices?
- What are the requirements for a seat on the supreme court?

- Does the state allow for direct appeal of cases to the supreme court or is there an intermediary level of appellate courts?
- What is the impeachment or removal process?
- What is the process of naming a successor in the case of death or disability?

10.2 Lower Courts

Most states provide for at least one tier of state courts below the supreme court, normally a court of appeals roughly akin to the U.S. Courts of Appeals. A few states, including Texas and Oklahoma, have two separate appellate levels below the supreme court — a court of criminal appeals and a court of civil appeals. Following the model of the U.S. Constitution, states uniformly allow their legislatures to create, expand, or abolish courts inferior to the supreme court as deemed necessary.

The number and nature of lower level state and local courts covers a broad spectrum. A few states, such as Alaska, have nothing below the state court level; there are no municipal or county courts at all. Most other states however provide for local courts, especially at the trial level. The names of these courts include superior court, district court, municipal court, and county court. Many states and local jurisdictions separate civil and criminal courts, giving them different names and allowing them to follow different rules with regard to jury size, conditions for jury trials, evidence, rules, and procedures.

A significant number of states have separate probate courts to deal with wills and estates.

Some local jurisdictions have family courts or domestic relations courts charged with considering a spectrum of cases including divorce, marital separation, adoption, domestic violence, child neglect, and other domestic relations issues.

Many states have a potpourri of courts below the trial court level and courts of special jurisdiction. These include justices of the peace, magistrates, traffic courts, tax courts, bankruptcy courts, and small claims courts (limited to settling damage claims, debts, and financial claims usually of no more than $500 and often significantly less, depending on local law).

Some states, including Illinois, Michigan, New York, and Ohio, have established courts of claims with jurisdiction to adjudicate cases seeking civil damages and/or involving contract claims against the state. Several other states are considering the creation of courts of claims.

Throughout the various systems a variety of other courts, sometimes with arcane names appear, including chancery courts and equity courts (that, for the most part, hear civil cases) and orphan's courts (primarily probate courts).

The states are split with regard to the election or appointment of lower court judges. Most states have shorter terms for lower court judges than for their supreme courts. And all states have minimum requirements for judges including state residency, usually residency in the district, county, or municipality in which they sit, and membership in the state's bar.

Key Points

- Most states have at least one appellate level of state courts below the state supreme court, with some employing a dual structure separating criminal and civil appeals.
- Very few states have only state courts providing for criminal and civil trials, an appellate level, and the state's highest or supreme court.
- Most states have county and/or municipal courts that have original jurisdiction over civil and criminal cases.
- Other common state and local courts include probate courts, tax courts, traffic courts, family courts, and small claims courts.
- The states are divided regarding election or appointment of judges.

Variations and Differences — Questions for Reporters

- What are the names and functions of the state courts below the state's highest court?
- What are the names and functions of county and/or municipal courts?
- Is there a separate civil and criminal division either at the appellate or trial level?
- Are there courts of special jurisdiction at the state or local level?
- Are judges elected or appointed?
- What are the qualifications for judges?
- How long are judges' terms?

10.3 Lawyers, Prosecutors, and Juries

Each of the fifty states has requirements for admission to the state bar in order to practice law in that particular state. The "bar" is the legal term meaning the collective group of lawyers licensed to practice in the state. Bar admission is usually conditioned on completion of law school and passage of a state bar examination. A very few states provide for a legal apprenticeship in lieu of law school. Some, but not all, states allow for admission to the bar by reciprocity (waiver of the bar exam based on certain conditions, for example if a lawyer has been in practice for a specific period of time in another state).

In most state criminal cases the chief prosecutor is known as the district attorney or state's attorney. Criminal charges are always filed by the state or local jurisdiction on behalf of the public.

State's attorneys are often appointed by the state attorney general or the governor. The local office of district attorney is usually an elective position. In most jurisdictions, the bulk of the actual trial work is handled by assistant district attorneys or assistant state's attorneys. Some big cities and counties have hundreds of assistant DAs, even going so far as to have them specialize, such as in prosecuting murder cases, rape cases, arson, assault cases, white collar crimes, and so on.

It is the district attorney's office that decides which cases merit presentation to grand juries, which to take to trial, and which cases to plea-bargain. Plea-bargaining goes on in all jurisdictions and involves a *quid pro quo* in which the prosecution offers a reduction in the charges against a defendant (such as reducing murder to manslaughter or aggravated assault to simple assault) in exchange for a guilty plea. This saves the state or local jurisdiction's resources by precluding the necessity for a trial. In addition the plea bargain may include other conditions such as testimony against another person or cooperation in an ongoing investigation.

In addition to DAs many jurisdictions have an office of public defender. Under the Sixth Amendment criminal defendants have a right to counsel, and in cases where the defendant cannot afford his/her own lawyer the courts assign one. The public defender's office is seldom an elective position. In some places there's no office of public defender at all. Instead the clerk of the court oversees a pool of local attorneys who are assigned, usually by rotation, to represent criminal defendants who cannot afford to pay for their own counsel.

District attorneys and public defenders are only part of the criminal judicial process. In civil cases — litigation between individuals — most states require that the litigants provide their own legal counsel or appear *pro se* (for him or herself).

State and local juries are picked in very much the same manner as federal court juries. (See Chapter 4, section 4.5.) A great many jurisdictions select their jury pools from voter registration lists. All states have laws that prohibit employers from firing, demoting, or otherwise punishing employees who are called for jury duty. States vary widely in the reasons someone called for jury duty will be excused. Some states automatically excuse lawyers, law students, judges, police officers, doctors-on-call, and those on whom jury duty would impose a serious personal hardship, such as nursing mothers. A few states and localities require a personal petition for a waiver of jury duty. In most states, deliberate and willful failure to answer a summons to jury duty can result in a contempt of court citation.

Once the jury pool is formed, small groups from it are called for individual trials. As in the U.S. District Courts, potential jurors are questioned in a process known as *voir dire*. Jurors may be challenged and excused. An unlimited number of jurors may be challenged for cause (excused for such reasons as knowing the defendant or a trial participant, having special knowledge or interest in the case, or otherwise being unable to render a fair verdict). In pre-trial agreements or as outlined in trial and procedural rules in some states, each side will have a set number of peremptory challenges. Jurors so challenged are excused for no reason at all.

Key Points

- All states set standards for the right to practice law, including completion of law school and passing the bar examination.
- In most state criminal cases, the prosecutor is known as the district attorney or the state's attorney.
- District attorneys are often elected officials, with a number of assistants who actually try the cases.
- Many localities have an office of public defender to provide legal counsel to criminal defendants who cannot afford it; in some places there is simply a pool of lawyers assigned to cases by rotation.

- In almost all civil cases the litigants must obtain their own attorneys or appear for themselves.
- In most jurisdictions the process of impaneling and selecting jurors for trials is very similar to the federal jury process.
- States have legal requirements that employers must give employees time off for jury service without jeopardizing their job or their seniority.

Variations and Differences — Questions for Reporters

- What are the requirements for admission to the state bar?
- What is the makeup of the district attorney's or state's attorney's office?
- Is DA an elective position?
- How does the state handle legal counsel for criminal suspects who can't afford their own attorney?
- What are the specifics of calling prospective jurors (is it done from voter rolls, how long do the prospective jurors have to serve)?

10.4 The Death Penalty

State and federal courts have wrestled with the issue of capital punishment for decades. In 1966, a U.S. Supreme Court decision resulted in a ten-year moratorium on executions. In 1976, the court revisited the issue in three death penalty cases — *Gregg v. Georgia*, *Jurek v. Texas*, and *Proffitt v. Florida*. Not only did the U.S. Supreme Court reverse itself and uphold the death penalty in those three cases (known together as *The Gregg Case*), the court held that capital punishment, itself, did not breach the Eighth Amendment's prohibition against "cruel and unusual punishments" and thus was constitutional.

In January 1977, Utah became the first state to avail itself of the high court's restoration of the death penalty. Gary Gilmore was executed by firing squad.

Thirty-eight states as well as the federal government and the U.S. military have provisions for capital punishment. Of those thirty-eight states that provide for capital punishment, seven — Connecticut, Kansas, New Hampshire, New Jersey, New Mexico, New York, and South Dakota — have not executed anyone since *The Gregg Case* was decided, although all but New Hampshire have people on death row awaiting execution. Twelve states — Alaska, Hawaii, Iowa, Maine,

Massachusetts, Michigan, Minnesota, North Dakota, Rhode Island, Vermont, West Virginia, and Wisconsin — do not have the death penalty.

Even where capital punishment has been used with regularity, the legal wrangling continues. In October 2001 the Georgia state supreme court ruled 4-3 that the electric chair is cruel and unusual punishment and thus is unconstitutional. Georgia immediately changed its execution method to lethal injection, and left Nebraska and Alabama as the only states to retain the electric chair as the sole method of executing prisoners. In those other states that still have the electric chair, prisoners are given an option of execution method — lethal injection or electrocution. The lethal injection option is also available to people convicted of capital crimes in states that retain the gas chamber as a method of execution.

Key Points

- In 1966, the Supreme Court struck down the death penalty and in 1976 restored it.
- Thirty-eight states, the federal government and the U.S. military currently have capital punishment laws, although seven states have not carried out an execution since the 1976 Supreme Court ruling.
- The legal battles surrounding the death penalty continue, with the Georgia state supreme court declaring the electric chair a cruel and unusual punishment in 2001.

Variations and Differences — Questions for Reporters

- Does my state have capital punishment and have there been any executions since 1976? How many?
- What is the method of execution?
- If the state has capital punishment, is there any political movement toward ending it by legislation or ballot initiative?
- If the state does not have capital punishment, is there any political movement toward enacting it by legislation or ballot initiative?

10.5 Cameras in Courts

Obviously, the issue of whether to allow broadcast coverage of judicial proceedings was never contemplated by the framers of the

Constitution. Colorado was the first state to experiment with cameras in its courts in the 1950s. While most states rejected the notion of cameras in courts in the '50s and '60s, a few, including Texas, launched early experiments in broadcast coverage of judicial proceedings.

In 1962, a wheeler-dealer named Billy Sol Estes was charged by the state of Texas with fraud and swindling in connection with an illegal pyramid scheme involving nonexistent fertilizer tanks. Estes was ultimately convicted. He appealed, claiming his right to a fair trial was abridged by a disruptive and prejudicial media presence. The local court allowed camera coverage of the pre-trial proceedings.

In the early 1960s, technology was primitive. TV cameras were as big as washing machines. Coaxial cable was the size of a fire hose. Microphones were like bowling pins. And still cameras clicked, flashed, and hissed like cicadas.

In 1965, the U.S. Supreme Court overturned Estes' conviction and with it rejected the notion of cameras in courtrooms. In his concurring opinion, widely cited by opponents of cameras in the courts, Chief Justice Earl Warren decried "photographers roaming at will through the courtroom."

Fifteen years later, the issue made its way back to the U.S. Supreme Court. The court agreed to hear an appeal from a pair of Miami cops convicted of a variety of charges in connection with a burglary at a local restaurant. Their trial was open to cameras under an experiment then underway in the Florida courts. The defendants appealed, citing *Estes v. Texas*. A unanimous Supreme Court effectively overturned the *Estes* decision.

Chief Justice Warren Burger wrote the opinion in *Chandler et al. v. Florida*: "An absolute constitutional ban on broadcast coverage of trials cannot be justified simply because there is a danger that, in some cases, prejudicial broadcast accounts of pretrial and trial events may impair the ability of jurors to decide the issue of guilt or innocence uninfluenced by extraneous matter. The risk of juror prejudice in some cases does not justify an absolute ban on news coverage of trials by the printed media; so also the risk of such prejudice does not warrant an absolute constitutional ban on all broadcast coverage."

The Supreme Court refused to invalidate the Florida experiment with cameras in the courts and the stage was set for much wider state acceptance of broadcast coverage of trials. The *Chandler* decision effectively left the issue of cameras with the individual states, the only caveat being a warning that the Supreme Court would intervene if states were to allow camera coverage that infringed on the fundamental constitutional rights of defendants.

Today all fifty states permit some kind of electronic coverage of their courts. In 2001 Mississippi and South Dakota — the last two states with absolute prohibitions on camera coverage — both approved camera coverage of courts on a limited basis. Five states still call camera coverage experimental; forty-five states have established permanent rules regarding cameras. The federal courts still prohibit camera coverage.

Reporters, especially radio and TV reporters, should know that the rules vary from state to state. In some states defendants may petition the trial court to have cameras removed; in some states it is up to the discretion of individual judges (both trial and appellate) whether to permit camera coverage; in Ohio, Oklahoma, and Maine any trial participant not wanting camera coverage can petition to have cameras prohibited. Some states, such as Illinois, New York, and Minnesota limit cameras to appellate courts only, prohibiting cameras in trial courts. And a few states, including Maryland and Maine, limit camera coverage of trial courts to civil cases only.

Key Points

- In 1981, the U.S. Supreme Court ruled that camera coverage of court proceedings was not inherently unconstitutional.
- The ruling allowed individual states to determine if, and how much, electronic coverage of judicial proceedings would be permitted.
- All fifty states now allow at least a minimum level of electronic coverage of their courts.
- The rules governing camera coverage and the circumstances under which cameras may be excluded vary widely from state to state.

Variations and Differences — Questions for Reporters

- What are the rules in my state for camera coverage of judicial proceedings?
- What courts (criminal, civil, trial and/or appellate) allow cameras?

- Under what circumstances may cameras and/or microphones be prohibited?
- Do defendants have the right to petition against electronic media coverage?
- Can trial participants other than defendants seek removal of cameras from courts?
- Do judges have the discretion to prohibit camera coverage of a specific trial?

10.6 Reporter Shield Laws

Journalists have long been at odds with various federal and state courts over whether and when they may be compelled to reveal the identities of confidential sources. The journalists' position, articulated by the Reporters Committee for Freedom of the Press, asserts that forcing journalists to disclose the names of their confidential sources undermines the newsgathering process, threatens the constitutional principle of a free press, and is likely to have a chilling effect on editorial decisions about whether to cover matters that might cause a reporter to be subpoenaed.

U.S. jurisprudence has long recognized the concept of privilege. Privilege is a right held by a person or class of persons that immunizes them from the normal course of law. Among the most generally recognized privileges are doctor-patient privilege (in which a doctor may not be compelled to disclose information about a patient), husband-wife privilege (in which one spouse may not be compelled to testify against the other), clergy-penitent privilege (in which a member of the clergy may not be compelled to disclose information divulged in "the sanctity of the confessional"), lawyer-client privilege (in which an attorney may not disclose communications with a client), and executive privilege (in which the president of the United States may not be required to provide confidential information or disclose the contents of confidential documents).

Thirty-one states have adopted a highly divergent catalogue of reporter shield laws, granting limited protection for journalists against being forced to identify confidential sources. Most of these shield laws direct the courts of the states to use variations on a three-pronged test regarding whether a journalist may be compelled to name his/her source. The test requires the courts to ask:

1. Whether the information sought is clearly relevant to the case;
2. Whether the information sought is essential to the proof of the crime; and
3. Whether the information was unable to be obtained in any other manner.

Most state shield laws specifically do not afford reporters any protection where the reporter actually witnessed criminal activity.

Advocates of a journalist's privilege (in which reporters are protected from being forced to identify confidential sources) often turn to *Branzburg v. Hayes* for legal support for at least a qualified or conditional privilege. Despite the fact that the *Branzburg* decision rejects the notion of journalist's privilege, the advocates for such a privilege rely on the reasoning set out in one concurring opinion and two dissents to suggest that a five-justice majority actually supported the idea of a conditional reporters' privilege. Justice William O. Douglas is frequently cited: "A reporter is no better than his source of information. Unless he has a privilege to withhold the identity of his source, he will be the victim of governmental intrigue or aggression."

Lawyers for the Reporters Committee for Freedom of the Press and other media attorneys warn that the courts have not consistently supported the interpretation of *Branzburg* that transforms the minority of justices into a majority, and they note that some courts specifically have rejected that interpretation. The fact is that courts around the country continue to subpoena reporters regarding the identities of their confidential sources.

If a reporter is subpoenaed to testify, either at trial or before a grand jury, refusal to testify can result in a contempt of court citation and the possibility of a fine or being sent to jail. Only a few state shield laws prohibit courts from issuing contempt citations for refusal to testify.

In addition, reporters may be faced with a legal dilemma. Journalists may be subject to lawsuits for contract violation if they divulge the names of confidential sources. In *Cohen v. Cowles Media*, the U.S. Supreme Court ruled in 1991 that the First Amendment does not immunize reporters from such suits. The court left it to the state legislatures to determine their own course regarding whether news organizations and reporters who grant anonymity to sources are subject to suit for breach of contract if they disclose the names of those sources. This has caused many news organizations to review their own policies regarding the use of confidential sources.

Key Points

- Thirty-one states and the federal courts recognize a limited privilege for reporters not to disclose the identities of their confidential sources.
- Most state and federal courts employ a three-part test with regard to compelling a journalist's testimony: relevance to the case, criticality to proof of the crime, and whether the information can be obtained elsewhere.
- Despite wide recognition of a qualified or limited journalists' privilege, courts continue to subpoena reporters and demand the identities of confidential sources.
- In some states and in the federal courts, reporters may he held in contempt of court if they are subpoenaed and refuse to testify.
- In 1991 the U.S. Supreme Court ruled that reporters are not immune from lawsuits for breach of contract if they disclose the names of confidential sources.

Variations and Differences — Questions for Reporters

- Does my state have a reporter shield law?
- If so, what are the express limits on a journalist's privilege not to identify confidential sources?
- Am I likely to be cited for contempt of court if I am subpoenaed and refuse to divulge the name of my confidential source?
- What is my news organization's policy with regard to granting anonymity to confidential sources?

11

Local Government

Local government is the most difficult civics area for reporters to grasp, because of the enormous variations — there are state-to-state, city-to-city, and county-to-county differences. They encompass a vast array of elements including government structure, regulatory authority, taxation, law enforcement authority and jurisdictions, zoning and land use, and schools. The differences include the names of the various agencies, the authority of those agencies, the law-making and enforcement scope of the local governments, and which local officials are elected versus those that are appointed.

This chapter will endeavor to highlight some general parallels and to raise some of the key questions journalists will need to ask if they are covering local government.

11.1 Makeup of Local Government

Every state has counties, geographic districts within the boundaries of the state. Delaware has the fewest counties — three. Rhode Island and Hawaii have five each. Large states have dozens of counties. California has 58. Texas has 254. Counties are called parishes in Louisiana.

Cities are incorporated areas and may be entirely within one county or overlap into more than one county. In some cases cities and counties are combined — Los Angeles and Denver are examples. The boundaries of the city of Jacksonville and Duval County, in Florida, are the same.

Towns are incorporated areas, usually within a single county. Most states differentiate cities and towns by size, with cities being the larger municipal designation. Some states add a third, even smaller, municipal level called villages. Some states define all these local divisions, including the counties, as municipalities, although there is generally a difference in the government structure, regulatory authority, and government organization between counties and cities, towns, and villages.

Most cities and towns have mayors. In some cases they are the chief executive officer of the city or town. In other cases the mayor is mainly a ceremonial officer with the real operational authority vested in a city manager or city administrator. Usually, but not always, mayors are elected and city managers and/or city administrators are appointed.

Generally the chair of the county commission is a county's chief executive, but in a significant number of counties the duties of the chair rotate among the members of the county commission on an annual or biennial basis. The chair is usually a voting member of the county commission.

Every local jurisdiction — county, city, town, and village — is responsible for a local budget, primary and secondary public schools, roads and bridges, zoning and land use, law enforcement, public safety and fire protection, and taxation. The names, structure, organization and officials of the offices, agencies, boards, and commissions responsible for these areas vary widely.

Key Points

- Every state has counties.
- Cities are incorporated areas that may be in one county or overlap more than one county.
- Towns are incorporated areas usually all within the borders of one county.
- Local governments generally have a chief executive officer. Most cities and towns have mayors, but some also have city managers or administrators.
- In some cases the office of mayor is purely a ceremonial position with the real authority of government vested in a city manager and council.
- Local governments are uniformly charged with responsibility for budgeting, schools, law enforcement, zoning, fire protection and taxation.

Variations and Differences — Questions for Reporters

- What are the county, city, town, municipal, and/or regional governments within my coverage area?
- What are the responsibilities of the various local governments in my area?
- Does the city or town have a mayor or city manager or both?
- What is the makeup of the county commission?
- What is the budgeting function of the local jurisdiction?
- What is the budgeting agency of the local jurisdiction?

11.2 State Authority and Control

Every local government — county, city, town or other municipality — gets its authority to function from the state constitution and state legislature, through a combination of constitutionally-set guidelines and statutory laws. Almost all state constitutions provide for the state legislatures to adopt two categories of legislation regarding local government: "General laws" which apply to all local jurisdictions, and local or "special laws" which apply to individual localities.

A vast majority of state constitutions have specific prohibitions on certain kinds of special laws. Many are extremely detailed, such as Delaware's: "The General Assembly shall not pass any local or special law relating to fences: the straying of livestock: ditches: the creation or changing the boundaries of school districts . . ." Indiana's constitution provides another example prohibiting special laws regarding "changing the venue in civil and criminal cases . . . changing the names of persons . . . [and] vacating roads, town plats, streets, alleys, and public squares . . ."

Many states have constitutional provisions allowing home rule for local governments. Home rule authorizes the local jurisdiction to set up its own government structure, within the broad parameters established in the state constitution and by the state legislature in general laws. Some states require adoption and voter approval of a home rule charter to codify the local government structure and scope. Home rule is often limited to cities, towns, and municipalities, with states retaining general authority over counties. The Pennsylvania constitution is typical: "Municipalities shall have the right and power to frame and adopt home rule charters." It goes on to state that the voters of the municipality must approve the home rule structure.

Other states, however, retain tight legislative control over local government. The constitution of Virginia, for example, is painstakingly specific about the guidelines for local government, including the officers, procedures, and dates of elections for counties, cities, and towns: "The General Assembly [state legislature] shall provide by general law for the organization, government, powers, change of boundaries, consolidation, and dissolution of counties, cities, towns, and regional governments."

Key Points

- All local governments get their authority to function from state constitutions and state legislatures.
- General laws are omnibus acts of a state legislature affecting all local jurisdictions.
- Special laws are limited acts of a state legislature affecting only one local jurisdiction.
- Some states retain tight control over the organization, powers, officers, and authority of local governments.
- Some states allow for home rule, especially in cities, towns and municipalities, in which the local jurisdiction sets up its own government structure within broad state legislative guidelines.

Variations and Differences — Questions for Reporters

- Does the state have home rule jurisdictions or are they all controlled by the state legislature?
- Must home rule charters be approved by voters?
- How much local control is exercised by the state legislature?
- What are the areas of authority granted by the state to the local governments?
- Are there limits on the state legislature with regard to enacting special laws?

11.3 Structure of Local Governments

Every local government has a central governing body. It is most frequently called the city, town, or village council; in counties it is generally the county commission or occasionally the county council. For the most part these bodies have both legislative and executive functions. Most enact laws (sometimes called ordinances) and regulations; and most have an administrative and enforcement authority to implement and enforce those laws and regulations.

The structure of county commissions and city councils is more similar to parliamentary models than to federal or state models. As in a parliamentary government, there is little distinction between the executive and legislative branches. The top executive (the chair of the county commission or the mayor) generally sits on the commission or council. In some cases the council, as in a parliamentary system, picks the chief executive from its ranks. There is frequently no executive veto power, as there is in the national or state structure.

While most big cities have only an elected mayor as the chief executive, some smaller cities and towns have both a mayor (usually a ceremonial office or the presiding officer of the city council) and a city manager, an appointed official who is the chief executive of the city or town. The city manager, sometimes called the city administrator, is charged with such things as implementing what the city council has enacted, preparing the budget, and overseeing the operation of agencies and departments of the municipality.

Schools are generally considered one of the principal areas of jurisdiction for local governments. Local governments uniformly have some kind of school board that administers geographic areas called school districts. A school district is often, but not always, contained within the same boundaries as a county. Some legal scholars equate local school systems to quasi-corporations in which the school board is effectively the board of directors, responsible to the voters of the school district. As in a corporate structure, most school districts have a superintendent as chief executive officer, generally appointed by the school board and responsible directly to the board.

School boards are usually elected. There is enormous variation among school boards as to the length of members' terms, whether terms are staggered, the number of members, members' qualifications, and whether the boards are elected in partisan or non-partisan elections.

The authority of school boards uniformly includes responsibility for the budget, curricula, administration, physical operation, staffing, security, and general policies of public primary and secondary schools. Most school boards have no taxing authority of their own and work closely with the local government to see that revenues raised are sufficient to operate the schools. Some states, such as New York, provide for local jurisdictions to have separate school taxes and require a separate vote on each budget proposed by the school board.

In addition to public education, many states delegate other state functions to local governments. For example, the administration of licensing (drivers' licenses, business licenses, commercial licenses, liquor licenses, and the like) is often delegated to counties or large cities, along with the authority to enforce licensing rules and regulations. These local jurisdictions are then empowered to impose and collect fines for breaching those rules and regulations.

Other local areas and offices common to counties and cities include tax collection, water and sewer, sanitation, public transportation (which may include buses, subways, commuter railroads, and/or ferries), ports and airports, registration of wills, recording real estate deeds, law enforcement, public prosecutors, public defenders, coroners, and clerks of the local courts.

In cases where these functions overlap jurisdictions, many states provide for regional authorities to be established. These regional authorities can encompass areas involving a city and one or more counties, more than one city, and/or more than one county. Denver's regional transit district is an example. It deals with public transportation in Denver and the surrounding suburbs. The Port Authority of New York and New Jersey, as another example, embraces several counties in two states. Its jurisdiction includes the three major airports in the New York metropolitan area as well as several maritime terminals, docks, and ports.

There is enormous variation among local jurisdictions regarding the number of members on commissions and councils, and who is entitled to vote. A few examples:

— Chicago: Has fifty members of the city council. Members of the city council are called aldermen, each representing a district called a ward. Aldermen are elected for four-year terms. The mayor is the presiding officer of the city council, but may vote only if there is a tie.

— Portland, Oregon: Has a four-member city commission and a mayor, each with one vote on the commission. They are each elected for four-year terms.

— Laramie, Wyoming: Has a nine-member city council, with members elected for four-year terms. The council picks the mayor every two years. The chief executive is the city manager, who reports directly to the city council.

— Live Oak, Florida: Has five members on the city council, each elected for a four-year term. The mayor is also elected for a four-year term, but serves primarily as a ceremonial figure. The mayor has no vote on the city council. The chief executive officer is the city administrator who reports directly to the city council.

Reporters also need to know when elections are scheduled. Some states require municipal elections to be held at times other than during the general election in November. Virginia's constitution, for example, requires municipal elections to be held in June.

In addition reporters must find out whether elections for mayor, school board, county commission, and city, town, or municipal council are partisan or non-partisan. In the case of non-partisan elections (where candidates are not identified with a political party) reporters should look into the background of the candidates and the electoral history of the locality. In some places, elections are non-partisan in name only and in reality are highly partisan. There may be ample evidence in a "non-partisan" election that the party affiliation of the candidates is widely publicized to the voters by interest groups and politically active organizations in an effort to sway the outcome of the election.

Key Points

- All local governments have a central governing body, usually called a county commission or a city, town, or municipal council.
- Almost all local governments have a body called a school board to oversee each school district and the operation of public primary and secondary schools within each district.
- Each school district has a chief executive, usually called the superintendent and usually appointed by the school board.
- States delegate a large number of other functions to local governments including licensing and enforcement of licensing laws.
- Other local government agencies deal with such issues as law enforcement, taxation, land use, water and sewer, public transportation, coroners, recording of wills and registration of real estate deeds.

Variations and Differences — Questions for Reporters

- What is the name, structure, authority, and make-up of the local governing body or bodies in my coverage area?
- Who are the members of the local governing body?
- Is there a mayor, city manager, or both?
- What is the actual role of the mayor and/or city manager?
- What is the makeup and nature of the local school board?
- What is the role of the superintendent of schools?
- What other legislative and administrative functions are the responsibility of the local governing body?
- Are municipal elections held as a part of the general election in November or at another time?
- Are elections partisan or non-partisan?
- If they are non-partisan, is it really non-political or is it a political election without party labels?

11.4 Local Lawmaking

Local governing bodies — county commissions and city or town councils — have a dual role. They have a legislative function, in that they enact local laws, ordinances, regulations, and resolutions; they also have the executive authority to implement and enforce the laws they pass. This combined legislative and executive function differs sharply from the federal and state models, which clearly separate those powers between two separate branches of government. Local governments derive their law-making and enforcement authority from state constitutions and state legislatures.

Local laws are enacted by a vote of the commission or council. The localities are split with regard to vetoes and overrides. In a significant number of cities with a history of strong mayors — such as New York, Louisville and Springfield, Massachusetts — the mayor has veto power. In some jurisdictions there are provisions for a popular referendum on whether to reject local laws enacted by councils and commissions (see Chapter 8, section 8.4). And some localities provide for ballot initiatives to enact new laws. As with referenda and initiatives at the state level, the process for both involves gathering signatures on petitions (usually between five and ten percent of registered voters in the jurisdiction affected), certifying the signatures, and placing the question on the ballot for voter approval or disapproval. Some states restrict the number of times an issue can go before the voters. Pennsylvania's state constitution, as an example, decrees that ballot questions "shall not be submitted more than once in five years."

Most state legislatures require local governing bodies to hold public hearings and open debate before a law or resolution (an official policy declaration) can be voted on and/or adopted. Most require the yeas and nays of commission or council members to be recorded in the minutes or journal of the governing body's proceedings. Furthermore, sunshine laws, also known as open meeting laws, in every state require law-making votes to be conducted in open, public session.

Many localities prohibit the introduction and adoption of a law or regulation during the same meeting; some require publication of proposed local legislation before a vote can be taken. Both provisions are designed to allow time for public comment and/or public opposition to be voiced. They have their roots in myriad historic examples of mayors gathering enough city council members in special session to constitute a majority, or quorum, and passing a law in the dead of night.

Key Points

- Most local governments have both legislative and executive functions with the authority to enact laws and enforce those laws.
- Most state constitutions require public hearings and debate and a publicly recorded vote for local laws to be enacted.
- Localities are divided with regard to vetoes and overrides of actions by local governing bodies.
- Some state constitutions provide for citizen rejection of local law-making actions through popular referenda and for proposal of new laws through ballot initiatives.
- Many states provide for a waiting period between introduction of a local law and action on the measure by the local governing body.

Variations and Differences — Questions for Reporters

- What is the process for introduction, enactment and implementation of laws, ordinances, regulations and resolutions in my county or municipality?
- What are the rules regarding open meetings, public hearings and debate, and recorded votes of the local governing body?

- Can a local law be introduced and enacted at the same meeting or is a waiting period required between introduction and enactment?
- Is there a provision for veto, override, and/or popular referendum to counter the action of the local governing body?
- Can citizens propose laws through ballot initiatives?

11.5 Law Enforcement and Local Courts

Law enforcement involves a great deal more than arresting criminal suspects. The law enforcement function of local government includes criminal investigation, detention of criminal suspects, public safety, traffic control and enforcement, emergency response, domestic relations and child protection, truancy, and animal control.

Most cities and towns have police departments that enforce the laws. Most have a police chief. The chief is generally appointed, sometimes by the city council, sometimes by the mayor with the approval of the city council, sometimes by a special police commission or board. In some cities the police chief reports to the city manager or mayor. In others the police chief reports directly to the city council. In still others the police chief reports to the police commissioner (if that office is vested in one person) or to the police commission or police board. A few cities have only a police commissioner and no overall police chief. New York and San Francisco are examples. The larger the city, the bigger the police force and thus the larger the command structure.

Most counties have a sheriff, usually an elective position. The function and structure of most sheriffs' departments is similar to that of city police departments.

Many cities have jails or holding facilities for criminal suspects. Most counties have a jail that serves as a holding facility, and which is occasionally shared by towns or cities within the county that do not have their own facility. County jails also serve as incarceration and correctional facilities for certain criminals whose crimes and/or sentences fall below the threshold, usually determined by the length of the sentence or the severity of the crime, that would send them to the state prison.

Every city and county has a prosecutor. In most cities the prosecutor is the district attorney, usually an elective position. DAs have primary authority for determining if a crime has been committed, if there is sufficient evidence a particular person committed the crime, and whether the case should be presented to a grand jury. (See Chapter 4, section 4.5 for the federal model.) Once an indictment has been handed up by a grand jury, it is the district attorney — or more commonly as a practical matter a deputy district attorney — who takes the case through the pre-trial process (including bail), discovery, trial, and, if necessary, appeal. If a plea bargain or plea agreement is to be brokered it is done by the district attorney or with the approval of the district attorney.

Some local jurisdictions have a state's attorney as prosecutor instead of a district attorney. State's attorneys are often appointed by the state attorney general's office or occasionally by a state commission empowered to make such appointments.

Many localities have an office of public defender, which is generally an appointed position. Most local governments also have an elected position called clerk of the court, an office that generally oversees the courts within that jurisdiction. Clerks of the court are responsible for such things as organizing the dockets (schedules) for each individual judge, overseeing court personnel, purchasing, and business affairs. In jurisdictions where there is no public defender's office, it often falls to the clerk of the court to oversee a pool of attorneys who are appointed in rotation to represent criminal defendants who cannot afford their own counsel.

All local courts derive their authority directly from the state legislatures. Most local jurisdictions have some form of civil and criminal trial courts — either as a single court or as coequal divisions. Many localities have a lower tier of courts, including justices of the peace or magistrate courts, traffic court, small claims court, and domestic relations or family court. Larger cities and counties often have probate courts, to dispose of wills and estates.

Whether judges are elected or appointed is generally defined by state law, which covers all jurisdictions within the state under either statutory law or in the form of a constitutional provision.

Reporters need to be aware that while law enforcement jurisdictions frequently overlap geographically, there are very clear lines that determine which law enforcement agency will have primary jurisdiction. Usually city and town police departments have primary jurisdiction within the boundaries of the city or town. The county sheriff's department has primary jurisdiction in unincorporated areas outside the cities and towns. A frequent problem for journalists is knowing where the geographic boundary lines are, where a city ends and a suburb begins, or where a town ends and the county begins. It is not uncommon for one side of the street to be in one jurisdiction and the other side to be in another.

Obtaining basic information from local law enforcement agencies is generally routine for legitimate newspeople. Some sheriffs' offices and police departments have a person who deals with the news media and acts as a spokesperson. In cases involving local law enforcement — including arrests, detentions, investigations, emergency actions, traffic accidents, civil disturbances, and matters concerning public health and safety — reporters can usually obtain basic information from the dispatcher or desk officer who answers the phone.

Key Points

- Most cities and towns have police departments, generally headed by police chiefs.
- Most counties have sheriffs offices, headed by an elected sheriff.
- Many, but not all, cities and towns have jails or holding facilities.
- Most counties have jails that are both holding facilities and correctional institutions for criminals whose sentences do not reach a state prison threshold.
- All localities have a prosecutor, often called the district attorney in cities and towns.
- Many localities have an office of public defender.
- Cities, towns, and counties generally have trial courts for criminal and civil cases.
- Other local courts include justices of the peace or magistrate courts, traffic court, small claims court, and domestic relations or family court.

Variations and Differences — Questions for Reporters

- What are the law enforcement agencies within my coverage area?
- What are the lines of jurisdiction?
- Who is the police chief, sheriff, and district attorney, and what is the structure of each office and/or department?
- Is there a city or town jail?

- What is the city or county court structure, including criminal, civ-il, and lower courts?
- Are cameras and microphones allowed in the local courts? (See Chapter 10, section 10.5.)
- Is there an information office from which I can obtain information about the local agencies?

11.6 Zoning, Land Use, and Building Regulations

States generally vest localities with broad authority regarding how land within their boundaries may be used. Many local jurisdictions have one or several of the following: a zoning commissioner, a zoning commission or board, a land use commission, and a planning commission or board. Members of these commissions and boards may be elected or appointed. These entities often serve legislative, executive, and quasi-judicial functions. They frequently make rules and regulations, enforce rules and regulations, and interpret or hear appeals of rules and regulations.

They determine the general uses of land, architectural design, and the uses for various buildings and structures. They are also frequently involved in planning for future real estate development, land use, and population growth. Zoning authorities are responsible for drawing usage boundaries, defining those geographic areas, restricting and regulating their use, and enforcing zoning codes, rules, and regulations. Zoning categories include agricultural, single family dwellings, multi-family dwellings, commercial use, or multiple use. (The list is not comprehensive.)

In addition the zoning authority has primary jurisdiction for enforcing the localities' zoning regulations. Zoning authorities can issue citations, cease and desist orders (telling somebody to stop doing something), and in some cases impose fines. Flagrant, willful, or repeated violators can be, and frequently are, referred to the district attorney's office for prosecution. While these are common zoning authority responsibilities and categories, they do not represent all zoning authority responsibilities and categories.

Zoning authorities also concern themselves with such land use issues as historic preservation, environment, aesthetics, green space, parks and recreational land, and public facilities.

Zoning authorities are occasionally called upon to act in a quasi-judicial manner in deciding such questions as whether to grant a variance, or exception, to established zoning rules and regulations. For example, if a resident wanted to add an extension to his/her house but the extension would encroach on the buffer zone between the resident's lot and his/her neighbor's lot, the person might seek a zoning variance. (In many places there are restrictions on how close to the property line a structure may be built. These are called buffer zones or setbacks.) In most jurisdictions variances and other exceptions and/or changes to zoning regulations require public hearings and usually a public vote by the zoning authority.

Some states prescribe an appeals process for decisions of the zoning authority. In some cases the first appellate level is the city or town council or county commission. In other cases the zoning authority's decision can be appealed directly to the level of the state appellate courts directly below the state supreme court. No states permit direct appeal from a local zoning authority to the state's highest court.

In a few rare cases, there are virtually no zoning restrictions within certain municipal areas. Houston, Texas, is an example of a large city with few, if any, zoning regulations. That gives rise to single family homes amid office buildings, commercial buildings next door to single or multi-family homes, and multi-family compounds in the heart of single family neighborhoods.

In addition to zoning and land use, local governments are usually given broad authority by the state legislatures to grant building and construction permits, authorize occupancy permits, and develop and enforce building and/or construction codes within guidelines established by the states. Most localities have at least one and usually several building inspectors who work for the building and/or construction department. Their job is to inspect construction projects and enforce building codes.

Reporters should be aware that land use, population growth, and real estate development are hot political issues in many places, especially in the Sun Belt and other high growth areas. Local politics in places like Florida, Nevada, Colorado, and southern California bubbles with questions regarding population density, environmental impact, and strain on the local infrastructure (including water consumption, electricity usage, adequate roads, and available educational facilities). The political discourse often highlights a clash of values between those who see growth as an economic boon and those who see it as socially, environmentally, and culturally destructive.

Key Points

- Localities generally have a zoning and/or land use authority either in the form of one zoning commissioner or in the form of a board or zoning commission.
- Zoning authorities are responsible for drawing usage boundaries within the locality and for defining what the authority deems to be the appropriate uses of the land.
- A variance is the formal name for an exception to zoning regulations.
- Local zoning authorities are empowered to grant variances within their area.
- Public hearings are generally required before a variance can be granted.
- Appeals go to the city council, county commission, or to the middle level of state appellate courts.
- Localities are also empowered to grant building and construction permits, occupancy permits, and to modify and enforce building and construction codes.

Variations and Differences — Questions for Reporters

- What is the structure and who are the key officials of the zoning authority or authorities in my coverage area?
- Where can I obtain the general zoning, land use, and construction regulations for my coverage area?
- What are the major land use and zoning issues?
- Is development and land use a major political issue and if so who are the important players on all sides?
- When and how are zoning questions addressed?

Appendix A

The Constitution of the United States

(Editor's Note: The punctuation and spelling of the text of the Constitution and Amendments as they appear here are consistent with those of the original documents. This version also indicates parenthetically the parts of the Constitution that have been changed or superseded by amendments.)

Preamble

We the People of the United States, in Order to form a more perfect Union, establish justice, insure domestic Tranquility, provide for the common defence, promote the general Welfare, and secure the Blessings of Liberty to ourselves and our Posterity, do ordain and establish this Constitution for the United States of America.

Article I

Section 1. All legislative Powers herein granted shall be vested in a Congress of the United States, which shall consist of a Senate and House of Representatives.

Section 2. The House of Representatives shall be composed of Members chosen every second Year by the People of the several States, and the Electors in each State shall have the Qualifications requisite for Electors of the most numerous Branch of the State Legislature.

No Person shall be a Representative who shall not have attained to the Age of twenty five Years, and been seven Years a Citizen of the United States, and who shall not, when elected, be an Inhabitant of that State in which he shall be chosen.

(Representatives and direct Taxes shall be apportioned among the several States which may be included within this Union, according to their respective Numbers, which shall be determined by adding to the whole Number of free Persons, including those bound to Service for a Term of Years, and excluding Indians not taxed, three-fifths of all other Persons.)[1] The actual Enumeration shall be made within three years after the first meeting of the Congress of the United States, and within every subsequent Term of ten Years, in such Manner as they shall by Law direct. The number of Representatives shall not exceed one for every thirty Thousand, but each State shall have at Least one Representative; and until such enumeration shall be made, the state of New Hampshire shall be entitled to chuse three, Massachusetts eight, Rhode-Island and Providence Plantation one, Connecticut five, New-York six, New Jersey four, Pennsylvania eight, Delaware one, Maryland six, Virginia ten, North Carolina five, South Carolina five, and Georgia three.

When vacancies happen in the Representation from any State, the Executive Authority thereof shall issue Writs of Election to fill such Vacancies.

The House of Representatives shall chuse their Speaker and other Officers; and shall have the sole Power of Impeachment.

Section 3.   The Senate of the United States shall be composed of two Senators from each State, (chosen by the legislature thereof,)[2] for six Years; and each Senator shall have one Vote.

Immediately after they shall be assembled in Consequence of the first election, they shall be divided as equally as may be into three Classes. The Seats of the Senators of the first Class shall be vacated at the Expiration of the second Year, of the second Class at the Expiration of the fourth Year, and of the third Class at the Expiration of the sixth Year, so that one third may be chosen every second Year; (and if vacancies happen by Resignation, or otherwise, during the Recess of the Legislature of any State, the Executive thereof may make temporary Appointments until the next Meeting of the Legislature, which shall then fill such Vacancies.)[3]

---

1. Changed by Section 2 of the Fourteenth Amendment.
2. Changed by the Seventeenth Amendment.
3. Changed by the Seventeenth Amendment.

No Person shall be a Senator who shall not have attained to the Age of thirty Years, and been nine Years a citizen of the United States and who shall not, when elected, be an Inhabitant of that State for which he shall be chosen.

The Vice President of the United States shall be President of the Senate, but shall have no Vote, unless they be equally divided.

The Senate shall chuse their other Officers, and also a President pro tempore, in the Absence of the Vice President, or when he shall exercise the Office of President of the United States.

The Senate shall have the sole Power to try all Impeachments. When sitting for that Purpose, they shall be on Oath or Affirmation. When the President of the United States is tried, the Chief Justice shall preside: And no Person shall be convicted without the Concurrence of two thirds of the Members present.

Judgment in Cases of Impeachment shall not extend further than to removal from Office, and disqualification to hold and enjoy any Office of honor, Trust or Profit under the United States: but the Party convicted shall nevertheless be liable and subject to Indictment, Trial, Judgment and Punishment, according to Law.

Section 4. The Times, Places and Manner of holding Elections for Senators and Representatives, shall be prescribed in each State by the Legislature thereof; but the Congress may at any time by Law make or alter such Regulations, except as to the Places of chusing Senators.

The Congress shall assemble at least once in every Year, and such Meeting shall be (on the first Monday in December,)[4] unless they shall by Law appoint a different Day.

Section 5. Each House shall be the Judge of the Elections, Returns and Qualifications of its own Members, and a Majority of each shall constitute a Quorum to do Business; but a smaller Number may adjourn from day to day, and may be authorized to compel the Attendance of absent Members, in such Manner, and under such Penalties as each House may provide.

Each House may determine the Rules of its Proceedings, punish its Members for disorderly Behaviour, and, with the Concurrence of two thirds, expel a Member.

---

4. Changed by Section 2 of the Twentieth Amendment.

Each House shall keep a Journal of its Proceedings, and from time to time publish the same, excepting such Parts as may in their Judgment require Secrecy; and the Yeas and Nays of the Members of either House on any question shall, at the Desire of one fifth of those Present, be entered on the Journal.

Neither House, during the session of Congress, shall, without the Consent of the other, adjourn for more than three days, nor to any other Place than that in which the two Houses shall be sitting.

Section 6. The Senators and Representatives shall receive a Compensation for their Services, to be ascertained by Law, and paid out of the Treasury of the United States. They shall in all Cases, except Treason, Felony and Breach of the Peace, be privileged from Arrest during their Attendance at the Session of their respective Houses, and in going from and returning from the same; and for any Speech or Debate in either House, they shall not be questioned in any other Place.

No Senator or Representative shall, during the Time for which he was elected, be appointed to any civil Office under the Authority of the United States, which shall have been created, or the Emoluments whereof shall have been encreased during such time: and no Person holding any Office under the United States, shall be a member of either House during his Continuance in Office.

Section 7. All Bills for raising Revenue shall originate in the House of Representatives; but the Senate may propose or concur with Amendments as on other Bills.

Every Bill which shall have passed the House of Representatives and the Senate, shall, before it becomes a Law, be presented to the President of the United States; If he approve he shall sign it, but if not he shall return it, with his Objections to that House in which it shall have originated, who shall enter the Objections at large on their Journal, and proceed to reconsider it. If after such Reconsideration two thirds of that House shall agree to pass the Bill, it shall be sent, together with the Objections, to the other House, by which it shall likewise be reconsidered, and if approved by two thirds of that House it shall become a Law. But in all such Cases the votes of both Houses shall be determined by Yeas and Nays, and the Names of the Persons voting for and against the Bill shall be entered on the Journal of each House respectively. If any Bill shall not be returned by the President within ten days (Sundays excepted) after it shall have been presented to him, the Same shall be a Law, in like Manner as if he had signed it, unless the Congress by their Adjournment prevent its Return, in which Case it shall not be a Law.

Every Order, Resolution, or Vote to which the Concurrence of the Senate and House of Representatives may be necessary (except on a question of Adjournment) shall be presented to the President of the United States; and before the Same shall take Effect, shall be approved by him, or being disapproved by him, shall be repassed by two thirds of the Senate and House of Representatives, according to the Rules and Limitations prescribed in the Case of a Bill.

Section 8. The Congress shall have the Power To lay and collect Taxes, Duties, Imposts and Excises, to pay the Debts and provide for the common Defence and general Welfare of the United States; but all Duties, Imposts and Excises shall be uniform throughout the United States;

To borrow Money on the credit of the United States;

To regulate Commerce with foreign Nations, and among the several States, and with the Indian Tribes;

To establish an uniform Rule of Naturalization, and uniform Laws on the subject of Bankruptcies throughout the United States;

To coin Money, regulate the Value thereof, and of foreign Coin, and fix the Standard of Weights and Measures;

To provide for the Punishment of counterfeiting the Securities and current Coin of the United States;

To establish Post Offices and post Roads;

To promote the Progress of Science and useful Arts, by securing for limited Times to Authors and Inventors the exclusive Right to their respective Writings and Discoveries;

To constitute Tribunals inferior to the supreme Court;

To define and punish Piracies and Felonies committed on the high Seas, and Offenses against the Law of Nations;

To declare War, grant Letters of Marque and Reprisal, and make Rules concerning Captures on Land and Water;

To raise and support Armies, but no Appropriation of Money to that Use shall be for a longer Term than two Years;

To provide and maintain a Navy;

To make Rules for the Government and Regulation of the land and naval Forces;

To provide for calling forth the Militia to execute the Laws of the Union, suppress Insurrections and repel Invasions;

To provide for organizing, arming, and disciplining, the Militia, and for governing such Part of them as may be employed in the Service of the United States, reserving to the States respectively, the Appointment of the Officers, and the Authority of training the Militia according to the discipline prescribed by Congress;

To exercise exclusive Legislation in all Cases whatsoever, over such District (not exceeding ten Miles square) as may, by Cession of particular States, and the Acceptance of Congress, become the seat of the Government of the United States, and to exercise like Authority over all Places purchased by the Consent of the Legislature of the State in which the Same shall be, for the Erection of Forts, Magazines, Arsenals, dock-Yards, and other needful Buildings; — And

To make all Laws which shall be necessary and proper for carrying into Execution the foregoing Powers, and all other Powers vested by this Constitution in the Government of the United States, or in any Department or Officer thereof.

Section 9. The Migration or Importation of such Persons as any of the States now existing shall think proper to admit, shall not be prohibited by the Congress prior to the Year one thousand eight hundred and eight, but a Tax or duty may be imposed on such Importation, not exceeding ten dollars for each Person.

The privilege of the Writ of Habeas Corpus shall not be suspended, unless when in Cases of Rebellion or Invasion the public Safety may require it.

No Bill of Attainder or ex post facto Law shall be passed.

No Capitation, or other direct, Tax shall be laid, unless in Proportion to the Census or Enumeration herein before directed to be taken.[5]

No Tax or Duty shall be laid on Articles exported from any State.

No Preference shall be given by any Regulation of Commerce or Revenue to the Ports of one State over those of another: nor shall

---

5. See Sixteenth Amendment.

Vessels bound to, or from, one State, be obliged to enter, clear or pay Duties in another.

No Money shall be drawn from the Treasury, but in Consequence of Appropriations made by Law; and a regular Statement and Account of the Receipts and Expenditures of all public Money shall be published from time to time.

No Title of Nobility shall be granted by the United States: and no Person holding any Office of Profit or Trust under them, shall, without the Consent of the Congress, accept of any present, Emolument, Office, or Title, of any kind whatever, from any King, Prince, or foreign State.

Section 10. No State shall enter into any Treaty, Alliance, or Confederation; grant Letters of Marque and Reprisal; coin Money; emit Bills of Credit; make any Thing but gold and silver Coin a Tender in Payment of Debts; pass any Bill of Attainder, ex post facto Law, or Law impairing the Obligation of Contracts, or grant any Title of Nobility.

No State shall, without the Consent of the Congress, lay any Imposts or Duties on Imports or Exports, except what may be absolutely necessary for executing its inspection Laws: and the net Produce of all Duties and Imposts, laid by any State on Imports or Exports, shall be for the Use of the Treasury of the United States; and all such Laws shall be subject to the Revision and Controul of the Congress.

No State shall, without the Consent of Congress, lay any Duty of Tonnage, keep Troops, or Ships of War in time of Peace, enter into any Agreement or Compact with another State, or with a foreign Power, or engage in War, unless actually invaded, or in such imminent Danger as will not admit of delay.

Article II

Section 1. The executive Power shall be vested in a President of the United States of America. He shall hold his Office during the Term of four years, and, together with the Vice President, chosen for the same Term, shall be elected as follows

Each State shall appoint, in such Manner as the Legislature thereof may direct, a Number of Electors, equal to the whole Number of

Senators and Representatives to which the State may be entitled in the Congress: but no Senator or Representative, or Person holding an Office of Trust or Profit under the United States, shall be appointed an Elector.

(The Electors shall meet in their respective States, and vote by Ballot for two persons, of whom one at least shall not be an Inhabitant of the same State with themselves. And they shall make a List of all the Persons voted for, and of the Number of Votes for each; which List they shall sign and certify, and transmit sealed to the Seat of the Government of the United States, directed to the President of the Senate. The President of the Senate shall, in the Presence of the Senate and House of Representatives, open all the Certificates, and the votes shall then be counted. The Person having the greatest Number of Votes shall be the President, if such Number be a Majority of the whole Number of Electors appointed; and if there be more than one who have such Majority, and have an equal Number of Votes, then the House of Representatives shall immediately chuse by Ballot one of them for President; and if no Person have a Majority, then from the five highest on the List the said House shall in like Manner chuse the President. But in chusing the President, the Votes shall be taken by States, the Representation from each State having one Vote; A quorum for this Purpose shall consist of a member or members from two thirds of the States, and a Majority of all the States shall be necessary to a Choice. In every case, after the choice of the President, the Person having the greatest Number of Votes of the Electors shall be the Vice President. But if there should remain two or more who have equal Votes, the Senate shall chuse from them by Ballot the Vice President.)[6]

The Congress may determine the Time of chusing the Electors, and the Day on which they shall give their Votes; which Day shall be the same throughout the United States.

No Person except a natural born Citizen, or a Citizen of the United States, at the time of the Adoption of this Constitution, shall be eligible to the Office of President; neither shall any person be eligible to that Office who shall not have attained to the Age of thirty five Years, and been fourteen Years a Resident of the United States.

(In Case of the Removal of the President from Office, or of his

---

6. Changed by the Twelfth Amendment.

Death, Resignation, or Inability to discharge the Powers and Duties of the said Office, the Same shall devolve on the Vice President, and the Congress may by Law provide for the Case of Removal, Death, Resignation or Inability, both of the President and Vice President, declaring what Officer shall then act as President, and such Officer shall act accordingly, until the Disability be removed, or a President shall be elected.)[7]

The President shall, at stated Times, receive for his Services, a Compensation, which shall neither be increased nor diminished during the Period for which he shall have been elected, and he shall not receive within that Period any other Emolument from the United States, or any of them.

Before he enter on the Execution of his Office, he shall take the following Oath or Affirmation: — "I do solemnly swear (or affirm) that I will faithfully execute the Office of President of the United States, and will to the best of my Ability, preserve, protect and defend the Constitution of the United States."

Section 2. The President shall be Commander in Chief of the Army and Navy of the United States, and of the Militia of the several States, when called into the actual Service of the United States; he may require the Opinion, in writing, of the principal Officer in each of the executive Departments, upon any Subject relating to the Duties of their respective Offices, and he shall have the Power to grant Reprieves and Pardons for Offenses against the United States, except in Cases of Impeachment.

He shall have Power, by and with the Advice and Consent of the Senate, to make Treaties, provided two thirds of the Senators present concur; and he shall nominate, and by and with the Advice and Consent of the Senate, shall appoint Ambassadors, other public Ministers and Consuls, Judges of the supreme Court, and all other Officers of the United States, whose Appointments are not herein otherwise provided for, and which shall be established by Law: but the Congress may by Law vest the Appointment of such inferior Officers, as they think proper, in the President alone, in the Courts of Law, or in the Heads of Departments.

---

7. Changed by the Twenty-fifth Amendment.

The President shall have Power to fill up all Vacancies that may happen during the Recess of the Senate, by granting Commissions which shall expire at the End of their next Session.

Section 3. He shall from time to time give to the Congress Information of the State of the Union, and recommend to their Consideration such Measures as he shall judge necessary and expedient; he may, on extraordinary Occasions, convene both Houses, or either of them, and in Case of Disagreement between them, with Respect to the Time of Adjournment, he may adjourn them to such Time as he shall think proper; he shall receive Ambassadors and other public Ministers; he shall take Care that the Laws be faithfully executed, and shall Commission all the Officers of the United States.

Section 4. The President, Vice President and all civil Officers of the United States, shall be removed from Office on Impeachment for, and Conviction of, Treason, Bribery, or other high Crimes and Misdemeanors.

Article III

Section 1. The judicial Power of the United States, shall be vested in one supreme Court, and in such inferior Courts as the Congress may from time to time ordain and establish. The Judges, both of the supreme and inferior Courts, shall hold their Offices during good Behavior, and shall, at stated Times, receive for their Services, a Compensation, which shall not be diminished during their Continuance in Office.

Section 2. The judicial Power shall extend to all Cases, in Law and Equity, arising under this Constitution, the Laws of the United States, and Treaties made, or which shall be made, under their Authority; — to all Cases affecting Ambassadors, other public Ministers and Consuls; — to all Cases of admiralty and maritime Jurisdiction; — to Controversies to which the United States shall be a Party; — to Controversies between two or more States; — (between a State and Citizens of another State; —)[8] between Citizens of different States; —

---

8. Changed by the Eleventh Amendment.

between Citizens of the same State claiming Lands under Grants of different States, (and between a State, or the Citizens thereof, and foreign States, Citizens or Subjects.)[9]

In all Cases affecting Ambassadors, other public Ministers and Consuls, and in those in which a State shall be Party, the supreme Court shall have original Jurisdiction. In all other Cases before mentioned, the supreme Court shall have appellate Jurisdiction, both as to Law and Fact, with such Exceptions, and under such Regulations as the Congress shall make.

The Trial of all Crimes, except in Cases of Impeachment, shall be by Jury; and such Trial shall be held in the State where the said Crimes shall have been committed; but when not committed within any State, the Trial shall be at such Place or Places as the Congress may by Law have directed.

Section 3. Treason against the United States, shall consist only in levying War against them, or in adhering to their Enemies, giving them Aid and Comfort. No Person shall be convicted of Treason unless on the Testimony of two Witnesses to the same overt Act, or on Confession in open Court.

The Congress shall have Power to declare the Punishment of Treason, but no Attainder of Treason shall work Corruption of Blood, or Forfeiture except during the Life of the Person attained.

Article IV

Section 1. Full Faith and Credit shall be given in each State to the public Acts, Records, and judicial Proceedings of every other State; And the Congress may by general Laws prescribe the Manner in which such Acts, Records, and Proceedings shall be proved, and the Effect thereof.

Section 2. The Citizens of each State shall be entitled to all Privileges and Immunities of Citizens in the several States.

A Person charged in any State with Treason, Felony, or other Crime, who shall flee from Justice, and be found in another State, shall on Demand of the executive Authority of the State from which he fled, be

---

9. Changed by the Eleventh Amendment.

delivered up, to be removed to the State having Jurisdiction of the Crime.

(No Person held to Service or Labor in one State, under the Laws thereof, escaping into another, shall, in Consequence of any Law or Regulation therein, be discharged from such Service or Labor, but shall be delivered up on Claim of the Party to whom such Service or Labor may be due.)[10]

Section 3. New States may be admitted by the Congress into this Union; but no new State shall be formed or erected within the Jurisdiction of any other State; nor any State be formed by the Junction of two or more States, or Parts of States, without the Consent of the Legislatures of the States concerned as well as of the Congress.

The Congress shall have Power to dispose of and make all needful Rules and Regulations respecting the Territory or other Property belonging to the United States; and nothing in this Constitution shall be so construed as to Prejudice any Claims of the United States, or of any particular State.

Section 4. The United States shall guarantee to every State in this Union a Republican Form of government, and shall protect each of them against Invasion; and on Application of the Legislature, or of the Executive (when the Legislature cannot be convened) against domestic Violence.

Article V

The Congress, whenever two thirds of both Houses shall deem it necessary, shall propose Amendments to this Constitution, or, on the Application of the Legislatures of two thirds of the several States, shall call a Convention for proposing Amendments, which, in either Case, shall be valid to all Intents and Purposes, as Part of this Constitution, when ratified by the Legislatures of three fourths of the several states, or by Conventions in three fourths thereof, as the one or the other Mode of Ratification may be proposed by the Congress; Provided that no Amendment which may be made prior to the Year One thousand eight hundred and eight shall in any Manner affect the first and fourth

---

10. Changed by the Thirteenth Amendment.

Clauses in the Ninth Section of the first Article; and that no State, without its

Consent, shall be deprived of its equal Suffrage in the Senate.

Article VI

All Debts contracted and Engagements entered into, before the Adoption of this Constitution, shall be as valid against the United States under this Constitution, as under the Confederation.

This Constitution, and the Laws of the United States which shall be made in Pursuance thereof; and all Treaties made, or which shall be made, under the Authority of the United States, shall be the supreme Law of the Land; and the Judges in every State shall be bound thereby, any Thing in the Constitution or Laws of any State to the Contrary notwithstanding.

The Senators and Representatives before mentioned, and the Members of the several State Legislatures, and all executive and judicial Officers, both of the United States and of the several States, shall be bound by Oath or Affirmation, to support this Constitution; but no religious Test shall ever be required as a Qualification to any Office or public Trust under the United States.

Article VII

The Ratification of the Conventions of nine States, shall be sufficient for the Establishment of this Constitution between the States so ratifying the Same.

done in Convention by the Unanimous Consent of the States present the Seventeenth Day of September in the Year of our Lord one thousand seven hundred and Eighty seven and of the Independence of the United States of America the Twelfth In Witness whereof We have hereunto subscribed our Names,

George Washington, President and deputy from Virginia
New Hampshire — John Langdon, Nicholas Gilman
Massachusetts — Nathaniel Gorham, Rufus King
Connecticut — Wm. Saml. Johnson, Roger Sherman
New York — Alexander Hamilton
New Jersey — Wil: Livingston, David Brearly, Wm. Paterson, Jona: Dayton
Pennsylvania — B. Franklin, Thomas Mifflin, Robt Morris, Geo.

Clymer, Thos. FitzSimons, Jared Ingersoll, James Wilson, Gouv Morris
   Delaware — Geo: Read, Gunning Bedford jun., John Dickinson, Richard Bassett, Jaco: Broom
   Maryland — James McHenry, Dan of St Thos. Jenifer, Danl Carroll
   Virginia — John Blair, James Madison Jr.
   North Carolina — Wm. Blount, Richd. Dobbs Spaight, Hu Williamson
   South Carolina — J. Rutledge, Charles Cotesworth Pinckney, Charles Pinckney, Pierce Butler
   Georgia — William Few, Abr Baldwin
   Attest: William Jackson Secretary

Amendment I (1791)

Congress shall make no law respecting an establishment of religion, or prohibiting the free exercise thereof; or abridging the freedom of speech, or of the press; or the right of the people peaceably to assemble, and to petition the Government for a redress of grievances.

Amendment II (1791)

A well regulated Militia, being necessary to the security of a free State, the right of the people to keep and bear Arms, shall not be infringed.

Amendment III (1791)

No Soldier shall, in time of peace be quartered in any house, without the consent of the Owner, nor in a time of war, but in a manner to be prescribed by law.

Amendment IV (1791)

The right of the people to be secure in their persons, houses, papers, and effects, against unreasonable searches and seizures, shall not be violated, and no Warrants shall issue, but upon probable cause, supported by Oath or affirmation, and particularly describing the place to be searched, and the persons or things to be seized.

Amendment V (1791)

No person shall be held to answer for a capital, or otherwise infamous crime, unless on a presentment or indictment of a Grand Jury, except in cases arising in the land or naval forces, or in the Militia, when in actual service in time of War or public danger; nor shall any person be subject for the same offense to be twice put in jeopardy of life or limb; nor shall be compelled in any criminal case to be a witness against himself, nor be deprived of life, liberty, or property, without due process of law; nor shall private property be taken for public use, without just compensation.

Amendment VI (1791)

In all criminal prosecutions, the accused shall enjoy the right to a speedy and public trial, by an impartial jury of the State and district wherein the crime shall have been committed; which district shall have been previously ascertained by law, and to be informed of the nature and cause of the accusation; to be confronted with witnesses against him; to have compulsory process for obtaining witnesses in his favor, and to have the assistance of counsel for his defence.

Amendment VII (1791)

In Suits at common law, where the value of the controversy shall exceed twenty dollars, the right of trial by jury shall be preserved, and no fact tried by a jury, shall be otherwise re-examined in any Court of the United States, than according to the rules of the common law.

Amendment VIII (1791)

Excessive bail shall not be required, nor excessive fines imposed, nor cruel and unusual punishments inflicted.

Amendment IX (1791)

The enumeration in the Constitution of certain rights, shall not be construed to deny or disparage others retained by the people.

Amendment X (1791)

The powers not delegated to the United States by the Constitution, nor prohibited by it to the States, are reserved to the States respectively, or to the people.

Amendment XI (1798)

The Judicial power of the United States shall not be construed to extend to any suit in law or equity, commenced or prosecuted against one of the United States by Citizens of another State, or by Citizens or Subjects of any Foreign State.

Amendment XII (1804)

The Electors shall meet in their respective states and vote by ballot for President and Vice President, one of whom, at least, shall not be an inhabitant of the same state with themselves; they shall name in their ballots the person voted for as President, and in distinct ballots the person voted for as Vice President, and they shall make distinct lists of all persons voted for as President, and of all persons voted for as Vice President, and of the number of votes for each, which lists they shall sign and certify, and transmit sealed to the seat of the government of the United States, directed to the President of the Senate; — The President of the Senate shall, in the presence of the Senate and House of Representatives, open all the certificates and the votes shall then be counted; — the person having the greatest number of votes for President, shall be the President, if such number be a majority of the whole number of Electors appointed; and if no person have such majority, then from the persons having the highest number not exceeding three on the list of those voted for as President, the House of Representatives shall choose immediately, by ballot, the President. But in choosing the President the votes shall be taken by states, the representation from each state having one vote; a quorum for this purpose shall consist of a member or members from two-thirds of the states, and a majority of all the states shall be necessary to a choice. And if the House of Representatives shall not choose a President whenever the right of choice shall devolve upon them, before the fourth day of March next following, then the Vice President shall act as President, as in the case of the death or other constitutional disability of the President.

The person having the greatest number of votes as Vice President, shall be the Vice President, if such number be a majority of the whole number of Electors appointed, and if no person have a majority, then from the two highest numbers on the list, the Senate shall choose the Vice President; a quorum for the purpose shall consist of two-thirds of the whole number of Senators, and a majority of the whole number shall be necessary to a choice. But no person constitutionally ineligible to the office of President shall be eligible to that of Vice President of the United States.

Amendment XIII (1865)

Section 1. Neither slavery nor involuntary servitude, except as a punishment for crime whereof the party shall have been duly convicted, shall exist within the United States, or any place subject to their jurisdiction.

Section 2. Congress shall have the power to enforce this article by appropriate legislation.

Amendment XIV (1868)

Section 1. All persons born or naturalized in the United States, and subject to the jurisdiction thereof, are citizens of the United States and of the State wherein they reside. No State shall make or enforce any law which shall abridge the privileges or immunities of citizens of the United States; nor shall any State deprive any person of life, liberty, or property, without due process of law; nor deny to any person within its jurisdiction the equal protection of the laws.

Section 2. Representatives shall be apportioned among the several States according to their respective numbers, counting the whole number of persons in each State, excluding Indians not taxed. But when the right to vote at any election for the choice of electors for President and Vice President of the United States, Representatives in Congress, the Executive and Judicial officers of a State, or the members of the Legislature thereof, is denied to any male inhabitants of such State, being twenty-one years of age, and citizens of the United States, or in any way abridged, except for participation in rebellion, or any other crime, the basis of representation therein shall be reduced in the proportion which the number of such male citizens shall bear to the whole number of male citizens twenty-one years of age in such State.

Section 3. No person shall be a Senator or Representative in Congress, or elector of President and Vice President, or hold any office, civil or military, under the United States, or under any State, who, having previously taken an oath, as a member of Congress, or as an officer of the United States, or as a member of any State legislature, or as an executive or judicial officer of any State, to support the Constitution of the United States, shall have engaged in insurrection or rebellion against the same, or given aid or comfort to the enemies thereof. But Congress may by a vote of two-thirds of each House, remove such disability.

Section 4. The validity of the public debt of the United States, authorized by law, including debts incurred in payment of pensions and bounties for services in suppressing insurrection or rebellion, shall not be questioned. But neither the United States nor any State shall assume or pay any debt or obligation incurred in aid of insurrection or rebellion against the United States, or any claim for the loss or emancipation of any slave, but all such debts, obligations and claims shall be held illegal and void.

Section 5. The Congress shall have power to enforce, by appropriate legislation, the provisions of this article.

Amendment XV (1870)

Section 1. The right of citizens of the United States to vote shall not be denied or abridged by the United States or by any State on account of race, color, or previous condition of servitude.

Section 2. The Congress shall have the power to enforce this article by appropriate legislation.

Amendment XVI (1913)

The Congress shall have the power to lay and collect taxes on incomes, from whatever source derived, without apportionment among the several States, and without regard to any census enumeration.

Amendment XVII (1913)

The Senate of the United States shall be composed of two Senators from each State, elected by the people thereof, for six years; and each Senator shall have one vote. The electors in each State shall have the qualifications requisite for electors of the most numerous branch of the State legislatures.

When vacancies happen in the representation of any State in the Senate, the executive authority of such State shall issue writs of election to fill such vacancies: *Provided,* That the legislature of any State may empower the executive thereof to make temporary appointments until the people fill the vacancies by election as the legislature may direct.

This amendment shall not be so construed as to affect the election or term of any Senator chosen before it becomes valid as part of the Constitution.

Amendment XVIII (1919)

Section 1. After one year from ratification of this article the manufacture, sale, or transportation of intoxicating liquors within, the importation thereof into, or the exportation thereof from the United States and all territory subject to the jurisdiction thereof for beverage purposes is hereby prohibited.

Section 2. The Congress and the several States shall have concurrent power to enforce this article by appropriate legislation.

Section 3. This article shall be inoperative unless it shall have been ratified as an amendment to the Constitution by the legislatures of the several States, as provided in the Constitution, within seven years from the date of the submission hereof to the States by the Congress.

Amendment XIX (1920)

The right of citizens of the United States to vote shall not be denied or abridged by the United States or by any state on account of sex.

Congress shall have power to enforce this article by appropriate legislation.

Amendment XX (1933)

Section 1. The terms of the President and Vice President shall end at noon on the 20th day of January, and the terms of Senators and Representatives at noon on the 3d day of January, of the years in which such terms would have ended if this article had not been ratified; and the terms of their successors shall begin.

Section 2. The Congress shall assemble at least once every year, and such meeting shall begin at noon on the 3d day of January, unless they shall by law appoint a different day.

Section 3. If, at the time fixed for the beginning of the term of the President, the President elect shall have died, the Vice President elect shall become President. If a President shall not have been chosen before the time fixed for the beginning of his term, or if the President elect shall have failed to qualify, then the Vice President elect shall act as President until a President shall have qualified; and the Congress may by law provide for the case wherein neither a President elect nor a Vice President elect shall have qualified, declaring who shall then act as President, or in the manner in which one who is to act shall be selected, and such person shall act accordingly until a President or Vice President shall have qualified.

Section 4. The Congress may by law provide for the case of the death of any of the persons from whom the House of Representatives may choose a President whenever the right of choice shall have devolved upon them, and for the case of the death of any of the persons from whom the Senate may choose a Vice President whenever the right of choice shall have devolved upon them.

Section 5. Sections 1 and 2 shall take effect on the 15th day of October following the ratification of this article.

Section 6. This article shall be inoperative unless it shall have been ratified as an amendment to the Constitution by the legislatures of three-fourths of the several States within seven years from the date of its submission.

Amendment XXI (1933)

Section 1. The eighteenth amendment to the Constitution of the United States is hereby repealed.

Section 2. The transportation into any State, Territory, or possession of the United States for delivery or use therein of intoxicating liquors, in violation of the laws thereof, is hereby prohibited.

Section 3. This article shall be inoperative unless it shall have been ratified as an amendment to the Constitution by conventions in the several States, as provided in the Constitution, within seven years from the date of the submission hereof to the states by the Congress.

Amendment XXII (1951)

Section 1. No person shall be elected to the office of the President more than twice, and no person who has held the office of President, or acted as President, for more than two years of a term to which some other person was elected President shall be elected to the office of the President more than once. But this article shall not apply to any person holding the office of President when this article was proposed by the Congress, and shall not prevent any person who may be holding the office of President, or acting as President, during the term within which this article becomes operative from holding the office of President or acting as President during the remainder of such term.

Section 2. This article shall be inoperative unless it shall have been ratified as an amendment within seven years from the date of its submission to the states by the Congress.

Amendment XXIII (1961)

Section 1. The District constituting the seat of Government of the United States shall appoint in such manner as Congress may direct:

A number of electors of President and Vice President equal to the whole number of Senators and Representatives in Congress to which the District would be entitled if it were a State, but in no event more than the least populous State; they shall be in addition to those appointed by the States, but they shall be considered, for the purpose of the election of President and Vice President, to be electors appointed by a State; and they shall meet in the District and perform such duties as provided by the twelfth article of amendment.

Section 2. The Congress shall have the power to enforce this article by appropriate legislation.

Amendment XXIV (1964)

Section 1. The right of citizens of the United States to vote in any primary or other election for President of Vice President, for electors for President or Vice President, or for Senator or Representative in Congress, shall not be denied or abridged by the United States or any state by reason of failure to pay any poll tax or other tax.

Section 2. The Congress shall have the power to enforce this article by appropriate legislation.

Amendment XXV (1967)

Section 1. In case of the removal of the President from office or of his death or resignation, the Vice President shall become President.

Section 2. Whenever there is a vacancy in the office of the Vice President, the President shall nominate a Vice President who shall take office upon confirmation by a majority vote of both Houses of Congress.

Section 3. Whenever the President transmits to the President pro tempore of the Senate and the Speaker of the House of Representatives his written declaration that he is unable to discharge the powers and duties of his office, and until he transmits to them a written declaration to the contrary, such powers and duties shall be discharged by the Vice President as Acting President.

Section 4. Whenever the Vice President and a majority of either the principal officers of the executive department or of such other body as Congress may by law provide, transmit to the President pro tempore of the Senate and the Speaker of the House of Representatives their written declaration that the President is unable to discharge the powers and duties of his office, the Vice President shall immediately assume the powers and duties of the office as Acting President.

Thereafter, when the President transmits to the President pro tempore of the Senate and the Speaker of the House of Representatives his written declaration that no inability exists, he shall resume the powers and duties of his office unless the Vice President and a majority of either the principal officers of the executive department or of such other body as Congress may by law provide, transmit within four days to the President pro tempore of the Senate and the Speaker of the House of Representatives their written declaration that the President is unable to discharge the powers and duties of his office. Thereupon Congress shall decide the issue, assembling within forty-eight hours for that purpose if not in session. If the Congress within twenty-one days after receipt of the latter written declaration, of, if Congress is not in session, within twenty-one days after Congress is required to assemble, determines by two-thirds vote of both Houses that the President is unable to discharge the powers and duties of his office, the Vice President shall continue to discharge the same as Acting President; otherwise, the President shall resume the powers and duties of his office.

Amendment XXVI (1971)

Section 1. The right of citizens of the United States, who are eighteen years of age or older, to vote, shall not be denied by the United States or by any State on account of age.

Section 2. The Congress shall have the power to enforce this article by appropriate legislation.

Amendment XXVII (1992)

No law varying the compensation for the services of the Senators and Representatives shall take effect until an election of Representatives shall have intervened.

Appendix B

Useful Web Sites for Journalists

NOTE: While the Internet is a wonderful journalistic tool, it is impermanent. Web sites change or cease to exist. Web addresses change or become invalid. These web sites and addresses are accurate as we go to press.

Agencies

www.[agency abbreviation].gov	Most federal agencies have web sites
www.bls.gov	Bureau of Labor Statistics, employment data
www.cdc.gov	Centers for Disease Control, bounty of health statistics and data
www.epa.gov	Environmental Protection Agency
www.fcc.gov	Federal Communications Commission
www.fda.gov	Food and Drug Administration
www.fema.gov	Federal Emergency Management Agency
www.ftc.gov	Federal Trade Commission
www.irs.ustreas.gov/prod/	Internal Revenue Service, how much tax money is being raised and where it's being spent
www.odci.gov	Central Intelligence Agency

Civil Rights

www.aclu.org	American Civil Liberties Union
www.thecrisismagazine.com	Magazine of the NAACP, excellent site for civil rights issues

www.maynardije.org	Maynard Institute, information about diversity in business and journalism
www.splcenter.org	Southern Poverty Law Center, excellent information on racism, anti-Semitism and hate groups

Congress

www.cbo.gov	Congressional Budget Office
www.cq.com	Congressional Quarterly's site is a fount of information about the federal government
www.c-span.org	C-SPAN web page with information about congressional activities, pending business, schedules
www.house.gov/[enter name of committee]	House committees
www.house.gov/rules	House Rules Committee web site, excellent resource for House operations and procedures
www.nationaljournal. com	Congress Daily and other information about Congress
www.senate.gov/[enter name of committee]	Senate committees
http://thomas.loc.gov	Excellent source of Federal government information, particularly about Congress (named for Thomas Jefferson)

General Government Information

www.access.gpo.gov	The Government Printing Office web site, excellent in searching for official government publications and documents
www.brook.edu	The Brookings Institution
www.census.gov	A cornucopia of data about us, and about the states, cities and counties in which we live
www.citizen.org	Freedom of Information Clearinghouse (look for link to FOI)
www.gao.gov	General Accounting Office, documents on government oversight and investigations

http://govinfo.kerr.orst. edu	Oregon State University information-sharing web site with a wealth of government data
www.heritage.org	The Heritage Foundation
www.lcweb.loc.gov	Library of Congress web site, excellent for entire federal government
www.nfoic.org	National Freedom of Information Coalition

Executive Branch

www.[agency acronym]. gov	Web sites for federal cabinet departments and executive agencies (example: Department of Agriculture *www.usda.gov*)
www.whitehouse.gov	Official web site of the president, good for current White House statements especially the window for The Briefing Room

Journalism

www.asne.org	American Society of Newspaper Editors
www.cjr.org	Columbia Journalism Review, good site for journalism criticism and the magazine's archives
www.ire.org	National Institute for Computer-Assisted Reporting at the University of Missouri School of Journalism
www.jou.ufl.edu/ brechner	Brechner Center for Freedom of Information at the University of Florida, repository for First Amendment and media law
www.muckraker.org	Center for Investigative Reporting
www.nab.org/irc	National Association of Broadcasters information resource center
www.newseum.org	The Newseum web page, good source of media/ government history
www.newslab.org	NewsLab, the project for excellence in journalism
www.pccj.org	Pew Center for Civic Journalism
www.poynter.org	Poynter Institute and journalistic think tank
www.rcfp.org	Reporters Committee for Freedom of the Press; superb web site for issues pertaining to news coverage such as shield laws, sunshine laws and FOIA

www.rtnda.org	Radio-Television News Directors Association and Foundation; excellent for civics issues as they apply to journalists
www.spj.org	Society of Professional Journalists
www.splc.org	Student Press Law Center, specifically for legal issues concerning high school and college journalists

Law and Courts

www.fbi.gov	Federal Bureau of Investigation
www.findlaw.com	An exceptional legal search engine for both federal and state issues
www.lawcrawler.com	Excellent legal search engine
www.usconstitution.net	Constitutional law at your fingertips

Military Affairs

www.defensedaily.com	Military affairs and current Pentagon information
www.defenselink.mil	The Pentagon's web site
www.armytimes.com	Army Times Magazine
www.ida.org	Institute for Defense Analysis, military policy think tank

Politics

www.commoncause.org	Common Cause, citizens lobbying organization with a particular interest in campaign finance reform and political ethics
www.democrats.org	Democratic National Committee
www.fec.gov	Federal Election Commission, official data but not particularly user friendly
www.lwv.org	League of Women Voters
www.rnc.org	Republican National Committee
www.tray.com/fecinfo	A superb, privately-operated web site with information about political candidates, campaign financing and soft money

Search Engines

www.askjeeves.com	Excellent general search engine
http://assignmenteditor.	
com	Good research site for reporters
www.google.com	Excellent general search engine
www.go.infoseek.com	Solid search engine
www.hotsheet.com	Great place to start looking for information
www.phonebook.com	Multi-linked phone source, including a reverse directory
www.worldemail.com	E-mail address finder (international)
http://webcrawler.com	Another good search engine

State and Local Government (General Sites)

www.capitolimpact.com	Good site for state and local government
www.co.[county].	To access most counties in the country (example:
[state].us	El Paso County, Texas, is *www.co.el-paso.tx.us*)
	If link fails try a search engine.
www.state.[abreviation].	To access the main web pages of the various states
us	(example: Alabama is www.state.al.us*)

Appendix C

Government Acronyms

NOTE: Official Washington (and many state governments) often use acronyms and abbreviations, especially in internal documents and communications. Most are not appropriate for use in formal print or broadcast news reports. Occasionally it is acceptable to use commonly known acronyms in second reference, such as CIA (Central Intelligence Agency) or USDA (Department of Agriculture).

AA — (Congressional) administrative assistant

ADA — Americans with Disabilities Act

AG — Attorney general

ATF — The Bureau of Alcohol, Tobacco and Firearms

Cert — Lawyer shorthand referring to a writ of certiorari

FTC — Commodity Futures Trading Commission

CIA — Central Intelligence Agency

CINC — (Military) commander-in-chief; the CINC is the president; there are others such as CINCLANT, commander-in-chief of the Atlantic fleet, and CINCPAC, commander-in-chief of the Pacific fleet, occasionally seen in second reference in specialized publications

COS — Chief of staff

DCI — Director of Central Intelligence

DefSec — Secretary of defense

DepSec — Deputy secretary (example: DepSec DOC is deputy secretary of the Commerce Department)

DOC — Department of Commerce

DOE — Usually Department of Energy (sometimes Department of Education)

DOJ — Department of Justice

DOT — Department of Transportation

EPA — Environmental Protection Agency

EEOC — Equal Employment Opportunity Commission

FCC — Federal Communications Commission

FEC — Federal Election Commission

FEMA — Federal Emergency Management Agency

FLOTUS — First lady of the United States, not used in formal print or broadcast reports

FOIA — Freedom of information acts, refers to both the federal FOIA and the various state acts

FTC — Federal Trade Commission

GSA — General Services Administration

HHS — Department of Health and Human Services

HUD — Department of Housing and Urban Development

HumInt — Intelligence gathered by humans (as opposed to satellites or through technology), usually spies or other operatives

InTelSat — An intelligence gathering satellite

JAG — (Military) judge advocate general

LA — (Congressional) legislative assistant

LD — (Congressional) legislative director

NASA — National Aeronautics and Space Administration

NSA — The National Security Agency, the highly secret and secretive intelligence agency generally charged with electronic, satellite, photographic, and technological intelligence gathering, decoding and analysis

OSHA — Occupational Safety and Health Administration

POTUS — President of the United States, not used in formal print or broadcast reports

SCOTUS — Supreme Court of the United States, not used in formal print or broadcast reports

SEC — Securities and Exchange Commission

USDA — U.S. Department of Agriculture

USPS — U.S. Postal Service

Veep — Shorthand for vice president, not used in formal print or broadcast reports

Glossary

Act — A law. (See Law, below.)

Administrative law — Rules, regulations, and orders not enacted by Congress but made, implemented, and enforced by executive departments and agencies with the force of law. For example, the FCC rules governing radio and TV licensing are administrative law. (See Chapter 3, section 3.8.)

Adjourn *sine die* — [Latin: without a day] The way the U.S. Congress ends a session, literally without setting a date or time at which to reconvene. Unless there is an intervening special session of Congress, the next time Congress will meet after adjourning *sine die* is to convene a new Congress.

Advice and consent — The constitutional requirement that the president seek the advice and consent of the Senate on nominations to top government jobs and for approval of international treaties. Nominations require a majority vote; treaties require a two-thirds majority. (See Chapter 2, section 2.9.)

Aisle — Literally the walkway that leads from the back door to the dais in the U.S. Senate or House of Representatives. In both chambers members of the Republican Party sit on the right side of the aisle facing the presiding officer and members of the Democratic Party sit on the left.

Amend — 1. To change the Constitution of the United States. (See Chapter 5, section 5.3.) 2. To change the constitution of one of the fifty states. 3. To change, modify, alter, adjust, or otherwise add to or delete from a bill, resolution or other federal or state legislative action. (See Chapter 2, section 2.4.)

Appropriation — Legislative action to draw money from the treasury for spending on specific programs, departments, and agencies. (Federal, see Chapter 2, section 2.6; states, see Chapter 8, section 8.6.)

Authorization — Legislative earmarking where government money should be spent. (Federal, see Chapter 2, section 2.6; states, see Chapter 8, section 8.6.)

Ballot initiative — A state mechanism by which citizens are directly involved in drafting and enacting laws through a process of gathering the requisite number of signatures on petitions, having those signatures certified as authentic and qualified to sign, and placing the proposed law on an election ballot. (See Chapter 8, section 8.4.)

Bicameral — Having two chambers, such as a bicameral legislature which has an upper and lower chamber. (See Chapter 8, section 8.1.)

Biennial — Every two years. A biennial budget, for example, is one that covers two fiscal years.

Bill — A measure pending legislative action. (Federal, see Chapter 2, section 2.4; states, see Chapter 8, section 8.3.)

Chair — 1. The person presiding over a meeting or hearing. 2. The ranking majority member of a committee of the U.S. Congress or state legislature.

Chamber — 1. Either body of Congress or of a state legislature. 2. The room in which the House, Senate, or Supreme Court meets.

Change of venue — A change in the location of a judicial proceeding from one place to another.

Clerk — 1. In Congress, a support official who, among other things, calls the roll for roll call votes in the Senate and who reads aloud all or part of every bill to come before the House. 2. In court, the top judicial assistant to a judge or justice. 3. In local government, the clerk of the court is an elected official responsible for court administration.

Cloture — A rule in the U.S. Senate that allows a filibuster to be ended and debate cut off upon a three-fifths majority vote. (See Chapter 2, section 2.12.)

Concurrent resolution — A formal statement, without the force of law, passed by both the House and Senate stating a congressional consensus on a specific issue. It does not require the president's signature. (Example: the Concurrent Budget Resolution.) Applicable only to a few state legislatures.

Conference committee — A group consisting of members of the U.S. House and Senate named to iron out differences in a bill and to produce an identical measure that can be passed by both chambers and sent to the president for signature. (See Chapter 2, section 2.4.) Also used in state legislatures.

Continuing resolution — Legislation providing temporary funding for a program, department or agency for which Congress has not completed the appropriation process by the end of the fiscal year.

Deregulation — A policy of eliminating administrative rules and regulations that are considered unnecessary or burdensome.

Electoral College — The formal body, as defined in the Constitution, that elects the president and vice president. In the Electoral College, each state has as many votes as that state has members of the House and Senate combined. Under the Twenty-third Amendment, the District of Columbia was given three votes in the Electoral College, the same number as the smallest state in population. (See Chapter 3, section 3.1.)

Engrossed bill — The official version of a bill approved by either the U.S. House or Senate. Occasionally used in state legislatures.

Enrolled bill — The official version of a bill passed by both the U.S. House and Senate, to be sent to the president. The same term applies in many state legislatures.

Filibuster — A tactic in the U.S. Senate that allows any senator to speak for as long as he/she desires on a given piece of legislation, except the federal budget, which is governed by a time restriction. (See Chapter 2, section 2.12.)

Fiscal year — A twelve-month period for financial and accounting purposes if other than a calendar year; October 1 to September 30 for the federal government; varies state by state.

Franking privilege — Free use of the U.S. Postal Service by members of Congress and federal departments and agencies. The signature of a senator or representative acts in place of a stamp.

Freedom of Information Act — [Widely known by the acronym FOI Act or FOIA.] A federal or state statute designed to ease public and media access to government information, documents and records. Some states include open meeting provisions in their FOI laws. (See Chapter 8, section 8.10.)

General law — An act of a state legislature that applies to all localities and their local governments, as opposed to a special act, which applies to only one or a few localities or local governments. (See Chapter 11, section 11.1.)

Grand jury — In federal and state law, a panel of citizens that hears evidence presented by the prosecution and determines whether there is probable cause to hand up an indictment against someone accused of a crime and thus bind that person over for trial. (See Chapter 4, section 4.4.)

Hopper — The box into which proposed bills are placed to formally introduce them and start them on the legislative process in the U.S. Congress. The term is also used in some state legislatures.

Joint committee — A congressional committee with an equal number of senators and representatives. Chairmanship rotates every two years with the change of Congress. Joint committees are usually not authorized to move legislation or appropriate money. (Example: Joint Economic Committee.) There also are joint committees in many state legislatures.

Joint resolution — A formal statement, without the force of law but establishing a congressional position on a specific issue, passed by both the U.S. House and Senate and sent to the president for signature. The same term applies in many state legislatures, and may or may not require a governor's signature.

Judicial review — The authority of the Supreme Court to rule on the constitutionality of actions of the other two branches of government, established in the case *Marbury v. Madison*. (See Chapter 4, section 4.2.)

Justice of the peace — A local judge below the level of trial court judge in some county or municipal court systems.

Law — A bill that has been passed by Congress and signed by the president or approved by Congress over his veto. Similarly in state government, a bill that has been passed by the state legislature and signed by the governor or approved by the legislature over the governor's veto. In addition some states provide for laws to be enacted by the voters in a process called a "ballot initiative." Law and act are interchangeable terms.

Line-item veto — A state law which allows governors to strike specific items, usually from appropriation bills; a federal line-item veto law was struck down as unconstitutional by the Supreme Court in 1998. (See Chapter 8.)

Lobbyist — A person hired by a corporation, interest group, labor union, or foreign government to influence legislation, regulations, or public policy. (See Chapter 2, section 2.14.)

Magistrate judge — (See U.S. Magistrate Judge below.)

Markup — The last committee action before a bill goes to the House or Senate floor or to the floor of either chamber of a state legislature. The bill is reviewed word by word for accuracy.

Move the previous question — In the U.S. House, a procedural action to stop debate and vote on a pending matter. There is no corollary motion under U.S. Senate rules. It often applies to the procedures of the state legislatures.

Point of order — In parliamentary procedure, an objection from the floor to the presiding officer claiming that a rule has been broken.

Pool — A news gathering process used regularly at the White House and occasionally on Capitol Hill when space is limited. In a pool one or a few reporters, photographers, and broadcast technicians will cover an event and then will provide details, photos, audio, and video to all other news organizations before using it themselves. Pools have also been used to cover military operations. (See Chapter 6, section 6.1.)

Popular referendum — A state mechanism by which voters can exercise a veto over legislation passed by the state legislature. The process is similar to that of a ballot initiative in that petitions are signed, the signatures are certified, and the referendum is put on an election ballot. (See Chapter 8, section 8.4.)

President pro tempore — A Senate office named by the Constitution. Also referred to as president pro tem, it is the person who replaces the vice president when the vice president is not there to preside. In modern times the president pro tem is the longest-serving senator in the majority party. (See Chapter 2, section 2.2.)

Prior restraint — A prohibition of a broadcast or publication before the actual broadcast or publishing has happened. Prior restraint was declared unconstitutional in the 1931 case *Near v. Minnesota.*

Privilege — A right held by a person or class of persons that immunizes them from the normal course of law. Among the most generally recognized are: doctor-patient privilege (in which a doctor may not be compelled to disclose information about a patient); husband-wife privilege (in which one spouse may not be compelled to testify against the other); clergy-penitent privilege (in which a member of the clergy may not be compelled to disclose information divulged in "the sanctity of the confessional"); lawyer-client privilege (in which an attorney may not disclose communications with a client); executive privilege (in which the president of the United States may not be required to provide confidential information or contents of confidential documents or communications); and journalist's privilege (in which some laws recognize a limited privilege for journalists to protect the identity of confidential sources).

Quorum — The number of members who must be present for business to be conducted in a legislative body (usually, but not always, 50 percent plus one).

Ranking minority member — The longest-serving member of a U.S. House or Senate committee in the minority party. Also applies to state legislatures.

Recorded vote — 1) In the House, a vote taken by electronic voting device in which the result is shown on a giant electronic tote board above the House Chamber. 2) In the Senate, a roll call in which each senator announces his/her yea or nay that is recorded by the clerk on a tabulation sheet. 3) A vote in either chamber of a state legislature or local governmental body in which members' votes are recorded in the journal of the body's proceedings or minutes of the meeting.

Resolution — A formal statement, without the force of law, passed by either the House or the Senate. Also applies to state legislatures and in some cases to county and/or municipal governments.

Roll call vote — The U.S. Senate voting procedure by which the name of every senator is called and each responds "aye" or "nay" to record his/her vote.

Shield laws — State and federal laws giving journalists a limited right to protect their confidential sources, sometimes called a "limited journalist's privilege." Thirty states have shield laws giving reporters varying degrees of protection against being forced to reveal the identities of confidential sources.

Sine die — Latin meaning "without a day." (See above Adjourn *sine die.)*

Speaker of the House — Constitutionally the presiding officer in the House, leader of the majority in the House and next after the vice president in line of succession to the presidency. (See Chapter 2, section 2.1.) Many state legislatures also refer to the presiding officer in the lower chamber as the speaker.

Special act — A law passed by a state legislature that applies to one or a few local governments or jurisdictions.

Special and/or select committee — A committee, usually temporary, set up by Congress for a specific purpose or to investigate or oversee a specific issue. (The Senate set up the Special Select Committee on Watergate in 1973.) Occasionally applies to state legislatures.

Special session — 1) A session of Congress convened by the president during a recess, adjournment, or after adjournment *sine die* to consider some extraordinary measure, such as declaring war. 2) A session of a state legislature convened either by the governor or in some states by the legislature's top leaders to deal with an emergency or extraordinary circumstance.

Subpoena — 1) In judicial proceedings, including trials, court hearings, discovery proceedings, grand jury proceedings, and criminal and civil depositions, a summons to appear and give testimony, with legal sanctions, up to and including incarceration, for failure to appear. 2) In Congress, a summons to appear and give testimony before a committee or subcommittee, with legal sanctions, up to and including incarceration, for failure to appear.

Sunshine laws — Also known as open meeting laws. State and federal laws that govern media and public access to meetings, hearings, and conferences of government officials and government agencies, departments and bureaus. (See Chapter 8, section 8.10.)

Table [a bill or other measure pending House or Senate consideration] — A procedural action that removes the item being tabled from further consideration. It is a method of killing legislation and requires a majority vote.

Tort — A private or civil wrong, such as libel, slander, or trespassing, for which a civil court will provide a remedy, usually but not always in monetary terms, referred to as damages. (See Chapter 4, section 4.6.)

Unicameral — Having one chamber, such as the Nebraska legislature. (See Chapter 8, section 8.1.)

U.S. magistrate judge — An official of the U.S. District Court, subordinate to District Court judges, appointed for an eight-year term to try misdemeanors and perform pre-trial and procedural duties, such as granting search warrants and conducting arraignments. (See Chapter 4, section 4.9.) Some states also have judges with the title magistrate.

Voice vote — In the U.S. House or Senate, state legislature, county commission, city council, or any committee of these legislative bodies, a collective vocalized oral statement, not recorded or written, of yea and nay in which the presiding officer determines the winning side by the loudness of those voting.

West Wing — The section of the White House in which the Oval Office and other executive offices are located. (The first lady's office is in the East Wing.)

Writ of certiorari — An appeal to the Supreme Court. The court has absolute discretion whether to grant petitions for writs of certiorari. (See Chapter 4, section 4.7.)

Zoning variance — An exception to a local zoning regulation, granted or denied by the local zoning authority. (See Chapter 11, section 11.5.)

Index

CPSIA information can be obtained at www.ICGtesting.com
Printed in the USA
LVOW12s0351100714

393605LV00001B/27/P